LAND REVENUE POLICY

LAND REVENUE POLICY

OF THE

INDIAN GOVERNMENT.

PUBLISHED BY ORDER OF THE
GOVERNOR GENERAL OF INDIA IN COUNCIL.

BY

Dept. of Revenue and Agriculture

GYAN

Published by

GYAN

Gyan Publishing House
5, Ansari Road
Daryaganj, New Delhi-110002
Phone: 011-47034999, 9811692060
E-mail: books@gyanbooks.com

Distribution Network
gyanbooks.com
India, USA, Canada, UK, Australia, France

ISBN: 978-81-212-8728-9 (PB)
First Published, 1902

2nd Impression 2023

Printed at: Gyan Press, Delhi.

LAND REVENUE POLICY

Creattor: Dept. of Revenue and Agriculture

LAND REVENUE POLICY

OF THE

INDIAN GOVERNMENT.

PUBLISHED BY ORDER OF THE GOVERNOR GENERAL OF INDIA IN COUNCIL.

CALCUTTA:
OFFICE OF THE SUPERINTENDENT, GOVERNMENT PRINTING, INDIA.
1902.

Agents for the sale of Books published by the Superintendent of Government Printing, India, Calcutta.

IN ENGLAND.

E. A. Arnold, 37, Bedford Street, Strand, London, W. C.

Constable & Co., 2, Whitehall Gardens, London, S. W.

Sampson Low, Marston & Co., St. Dunstan's House, Fetter Lane, London, E. C.

P. S. King & Son, 2 & 4, Great Smith Street, Westminster, London, S. W.

Luzac & Co., 46, Great Russell Street. London. W. C.

Kegan Paul, Trench, Trübner, & Co., Charing Cross Road, London, W. C.

B. A. Quaritch, Esq., 15, Piccadilly, W.

Williams and Norgate, Oxford.

Deighton Bell & Co., Cambridge.

ON THE CONTINENT.

R. Friedländer & Sohn, 11, Carlstrasse, Berlin.

Otto Harrassowitz, Leipzig.

Karl W. Hiersemann, Leipzig.

Ernest Leroux, Esq., 28, Rue Bonaparte, Paris.

Martinus Nijhoff, The Hague.

IN INDIA.

Thacker, Spink & Co., Calcutta and Simla.

Newman & Co., Calcutta.

Thacker & Co., Ld., Bombay.

Higginbotham & Co., Madras, and Bangalore.

Superintendent, American Baptist Mission Press, Rangoon.

Rai Sahib M. Golab Singh and Sons, Mufid-i-Am Press, Lahore.

A. J. Combridge & Co., Bombay.

CONTENTS.

PREFATORY NOTE.

THIS volume contains the Resolution recorded by the Governor General of India in Council on the 16th January 1902 and published in the *Gazette of India* of the 18th idem, on the Land Revenue Policy of the Government. It also contains a series of reports by Local Governments on the same subject. The circumstances which led to the preparation of these reports, and to the promulgation of the views of the Government of India, are explained in the opening paragraphs of the Resolution.

The Resolution is an authoritative exposition of the principles on which the Land Revenue Administration in India has been based in the past, and by which it will be guided in the future. The reports of Local Governments not only afford a reply to criticisms which have recently been levelled at the administration of the Land Revenue in this country; they furnish valuable materials for a detailed study of the history and methods of the different systems of assessment which have been evolved to meet the widely differing circumstances of the various provinces. It is considered desirable that these papers should be given a wide publication and be made easily accessible both to the officers of Government and to the public: and with this object it has been decided to issue them in a cheap book form.

The papers have been arranged in chapters and supplied with an index and marginal abstracts to paragraphs for the convenience of those consulting the volume. Arrangements are in progress for the issue in each Province of a translation in the vernacular of the Resolution and of the particular report which concerns the Province.

J. B. FULLER,
Secretary to the Government of India.

CALCUTTA:
DEPARTMENT OF
REVENUE AND AGRICULTURE.
Dated 18th March 1902.

LAND REVENUE POLICY

LAND REVENUE POLICY

OF THE

INDIAN GOVERNMENT.

(BEING THE RESOLUTION ISSUED BY THE GOVERNOR GENERAL IN COUNCIL ON THE 16TH JANUARY, 1902.)

CHAPTER I.—INDIA.

THE attention of the Government of India has lately been called, in a special manner, to the subject of the Land Revenue administration of this country, partly by the series of almost unprecedented calamities which have in recent years assailed the agricultural population, partly by a number of representations which have reached them from sympathetic friends of India, who have devoted careful study to the above-named problem. In the course of 1900, Mr. R. C. Dutt, C.I.E., formerly Acting Commissioner of Burdwan, addressed to His Excellency the Viceroy a series of letters (subsequently published in the form of a book) concerning the Land Revenue system of the different provinces, and he submitted certain recommendations as to future policy and action. At a little later date the Secretary of State transmitted to the Government of India a memorial signed by certain retired officers of the Indian Civil Service, formulating a somewhat similar list of suggestions.

Origin and importance of the enquiry.

INDIA. 2. The Government of India welcomed the opportunity thus afforded to them of instituting renewed enquiries into a matter that has, for more than a century, been the subject of anxious discussion. The well-being of the agricultural community in India, constituting as it does so overwhelming a proportion of the entire population of the Indian continent, and contributing so large a quota to the Indian revenues, cannot fail to be to the Government a matter of the most intimate concern; nor can it be denied that upon the incidence of the land revenue collections must the prosperity of those classes in a great measure depend. The question may be recognized therefore as one of the highest national importance, transcending the sphere of party or sectional controversy, and demanding at once the most exhaustive scrutiny and the most liberal treatment. When further it appeared that the main contention submitted to the Government by certain of its critics was that the intensity and frequency of recent famines are largely due to poverty caused by over-assessment—a contention the gravity of which cannot be disputed, seeing that it is tantamount to an arraignment of the policy that has been pursued by successive Indian administrations for an entire century—and when this general proposition was accompanied by a series of detailed allegations as regards the system of assessment in vogue in the various parts of the country, it seemed to the Government of India that the opportunity should not be lost of definitely examining the grounds for these assertions; and the letters above referred to were accordingly referred to the Local Governments for their consideration and report. Their replies have been received and are annexed to this Resolution. The Governor General in Council is grateful for the labour which has been bestwed upon their preparation, and he hopes that in the comprehensive review of land revenue policy throughout India which has thereby been obtained, may be found a corrective to many current misapprehensions and a source of more trustworthy knowledge in the future. **INDIA.**

3. On the present occasion he is, however, less concerned with the individual statements or misstatements that may have been made with regard to particular areas—the replies of the Local Governments which show that an imperfect acquaintance with facts has been the source of much confusion and misunderstanding—than he is with the larger questions affecting our land revenue policy as a whole, and the connection which it is alleged to have with the recurrence and intensity of famine in India. It does not seem necessary to discuss the economic fallacy that any alteration in the system or scale of assessments can permanently save an agricultural population from the effects of climatic disaster. The relation of cause and effect between a good rainfall, abundant crops, and agricultural prosperity, is not more obvious than is that between a bad monsoon, deficient produce, and a suffering people. When the vast majority of the inhabitants of a country are dependent upon an industry which is itself dependent upon the rainfall, it is clear that a failure of the latter must unfavourably, and in extreme cases calamitously, affect the entire agricultural community. The suspension of the rains means a suspension of labour; the suspension of labour means a drying

Alleged connection between revenue policy and famine.

INDIA. up of the means of subsistence; and the latter is necessarily followed by distress and destitution. There is no industry in the world the sudden interruption or the temporary destruction of which is not attended by impoverishment and suffering; and there is no country in the world, where the meteorological and economic conditions are at all similar to those prevailing in India, that could by any land revenue system that might possibly be devised escape the same results.

4. Nevertheless, if prevention of the inevitable consequences of drought be an ideal incapable of attainment, mitigation is manifestly an object worthy of the closest attention of the Government. It cannot but be their desire that assessments should be equitable in character and moderate in incidence; and that there should be left to the proprietor or to the cultivator of the soil—as the case may be—that margin of profit that will enable him to save in ordinary seasons and to meet the strain of exceptional misfortune. Such aspirations must be even more forcibly impressed upon the Government at a time when, owing to the prolonged continuance of adverse circumstances, the agricultural population has passed through a phase of almost unequalled depression, and needs the fullest measure of encouragement that it is possible to afford. It is with the object of demonstrating how far these objects are capable of being realised under the existing system, or to what extent the latter is susceptible of improvement, that the Governor General in Council now proceeds to examine the general charges that have been brought against it, and the individual modifications that are proposed.

INDIA.

The two kinds of settlement: Permanent and Temporary.

5. By the ancient law of the country—to quote the opening words of Regulation XIX of 1793, by which the Permanent Settlement was created in Bengal—the ruling power is entitled to a certain proportion of the produce of every acre of land unless it has transferred or limited its rights thereto. The procedure by which that proportion is determined is styled a Settlement of the Land Revenue. A Settlement is of two kinds: permanent, by which the demand of the State is made fixed and unalterable for ever; temporary, under which the State demand is revised at recurring periods of greater or less duration. Inasmuch as all agricultural land in India must fall within either the permanently-settled or the temporarily-settled areas, it is desirable to consider what are the criticisms or proposals that have been made with reference to each of these two classes. The permanently-settled districts, as is well known, cover the greater part of Bengal, parts of the North-Western Provinces and Madras, and a few other isolated tracts. At an earlier period the school of thought that is represented by the present critics of the Government of India, advocated the extension of the Permanent Settlement throughout India; and although this panacea is no longer proposed, the Government of India are invited by Mr. Dutt to believe that had such a policy been carried into effect 40 years ago, "India would have been spared those more dreadful and desolating famines which we have witnessed in recent years." It is also stated by the latter in his letter upon Land Settlements in Bengal that in consequence of the Permanent

INDIA. Settlement in that province the cultivators are more prosperous, more resourceful, and better able to help themselves in years of bad harvest, than cultivators in any other part of India, that agricultural enterprise has been fostered, cultivation extended, and private capital accumulated, which is devoted to useful industries, and to public works and institutions. The hypothetical forecast above recorded is not rendered more plausible to the Government of India by their complete inability to endorse the accompanying allegations of fact. Bengal, and particularly Eastern Bengal, possesses exceptional advantages in its fertility, in its comparative immunity from the vicissitudes of climate to which other parts of the country are liable, in its excellent means of communication, in its enjoyment of a practical monopoly of the production of jute, and in the general trade and enterprise which radiate from its capital city. But neither these advantages nor the Permanent Settlement have availed to save Bengal from serious drought when the monsoon failure, from which it is ordinarily free, has spread to that part of India. Omitting

Failure of the Permanent Settlement to prevent famine in Bengal.

to notice the frequent earlier famines, that known as the Behar famine of 1873-74 (so called from the part of the Bengal Province most seriously affected) cost the State £6,000,000; while it can be shown that in the famine of 1897 there were at the height of the distress considerably more than ¾ million persons on relief in the permanently settled districts of Bengal, and that the total cost of that famine to the Bengal Administration was R1,08,04,000, or

£720,266 (as compared with a famine expenditure of R98,28,000, or £655,200, in Madras, and R1,26,37,000, or £842,466, in Bombay), and this although the daily cost of relief for each person was less (Re. ·081 in Bengal as compared with Re. ·104 in Madras and Re. ·106 in Bombay). If the figures of persons in receipt of relief in the permanently settled districts of Western Bengal were compared with those of the adjoining temporarily settled districts of the North-Western Provinces, where the conditions were closely similar, it would also be found that the percentage was more than half as high again in Behar as in the North-Western Provinces. The Government of India indeed know of no ground whatever for the contention that Bengal has been saved from famine by the Permanent Settlement, a contention which appears to them to be disproved by history: and they are not therefore disposed to attach much value to predictions as to the benefits that might have ensued had a similar settlement been extended elsewhere. **INDIA.**

Its influence on the condition of the tenantry in Bengal.

6. As regards the condition of cultivators in Bengal, who are the tenants of the landowners instituted as a class in the last century by the British Government, there is still less ground for the contention that their position, owing to the Permanent Settlement, has been converted into one of exceptional comfort and prosperity. It is precisely because this was not the case, and because, so far from being generously treated by the zemindars, the Bengal cultivator was rack-rented, impoverished, and oppressed, that the Government of India felt compelled to intervene on his

INDIA. behalf, and by the series of legislative measures that commenced with the Bengal Tenancy Act of 1859 and culminated in the Act of 1885, to place him in the position of greater security which he now enjoys. To confound this legislation with the Permanent Settlement, and to ascribe even in part to the latter the benefits which it had conspicuously failed to confer, and which would never have accrued but for the former, is strangely to misread history. As for the allegation that the Permanent Settlement has been the means of developing in Bengal an exceptional flow of public-spirited and charitable investment, while the Government of India are proud of the fact that there are many worthy and liberal-minded landlords in Bengal—as there also are in other parts of India—they know that the evils of absenteeism, of management of estates by unsympathetic agents, of unhappy relations between landlord and tenant, and of the multiplication of tenure-holders, or middlemen, between the zemindar and the cultivator in many and various degrees—are at least as marked and as much on the increase there as elsewhere ; and they cannot conscientiously endorse the proposition that, in the interests of the cultivator, that system of agrarian tenure should be held up as a public model, which is not supported by the experience of any civilised country, which is not justified by the single great experiment that has been made in India, and which was found in the latter case to place the tenant so unreservedly at the mercy of the landlord that the State has been compelled to employ for his protecton a more stringent measure of legislation than has been found necessary in temporarily settled areas. It is not in fine in the Permanent Settlement of Bengal that the ryot has found his salvation; it has been in the laws which have been passed by the Supreme Government to check its license and to moderate its abuses. **INDIA.**

7. It is, however, to the temporarily settled districts that the bulk of criticism has been directed, and to this branch of the subject the Governor General in Council will now turn. The two sub-divisions of this category will be successively examined; the zemindari tracts (in some provinces called malguzari and talukdari), where the landlord pays the land revenue to the State, whether he cultivates the land himself or by means of rent-paying tenants; and the ryotwari tracts, where the cultivator pays directly to the State.

The two classes of Temporary Settlements: Zemindari and Ryotwari.

8. The zemindari tenure is the prevailing form of land tenure in the Central Provinces, the North-Western Provinces and Oudh, and the Punjab. The suggestions with regard to it which the Government of India have been invited to consider, are as follows:—

9. It is nowhere clearly stated, but it may be inferred, that in the opinion of their critics some limit should be placed to the amount of rent which the landlord may take from his tenant. The Government of India would have been better pleased had greater prominence and a more indisputable enunciation been given to this proposition, since it is one with which they are in cordial agreement. It does not seem to

Suggested reforms in Zemindari Settlements examined.

(1) Limitation of landlord's enhancement of tenants' rents.

INDIA. them to be consistent that great stress should be laid upon the share of the produce which should be taken by the Government, when it deals directly with the tenant, or with the share of the rental that it should take from the landlord when the latter is the intermediary, while little or no attention is devoted to the rent paid by the cultivator in cases where he happens to pay it to a zemindar. If it is the interests of the ryot that are at stake, and that stand in most urgent need of protection, that protection is not less necessary when his payments are made to a native landlord in the form of rent than when they are made in the form of land revenue to the British Government. Such being the logic of the case, it is with satisfaction that the Government of India can point to the fact that the principles here laid down have been, and are still, the basis of the numerous Tenancy Laws which have been enacted by them in recent years. Mention has already been made of the Tenancy Acts in Bengal. Similar legislation has been carried through for the Central Provinces, and in the North-Western Provinces a Tenancy Law has recently been strengthened in the interest of the ryots. The Government of India will welcome from their critics, upon future occasions, a co-operation in these attempts to improve and to safeguard the position of the tenant which they have not hitherto as a rule been so fortunate as to receive.

(2) Limitation of the State's demand on landlords.

10. The next contention is that where the land revenue is paid to the State by the landlord, the principle adopted in the Saharanpur Rules of 1855, limiting the State demand to one-half

of the rent or assets of the landlord, should be universally applied. Here it seems to the Governor General in Council to be necessary to utter a word of caution, which will be found to apply both to the present and still more to some of the subsequent proposals that will come under examination. These proposals contain the common suggestion of definite mathematical fractions of rent or produce, as the maximum share of Government. The Governor General in Council, while far from denying the possible utility of such standards as general principles of guidance, must guard himself from any acceptance of them as hard-and-fast rules of practice. It is impossible to apply any one criterion to all parts or classes in one province, much more so to the whole of India. The conditions of uniformity which would alone justify uniformity of treatment, are in many cases lacking. A rule of division which would be light in one case might be harsh in another; a proportion of rent or of produce which would leave a wide margin of profit in one part of India might be vexatious elsewhere. While, therefore, general principles may reasonably be formulated in order, as far as possible, to secure unity and continuity of policy, the Government of India would deprecate, in any case, the hasty acceptance of too precise mathematical formulæ, as likely to tie the hands of their officers, and to produce rigidity, instead of elasticity, in Land Revenue administration. **INDIA.**

11. Subject to the above qualification, the Governor General in Council now proceeds to examine the suggestion of a 50 per cent. limitation of the Government

INDIA. share in the landlord's rental. It has already been stated on the authority of Regulation XIX of 1793 that the ruling power in India has always, by the ancient law of the country, been entitled to share in the produce of the soil. Regulation II of 1793 pointed out that the Government share of that produce was fixed by estimating the rents paid by the tenants, deducting therefrom the cost of collection, allowing to the landlords one-eleventh of the remainder as their share, and appropriating the balance or ten-elevenths, as the share of the State. But if this was the ostensible basis upon which the Permanent Settlement in Bengal was originally made, and if, at the commencement of their fiscal administration, the Government of India thus followed indigenous custom in assessing the revenue they soon began to moderate the severity of the practice. It is unnecessary to trace here in detail the process of mitigation. It will suffice to say that long before the late century had reached its midway point the demand of the State upon the landlord had been limited to two-thirds of the net assets. About the middle of the century, *i.e.*, before the Mutiny, the question of the relative shares of the State and of the landlords in the net produce of the soil came again under careful review in Northern India; and the result of this further consideration of the matter was embodied in what are known as the "Saharanpur Rules" (so called because they were issued in connection with the resettlement of the land revenue of the Saharanpur district of the North-Western Provinces). The Settlement Rules previously in force authorised the

Ancient right of the State to a share of the produce of the soil.

demand of two-thirds of the net produce of an estate, or **INDIA.** rather of its value in money, as the Government share in respect of land revenue. The Saharanpur Rules, issued in

The Saharanpur Rules.

1855, laid down "not that the revenue of each estate is to be fixed as one-half of the net average assets, but that in taking these assets with other data into consideration, the Collector will bear in mind that about one-half, and not two-thirds as heretofore, of the well-ascertained net assets should be the Government demand." These orders have since remained the accepted canon of assessment on landlords' estates in the North-Western Provinces, and they continued to govern assessments in the adjacent districts of the Central Provinces, until the constitution of the latter as a separate administration in 1862. But for the assessment of the Nagpur district of the Central Provinces, which had been escheated to the Government of India in 1854, assessment up to 60 per cent. of the gross rental had been permitted by separate orders issued in 1860, owing partly to the undesirability of introducing too sharp a revulsion from the practice of the previously existing native administration, partly to the great extent of uncultivated land, which enabled the landlords largely to increase their incomes while the Settlement was running its course.

Progressive reduction of the State's share under British rule.

12. It is, therefore, an erroneous assumption that what is known as the "half assets rule" anywhere bound the Government to take as its land revenue from a district as a whole no more than 50 per cent. of the actual

INDIA. rental of the land owners. Not only were there no compulsory orders in the matter, but the construction placed on the word "assets" at the time, and for many years later, permitted the Settlement Officer to look beyond the actual cash rental, and to take into consideration prospective increases of income, to assume a fair rent for land held by tenants enjoying privileges as against the landlord, and to consider the profits of *sir* or home-farm cultivation (where the land was held entirely by cultivating proprietors) as well as the rental value of home-farm lands. Hence it arose that the assessments taken, though amounting only to about 50 per cent. of the nominal assets, absorbed as a rule a considerably higher proportion of the realised rental. In recent years, however, there has been a steady movement in the downward direction. In the North-Western and other zemindari provinces prospective assets have been excluded from consideration; allowances have been made for improvements made by the landlord, for precariousness of cultivation, and for local circumstances; and the revenue has been fixed at a share of the actual income of the proprietor, his income including a fair rental value for the lands which he farms himself, or assigns on privileged terms to tenants. The share to be taken as land revenue by Government is thus being brought down in the North-Western Provinces—in the interests of the proprietor—to an average of less than 50 per cent., while in the re-settlement of Oudh, now on the point of completion, the average falls below 47 per cent. In the Central Provinces, which have been for a shorter period under British rule, and where much higher assessments, amounting in some cases to over 75 per cent. of the actual income, were inherited from the Mahratta Government, there has been a progressive reduction of assessment; but it has not yet reached the very moderate level that is common in the North-Western Provinces. In time, as population increases, and more labour and expenditure are devoted to cultivation, the share taken by Government may be expected still further to diminish, and already (as pointed out in the Report from the Central Provinces) three of the districts in the north of the provinces have recently been re-assessed (from a desire to limit the sudden enhancements that result from long-term settlements) at less than 50 per cent. of the rental. In Orissa the gradual reduction of the Government proportion has been even more striking. In 1822 it was authoritatively declared to be 83·3 of the assets; in 1833 it was lowered to 70—75 per cent.; in 1840 to 65 per cent., with a permissive reduction to 60 per cent., while at the re-settlement just concluded, it has been brought down to 54 per cent. In the Punjab, where proprietary cultivation is common, and where the maximum land revenue that may be taken is the "estimated value of half the net produce"—the principal guide to this being the rents that are paid by neighbouring tenants-at-will—the calculations given in the official reply reveal yet lower proportions. Assessments of 45, 39, 35, and 25 per cent. are recorded in particular cases, and the general average is shown not to exceed 45 per cent. of the net income. INDIA.

13. From this summary it results that while the standard of 50 per cent. has nowhere been laid down as a

INDIA. fixed and immutable prescription, there has been, and there is, a growing tendency throughout temporarily settled zemindari districts to approximate to it, and in special circumstances a very much lower share is taken. It does not appear to the Government of India to be necessary to issue fresh regulations upon a matter in which their general policy is so clear and where, save in exceptional cases, to be justified by local conditions, uniformity of practice is now so common.

Suggested reforms in Ryotwari Settlements: Revenue to be a definite share of gross produce.

14. The Governor General in Council now passes to the consideration of those parts of the country where, under temporary settlements, the ryotwari or peasant proprietary form of tenure prevails, and where the cultivator pays directly to the State. The principal illustrations of this category are the greater parts of the Presidencies of Madras and Bombay, and the Provinces of Burma and Assam. The recommendations that have been made with regard to these areas will now be examined. It should be noted, however, that there is not complete identity between the two forms of the first recommendation that falls to be noticed; for whereas the memorial sets forward the proposition that "the Government demand should be limited to 50 per cent. of the value of the net produce, after a liberal deduction for cultivation expenses has been made, and should not ordinarily exceed one-fifth of the gross produce, even in those parts of the country where, in theory, one-half of the net is assumed to approximate to one-third of the gross produce," Mr. Dutt, when speaking

for himself, urges that "the impracticable rule of realising one-half the net produce or one-third the gross produce be abandoned, and the rule of fixing one-fifth the gross produce as the maximum of rent be adopted." It appears, therefore, that whereas Mr. Dutt as a signatory of the memorial does not contemplate the complete abandonment of the net produce standard, he yet, when petitioning on his own behalf, describes it as impracticable, and urges its disappearance. Moreover, in the latter capacity, he advocates a further mathematical criterion, namely, that while the maximum of one-fifth the produce should not be exceeded in the case of any single holding, the average land revenue for a whole district, including wet and dry lands, should be limited to one-tenth, as alleged to be the case in Northern India. **INDIA.**

Danger of arithmetical standards.

15. These fractional standards illustrate the remarks which were made a little earlier as to the danger of laying down hard-and-fast lines; and they also indicate the arbitrary and inelastic nature of the system which the Government of India are now invited to introduce. When Mr. Dutt suggests the analogy of Northern India, which is under an entirely different form of tenure, he appears to confuse rent with revenue, for he has elsewhere said that in Bengal and Northern India the average rents paid by the cultivator to the landlord are equivalent to one-fifth or 20 per cent. (not 10 per cent.) of the gross produce; whereas he here recommends that in Southern India the average proportion should be limited to one-tenth, or 10 per cent. Why there should be this distinction is not made clear.

INDIA.

Impracticability of the suggestion that the land revenue should be fixed at a share of the gross produce.

16. The Government of India believe it to be an entirely erroneous idea that it is either possible or equitable to fix the demand of the State at a definite share of the gross produce of the land. There is great practical difficulty in ascertaining what the average produce is. It is dependent upon a number of varying factors, such as the industry and resources of the cultivator, the nature of the crop, the capacity, security, and situation of the holding, and the chance of the seasons. The share of the gross produce which a crop can afford to pay must stand in close relation and in inverse proportion to the amount of expenditure which has been required to grow it, and this will vary very greatly, for instance, in the cases of sugarcane and of wheat. In zemindari districts, accordingly, rental value, and not produce, has for the last 50 years been adopted as the basis of assessments, although the latter have commonly been checked by comparison with produce, with the result, as a rule, of showing that, judged by that standard, they were unreasonably low. In the ryotwari provinces of Madras and Burma, the attempt has been made to fix assessment rates in accordance with produce, but the rules giving effect to this principle fence it round with so many qualifications as practically to involve its abandonment. It is now nearly 40 years since the alternative standard of half the net produce was introduced in Madras, the reason being that the gross produce standard, while it favoured the more fertile, pressed with extreme severity upon the poorer lands. But even the standard thus adopted has not been worked up to in practice. There and elsewhere the

net produce has been valued at much less than the current money rates, the outturn per acre deduced from crop experiments has been notoriously underestimated, and liberal deductions have been made for unprofitable cultivation, distance from markets, and vicissitudes of season, so that the rates in actual use for assessment are considerably below the nominal share. There has been a similar reduction in the theoretical measure of assessment, which is also one-half of the net produce, in Burma; and the last assessment report received from the Hanthawaddy district shows that the assessment actually imposed fell short of a quarter (not one-half) of the net produce by nearly 20 per cent. The truth is that assessment of land revenue is subject to so many complicated and varying conditions that any attempt to reduce it to an exact mathematical proportion either of gross or of net produce would not only be impracticable, but would lead to the placing of burdens upon the shoulders of the people, from which, under a less rigid system, if sympathetically administered, they are exempt. Nor must the influence of the personal equation be ignored. Those who are familiar with the realities of assessment know well that among Settlement Officers there is a growing inclination towards leniency of assessment; and that this spirit is encouraged by the avowed policy of Government, of the considerateness of which the progressive reduction of the State demand already indicated affords conclusive proof. The more the officers of Government know of the people, and the more intimate their mutual relations become, the less likelihood is there of severity in the enforcement of public dues. In no official **INDIA.**

INDIA. relation does a member of the Public Service come into such close contact with the people as in Settlement work; and it cannot be his desire to aggrieve those among whom he is spending some of the most laborious years of his life, or to initiate a Settlement which, after a short interval, will break down. Every natural instinct and every recent injunction of the Supreme Government urge him to reasonableness and moderation.

Its effects if adopted.

17. Nothing, indeed, can be more clear than that, while the net produce rule itself calls for, and is habitually subject to, modifications in the interest of the cultivator, the gross produce standard recommended by the memorialists would, if systematically applied, lead to an increase of assessments all round. The Report from the Central Provinces shows that the proportion to produce of the gross rental ranges from one-sixth to one-fourteenth, and that the enforcement of any such standard would double the liabilities of the ryots. The Bengal Report gives statistical reasons for believing that rents are generally much below one-fifth of the gross produce, and indicates that ryots on Government temporarily settled estates are, judged by this standard, better off than under proprietors with a permanent settlement. The Madras reply says that, "if Government took one-fifth of the real gross produce from its ryots, it would fully double its present land revenue, exclusive of cesses, but inclusive of the total charge for water." In the ryotwari tracts of the Punjab the proportion taken by Government nowhere exceeds one-fifth of the gross produce, and is more often one-seventh or one-eighth, or

even less. Similar conclusions are borne out by the Report of the recent Famine Commission (paragraphs 261—268), in which it is stated, as the result of special enquiries, that in the Central Provinces the incidence of land revenue is less than 4 per cent. of the average value of the produce, that in Berar it is about 7 per cent., in Ajmer about 10 per cent., in the Hissar district of the Punjab 3½ per cent., in other parts of the Punjab 7 per cent., except in the Delhi district, where it is 10 per cent.; in the Deccan probably above 7 per cent., in the Panch Mahals 5 per cent.; and in Gujarat alone (where the profits on cultivation are very high) 20 per cent., or the equivalent of the one-fifth pleaded for in the memorial. Since then it has been conclusively established that, under the existing practice, the Government is already taking much less than it is now invited to exact, and since the average rate, so far from showing an inclination to enhancement, is everywhere on the downward grade, the Governor General in Council is unable to accept a proposal which could only have consequences the very opposite of those which are anticipated by its authors. **INDIA.**

The term of settlement. Suggested minimum of 30 years.

18. The next recommendation to which the attention of the Government of India has been drawn is that no term of settlement in temporarily settled districts should be for a shorter period than 30 years. The history of settlements may briefly be summarised as follows. In Bombay the 30 years' term was introduced by the Court of Directors so far back as 1837. From there it was extended to Madras and the North-Western Provinces, where it has been the standard period for the last half century. The

INDIA. same principle was followed in an extension of the Orissa Settlement in 1867, and in confirming most of the settlements made in the Central Provinces between 1860 and 1870. But it never came into general use in the Punjab, where, in the greater part of the province, the shorter term of 20 years has been the recognized rule. The question was exhaustively examined in 1895, when it was finally decided by the Secretary of State that 30 years should continue to be the ordinary term of settlement in Madras, Bombay, and the North-Western Provinces, that in the Punjab 20 years should be the general rule (30 years being admitted in some cases), and in the Central Provinces 20 years also. A 30 years' term has been adopted for the recent re-settlement of Orissa. In backward tracts, such as Burma and Assam, and in exceptional circumstances such as exist in Sind, shorter terms are permitted. The reasons for this differentiation are familiar and obvious. Where the land is fully cultivated, rents fair, and agricultural production not liable to violent oscillations, it is sufficient if the demands of Government are re-adjusted once in 30 years, *i.e.*, once in the lifetime of each generation. Where the opposite conditions prevail, where there are much waste land, low rents, and a fluctuating cultivation, or again where there is a rapid development of resources owing to the construction of roads, railways, or canals, to an increase of population, or to a rise in prices, the postponement of re-settlement for so long a period is both injurious to the people, who are unequal to the strain of a sharp enhancement, and unjust to the general tax-payer,

Considerations which determine the term of settlement.

who is temporarily deprived of the additional revenue to which he has a legitimate claim. Whether these considerations, justifying a shorter term of settlement than 30 years, apply with sufficient force to the Punjab and the Central Provinces at the present time; and, if they do apply at the present time, whether the force of their application will diminish with the passage of time, are weighty questions to which careful attention will be given by the Government of India upon a suitable occasion. **INDIA.**

Improvements in procedure rendering re-settlements less disturbing.

19. It may further be pointed out that many of the objections at one time urged to revisions of settlement have become, or are fast becoming, obsolete. The process of re-settlement itself is more rapid and less disturbing than was formerly the case. Where the re-settlement of a district thirty years ago lasted for six or eight years, the work is now, in a large district, usually completed in about four years and often in less. The improvement in the village records, and their punctual correction and maintenance up to date, have to a large extent obviated the necessity for detailed surveys, and for those local enquiries by subordinate officers which were in former times a fruitful source of harassment and extortion to the agricultural community. The aim of the existing policy is to exclude underlings from all connection either with the work of assessment or with the preliminary investigations leading up to it, and to devolve upon the Settlement Officer and his gazetted assistants all the negotiations with the people. The Government of India and the Local Governments will always be ready to carry this policy to further developments, their

INDIA.

object being to simplify the maintenance, correct and up to date, of the village papers, and thereby to secure an authentic record of the rights and privileges of the people, as well as a trustworthy instrument for the speedy determination of the fair claims of the Government on the land.

Exemption of improvements from assessment.

20. Again, the principle of exempting from assessments such improvements as have been made by private enterprise, though it finds no place in the traditions of the past, has been accepted by the British Government, and is provided for by definite rules, culminating, in the case of the Bombay Presidency, in legal enactments which secure to the cultivator in perpetuity the whole of the profit arising not only from such irrigation works as private wells or tanks, but from the minor improvements which would count for an increase in assessment under a system of reclassification of the soil. The Madras ryots have a recognized right to enjoy for ever the fruit of their improvements, and the exemption of wells, irrigation channels, and tanks which are private property is provided for by executive orders. Minor improvements are also protected, as in Bombay, by the permanent recognition of a land classification once fairly effected. In zemindari provinces, where the revenue is temporarily assessed on estates as a whole, and not on each particular plot of land composing them, the State has not similarly surrendered its right to all share in improvements in which the capacity of the soil plays a part with the industry or outlay of the cultivator. But the principle followed has been that additional assessments should not be imposed on these grounds until the private labour or capital expended upon them has

had time to reap a remunerative return. In the Punjab and Bengal the term of exemption has been fixed, without reference to the term of settlement, at 20 years for masonry wells, 5 years for canal distributaries, and 10 years for other irrigation works. In the North-Western Provinces and the Central Provinces, irrigation works not constructed by Government are freed for the term of settlement next following their construction, the average period of exemption being 45 years in the former and 30 years in the latter provinces. The rules of all provinces provide for the grant of longer terms of exemption in special cases. This summary of existing procedure reveals a variety in practice which it is not possible to reduce to complete uniformity. It is the intention, however, of the Government of India, in consultation with the Local Governments, to take the whole matter into consideration, with a view to the framing of rules that may stimulate the expenditure of private capital upon the improvement of the land, and secure to those who profit by such opportunities the legitimate reward of their enterprise.

Effect of long as against short settlements in increasing resources of the people.

21. The question of the effect upon the domestic life of the community of long as against short settlements has been the subject of much discussion. It may be regarded as certain that long-term settlements leave more money to the people, however large be the revenue enhancement at the close. On the other hand, short-term settlements, which are the familiar practice of Native Rulers, excite less discontent, when not associated with inquisitorial proceedings. An increase of liabilities which comes once in a generation

INDIA. is said by some to be more acutely resented than one which has been rendered familiar by more frequent repetition. Upon this point it is difficult and perhaps unnecessary to pronounce: attention should, however, be called to a concession made by the Government with a view to reducing its own share of the produce, and leaving more to the landholder. Formerly the basis of assessment was the anticipated average yield of the land during the coming period of settlement. Now it is the actual yield at the time of assessment, so that the landowner enjoys to the full any new advantages that may accrue either from his own outlay or from outside circumstances, in the interval before the next revision is made. Assessment upon actual, as distinct from prospective, assets has thus become a cardinal principle of the land revenue policy of Government.

Suggested limitation of Government enhancements to rise in value due to (1) State improvements, (2) rise in prices.

22. In the foregoing paragraphs a partial answer has been given to the next prayer of the memorialists that in ryotwari tracts "there should be no increase in assessments except in cases where the land has increased in value, (1) in consequence of improvements in irrigation works carried out at the expense of Government; (2) on account of a rise in the value of produce, based on the average prices of the thirty years next preceding such revision." The first of the above provisos is not included in Mr. Dutt's independent recommendation, which is to the effect that no enhancement be anywhere permitted at a new settlement except on the ground of an increase of prices. The entire contention will now be examined. The principle that the State in India has a right to share in the

produce of the land carries with it the right to share in any increment of the produce or its value. In the case of increments resulting from the expenditure of private labour or capital, this right, as has already been pointed out, has been altogether waived in some provinces, and materially limited in others. But it can scarcely be contended that such a surrender should equally apply to improvements produced by the growth of population, by the gradual development of the country, by the introduction of new staples or by an increase in the productivity of the soil and in the value of its produce, more particularly if the latter are themselves the result of an expenditure upon irrigation or communications that has been incurred by the State. The concession to the landlord or the tenant of a complete monopoly of the profits of all improvements of the soil in perpetuity, whether created by himself or not, would be a doctrine not merely economically unsound, but without any foundation in native custom or any precedent in history. What happens in practice is this: in zemindari areas the claims of Government to a share in the increasing value of the land are adjusted by a periodical settlement with the landlords for its portion of the rental, subject to a not infrequent sacrifice, in the interest of the tenants, of the fractions which might fairly be claimed. The possibility of making prices the basis of assessment in these tracts was carefully considered, and was finally negatived by the Secretary of State in 1885. Some interesting information may be derived from the Bengal Report as to the inequality of assessment which has resulted in that province from the non-interference of Government during the past century;

INDIA. and from this may be deduced how uneven a settlement would become that was only liable to revision by an all-round enhancement or deduction. Whatever be the case as regards zemindari districts, it is now, however, urged that in ryotwari areas no ground of enhancement but a rise in price should in future be allowed. Attention has already been called to the limitation that has been placed by Government upon the discretion of its officers in respect of changes in land classification as a possible basis of enhancement. In Bombay no change in a classification once definitely accepted is permitted by the law. In Madras, though the Government of India, acting under the instructions of the Secretary of State in 1885, have declined to give a pledge against future revisions of classification, they have intimated their cordial acceptance of the principle that the existing classification, if found to be in the main equitable, shall, on re-settlement, not be disturbed. In these circumstances, to deny the right of the State to a share in any increase of values except those which could be inferred from the general tables of price statistics—in itself a most fallacious and partial test—would be to surrender to a number of individuals an increment which they had not themselves earned, but which had resulted, partly from the outlay of Government money or great public works, such as canals and railways, partly from the general enhancement of values produced by expanding resources and a higher standard of civilisation.

Limitation of cesses on land.

23. The concluding proposal, which it is the duty of the Governor General in Council to examine, and which, in slightly different shapes, finds a place in both memorials, is that no cesses

should be imposed on the rental of land, except for purposes directly benefiting the land, and that a limit should be fixed beyond which it may not be permissible to surcharge the land tax with local taxation. These cesses, which are levied for the construction and repair of roads, the upkeep of schools and dispensaries, and other similar duties appertaining to Local Government Boards, are generally assessed on the assets or rental value, since the land revenue would, in many provinces, be an unfair basis of distribution. The rate in force in Bengal is 6¼ per cent. on the rental, and this rate is taken as a fair standard by Mr. Dutt when speaking for himself. When associated with the other memorialists, he admits that the maximum rate may be as high as 10 per cent., a proportion which, as a matter of fact, is nowhere exceeded. But before going into this question, the Governor General in Council desires to record an emphatic dissent from the opinion that primary education is not a proper object of local taxation, and that such taxation should be limited to objects directly connected with the land. The aim of local taxation is the benefit of the community, and the spread of elementary education amongst the cultivating classes is the surest preventive of the carelessness which allows so large a proportion of the increased value that settled government and improved communications have given to the produce of agricultural industry, to slip through the fingers of the people. INDIA.

Present incidence of Local Rates.

24. In the ryotwari provinces of Bombay and Madras and in Coorg the incidence of the Local Rates (for roads and schools) is precisely that in force in Bengal. This comparison

NDIA. involves the assumption that ryotwari revenue is the equivalent of rent; but, as a matter of fact, the extent to which sub-letting prevails in ryotwari provinces indicates that the revenue is substantially below the rental value, and the Local Rates are consequently below the Bengal level. In Lower Burma the Local Rates amount to 10 per cent. and in Assam to 8.3 per cent. on the ryotwari revenue. Though higher than elsewhere, they are within the maximum suggested in the memorial. In the Punjab they are equivalent to 5.2 per cent. on the rental value. In no other provinces do they exceed 4 per cent. In the North-Western Provinces they are charged at 6 per cent; but two-fifths of the proceeds are devoted to the maintenance of the village watch, which in Bengal and other parts is a charge upon special contributions assessed and collected apart from the Local Rates.

Responsibility of village communities for maintaining rural officers.

25. It may be objected, however, that the rates which are levied for Local Self-Government purposes are not the only extra charges imposed upon the population, and that count should also be taken of the sums payable by them for the remuneration of the village officers—the watchman, the headman, and the accountant. The support of this village staff has been a charge on the community from time immemorial. In the Central Provinces and Bombay watchmen are still remunerated, according to ancient custom, by grants of land and by fees collected by them directly from the people. Elsewhere they are

supported by the proceeds of a cess to which in some INDIA.
provinces non-agriculturists not unreasonably subscribe. The headman is a functionary of more importance in ryotwari than in zemindari villages, and, except in Madras, Sind, and Coorg, his remuneration in ryötwari provinces has been accepted in whole or in part as a charge upon the land revenue which he collects. In the zemindari provinces, the proprietor of a village is also its headman, but where there are several sharers in the proprietorship of a village, one or more of their number represent the remainder, and have a right to a commission on the revenue payable through them, the rate being generally 5 per cent. This represents a communal arrangement of very long standing. The village accountant's functions have been of late years considerably modified by his employment in the maintenance of a connected system of agricultural statistics for his village. This addition to his duties has been acknowledged in some provinces by grants towards his remuneration from the public revenues, but elsewhere than Bombay, Berar, Burma, and Assam, a cess provides, at all events, a part of his salary. The Governor General in Council does not consider that these customary contributions towards the maintenance of the staff of village officers can be classed as local taxation without some important qualifications. The commission paid in zemindari areas by proprietors to their representatives is in no sense a tax, and it is necessary, of course, to exclude from the watchman cess the contribution made in some provinces by non-agriculturists before adding it to the charges on the agricultural population. Assuming, however, that, subject

INDIA. to these deductions, the maintenance of village officers should be accounted as taxation, it is a noteworthy fact that in no provinces but Sind, Madras, and Coorg does local taxation exceed the maximum limit suggested in the memorial, the incidence in these provinces being respectively 12¼, 10¾, and 13½ per cent. on the ryotwari revenue. There can be little doubt that it would be substantially lower if calculated on the true rental value. The general conclusion of the Government of India is that there is no reason for thinking that local taxation, if properly distributed, is on the whole either onerous or excessive, while, as a general rule, it already falls short of the limit which the memorialists would propose to fix. But there are grounds for suspecting that the distribution is often unfair; and that the landlords shift on to the tenants that share of the burden which is imposed by the law upon themselves. In the present backward condition of so many of the people, it is not possible effectively to redress this injustice: and the question presents itself whether it is not better, as opportunities occur, to mitigate imposts which are made to press upon the cultivating classes more severely than the law intended. The Government of India would be glad to see their way to offer such relief.

General conclusions as to burden of local taxation.

26. But the burdens of which complaint is made are by no means confined to the legal cesses, which, after all, are few in number and strictly limited in amount. There are also, in some zemindari tracts, a number of practically unauthorized village cesses, of which no mention has been made by the

Illegal cesses exacted by landlords.

critics of the existing system, but which are well-known to all those who are familiar with the economy of rural life in India. In many cases these unrecognized and often undesirable imposts exceed the total of the cesses levied under the British administration. Their imposition was prohibited by the Regulation of 1793, and ever since that date has been steadily discountenanced by the Government of India, as vexatious to the ryot and detrimental to the successful cultivation of the soil. Their complete suppression by the action of Government is not practicable in the present state of education among the agricultural classes. But the subject is one to which the friends of the ryot might appropriately devote their concern, and in which their exertions might be of much use in supplementing the opposition of Government to a wholly illegitimate form of exaction. **INDIA.**

Detailed examination of alleged connection of revenue assessments with the famine-resisting resources of the people.

27. The Governor General in Council has now reviewed the particular suggestions of Mr. Dutt and the memorialists. There remains to be noticed the underlying idea by which they have all alike been animated, and which, in some parts of the former's writings, has found definite expression. It is the theory that the amount of the land revenue taken by the Government of India, in one form or another, from the people is mainly responsible for famine, with its corollary that, were the assessments diminished, famine would be less frequent, or that at least, when they do occur, they would cause infinitely less suffering. The Governor General in Council does not believe that countenance to this theory can be derived either from

INDIA. the recorded facts of history, or from the circumstances of the present day. The evidence that has been adduced in this Resolution testifies to a progressive reduction of assessments, extending throughout the last century, and becoming more instead of less active during its second half. If then the severity of famine be proportionate to the weight of assessments, the famines in the earlier part of the 19th century ought to have been incomparably more serious than towards its close; whereas the contention is familiar that the reverse has been the case. Again, the contention that in recent famines the parts of India that suffered most severely were the parts that were most highly assessed, finds (with the exception of Gujarat, which had not been seriously famine-stricken for a century and was soft and unprepared) no support in fact, and was expressly disowned by the recent Famine Commission. It is conclusively disproved in the case of the Central Provinces by the evidence of the Chief Commissioner that, in the famine of 1899-1900, the districts which felt the famine pressure most acutely were those which had been exempted from paying the revised assessments, introduced at the previous revision; while the districts that suffered most from the famine of 1896-1897 were those in which there had been no enhancement for 40 years.

Agricultural losses resulting from famine.

28 The fallacy in question is the result of an imperfect appreciation of the smallness of the land revenue compared with the enormous losses resulting from a widespread failure of crops. It has been estimated that in the Central Provinces the agricultural classes have lost 40 crores of

rupees, or more than 26 millions sterling, during the past **INDIA.** seven years—an amount equivalent to the total land revenue of 50 years; while seven years' land revenue would be required to recoup the State for its famine expenditure in these provinces since the year 1896. Similar calculations could be made with regard to the other famine-smitten provinces. It is clear that no reduction of the land revenue demand, short of its total abolition and not even its abolition itself, could enable any community to hold up its head against a calamity so vast and so appalling.

Probable effects of an abatement of the land revenue on the resources of the people.

29. It is not of course disputed that if the Government were largely to abate its demand, and if the amount of such abatement were fairly distributed amongst the cultivating classes and were saved up by them, instead of being thoughtlessly spent, or absorbed by an increase of population, or appropriated by a particular section, a reserve would be created that might enable those classes better to withstand the losses caused by failure of the rains. But, unfortunately, neither in the past nor in the present circumstances of the country can any warrant be found for the belief that the revenue so relinquished by Government would constitute a famine relief fund in the hands of the people. Experience has shown that excessive leniency of the kind in question re-acts prejudicially upon the industry of the agricultural classes, while it encourages the transfer of the soil to money-lenders and middlemen, who swallow the profits intended for the cultivators, and reduce the latter to a condition resembling serfdom. In illustration a reference may be made to Behar, which is permanently

INDIA. settled at a very light revenue, estimated as equivalent to a concession of at least 80 lakhs of rupees a year to the inhabitants. These advantages, however, have been monopolised by the land-owning section of the community, while the Behar tenants remain among the most heavily rented in India; and as the experience of two famines in the last 30 years has shown, have displayed the least capacity of resistance to the shock.

The classes which suffer from famine.

30. An additional source of error lies in the conception, which is erroneous, that it is from the rent-paying or revenue-paying classes of the agricultural community that the sufferers in famine and the recipients of famine relief are principally drawn. An inspection of any relief works on a large scale, while it will show that the poorer sections of the tenant class are not unrepresented, will also demonstrate that the great majority are not ryots, but labourers on the land, whom the land revenue assessment practically in no way affects.

Theory of connection between land revenue and famines rejected by Famine Commission, 1901.

31. It is noteworthy that the theory which has here been examined, meets with no encouragement at the hands of the latest expert body that has enquired into the facts of the case, *viz.*, the Famine Commission of 1901. After stating what was, in each of the provinces visited by them, the pressure of the land revenue on the soil—in figures which have already been cited—they concluded by saying that except in Bombay, where they regarded it as full, the incidence of land revenue is low in moderate years, and that it should in no way, *per se*, be the cause of indebtedness. It

is unnecessary, on the present occasion, to discuss what are **INDIA.** the secondary causes of famine—for as to the primary, there can be no dispute—and of the poverty and indebtedness which famine brings in its train. But it is manifest that anyone who shuts his eyes to the industrial and economic forces that are at work in India at the present time, and that are patent upon the surface of agrarian life, who does not take into account the ever-increasing subdivision of holdings (arising from the land-hunger of the peasant population and the inveterate reluctance of the ryot to move even to the smallest distance from his natal place), the decline of industrial occupations other than agriculture, the rack-renting to which tenants are subjected by the more inconsiderate class of landlords and especially by middlemen of various degrees, the usurious rates of interest demanded by the money-lending class, the speculative expenditure upon litigation, the proneness to extravagance on festival occasions, and the numerous payments, in the form of petty bribes, among the ryots themselves, but who concentrates his entire gaze upon one aspect alone of their poverty, will carry away a most distorted impression both of the malady which he has set himself to diagnose, and of the remedies which it is in the power or is the duty of Government to apply.

Three possible causes of hardship requiring attention.

32. Before concluding his examination of this problem, the Governor General in Council desires to notice three aspects of the land revenue question involving three possible causes of hardship to the poorer landholder, which seems to him to be of much greater importance than the criticisms which he

INDIA. has so far been engaged in examining. The first of these is the pitch of enhancement; the second is the levy of the same assessment in bad years as in good, on the assumption that savings in the one will meet the losses of the other; the third is the effect of local deterioration upon land revenue payments.

(1) Large and sudden enhancements of revenue.

33. That revenue enhancements must often be large is of course the direct consequence of long-term settlements, and it is, no doubt, because their disturbing effect furnishes an argument for shorter settlements, that a reference to it has not been found in the fore-front of attack. There can be no question of the hardship which a family must experience in finding its income suddenly reduced by a third or even more, as may happen, for instance, when at the end of a term of settlement it is enjoying 75 per cent. of the assets, and re-settlement is made at 50 per cent. The question in the aspect now under consideration is not really affected (as is sometimes assumed) by the grounds on which the enhancement is made: a heavy addition to the assessment is as disturbing if justified by a large increase of cultivation as if resulting from a rise in valuation rates. It may be argued that a family in such a case has profited largely by the enjoyment of income which it would have lost under a shorter term settlement; that it should have saved from its surplus to meet the eventual curtailment of its means; and that the State will find long term settlements exceedingly disadvantageous if it is not only to lose all increment during their currency, but is also to forego part of its dues at their close. But the question must be considered from a practical point

of view, and with reference to the conditions of human nature. The State cannot without hesitation call upon people suddenly to effect a great reduction in their domestic expenditure, however well justified in theory its demand may be. A man will look more to the actual increase of his obligations than he will to the arithmetical standards by which it is justified or determined. If for 30 years he has been paying a land revenue of R1,000 and is called upon to pay R2,000 upon re-settlement, it is small consolation to him to be told that, while the former sum represented 50 per cent. of his former assets, the latter only amounts to 47 per cent. of his assets as they now stand. A reduction in percentages is far from compensating him for an enhancement of burdens.

INDIA.

The remedy applied.

34. To meet such cases, the Government of India desire to lay much stress upon the principle of gradual and progressive enforcement of sudden increases of other than moderate dimensions. The mitigation of a large enhancement by spreading its imposition over a term of years has been a recognized feature in the settlement procedure of Upper India for a long time past, but has not till recently been brought systematically into practice. In 1895 the Government of India, with the concurrence of the Secretary of State, drew general attention to the advisability of making larger use of progressive enhancements. In the North-Western Provinces, very complete effect has already been given to this principle. Similar rules have recently been used in the re-settlement of the Seoni district in the Central Provinces, and the expediency will now be considered of prescribing it

INDIA. for general guidance in those provinces. The rules on this subject contained in the Bengal Settlement Code are of particular application to ryots and tenure-holders; but they admit the use of progressive assessments in the Orissa settlements, though they lay down no definite scheme of progression, and, as a matter of fact, progressive assessments were most liberally granted in those settlements at a loss to the State of nearly 8 lakhs of rupees. In the Punjab, the use of progressive assessments has been discouraged on the ground that, though an appropriate means of easing an enhancement to a large landholder, they are not suitable to the circumstances of the petty proprietors who hold a very large proportion of the land in that province. Large increases in the demand have been commonly avoided by under-assessment. But it seems open to question whether an expedient which has proved serviceable in other parts of India might not be usefully adopted in the Punjab, and the point will be considered, though the effect of progressive assessments in this province would be to raise, not to lower, the Government revenue. Turning now to ryotwari settlements, a rule of the Madras Settlement Code limits to 25 per cent. the enhancement which may be imposed at once, the balance being imposed by annual instalments, each not exceeding 12½ per cent. on the original assessment. This gives a ryot six years in which to accommodate himself to the doubling of his assessment. In the Bombay Presidency also the levy of substantial enhancements is distributed over a term of years, and the maximum enhancement may not exceed double the former amount. Deviations from these rules have, however, apparently been permitted. The procedure of ryotwari settlements renders it difficult for an assessing officer to pay close regard to the circumstances of individuals in framing his proposals, and there is, therefore, the greater need of general rules to obviate hardships in particular cases, even if it be conceded that men who cultivate their own land can support a heavier percentage enhancement than those who subsist upon rental receipts. The question is one that calls for, and will receive, further consideration. **INDIA.**

35. The question of varying the revenue demand to meet the character of the season is similar to the preceding, in that it involves departure from the theory of settlement at the cost of some revenue to the State. In theory the Government revenue represents the sum that may fairly be demanded on an average of seasons, and it is assessed in the belief that cultivators will save from the surplus of good years to meet the deficit in bad. It is manifest, however, that, in tracts where the chances of a bad harvest are high, it must be exceedingly difficult to make allowances for crop failure in framing the assessment rates. And it is also clear that the agricultural classes have not, as a rule, yet learnt to regard a good harvest, not as an occasion for larger expenditure, but as a means of insurance against failure of crops. In truth, to a poor family a short harvest must be a severe calamity. The assessment may absorb but a small share of the gross produce of its land. But its circumstances depend on the net produce, on which the assessment is in higher proportion, and it is obvious that on inferior land a substantial deficiency in the outturn may

(2) Exaction of a fixed demand where produce fluctuates.

INDIA. leave no net produce whatever, so that (in the absence of savings) the assessment can only be paid by borrowing or by stinting the necessaries of life. When such a deficiency is frequent, the rigid demand of the land revenue must add very materially to the hardships endured by a poor and uneducated people.

36. In tracts where great variations from the average of produce are not very frequent, such a demand may be suitable enough, its simplicity and educative effect compensating for the hardship that may be felt in individual cases.

Necessity for greater elasticity.

But where the produce of the land is liable to great and frequent fluctuations owing to failure of irrigation or vicissitudes of season, there is reason to apprehend that a fixed assessment may ruin people before it teaches them. The revenue system of several provinces—notably those of Madras and the Punjab—have recognized the necessity of special arrangements for the remission of revenue for failure of crops on lands capable of being supplied by State irrigation works. In Madras no revenue is charged upon irrigable land the produce of which has not matured owing to the failure of the water-supply; and in the Punjab this principle has received a further development, a deficiency of produce, not amounting to total failure, entitling the ryot to a proportionate abatement of the assessment rate. This system entails an elaborate procedure of crop inspection, and throws much responsibility upon native subordinates. But it has worked well, and is being extended. Unirrigated lands in the ryotwari provinces of Burma and Assam are ordinarily exempt from payment of assessment if left unsown; but these provinces afford almost the only exceptions to the rule that lands which are dependent upon the rainfall pay a fixed assessment irrespective of their produce. During the past twenty-five years the advantages, for lands of this description, of a more elastic system of collection have been urged at various times on the Government of India by very high authority, and have been carefully debated with Local Governments. The weight of opinion has been against change; but this seems to be due partly to the idea that remissions in some years would be balanced by an increase of assessment in others, and partly to the difficulty contemplated in appraising the loss sustained by each of thousands of small holdings. The Government of India freely admit that a fluctuating assessment, in the sense of an assessment without a definite maximum limit in cash, and annually varying with the outturn of the crops, is exceedingly difficult to work with fairness, throws an undesirable amount of power into the hands of subordinate officials, and lacks the influence for thrift which has been the desire of Government to secure in its land revenue policy. It would be a retrograde step, and would imply a reversion to the methods of native rule. But these objections would not apply so forcibly to a system under which the produce of particular harvests would be taken merely to justify the reduction of a standard demand, when such produce falls below a point at which relief is, for general reasons, pronounced to be necessary Experience, gained on a large scale during the past years of distress, indicates that when crop failure affects an entire village, or other separately

INDIA.

INDIA. assessed area, the difficulty of dealing with holdings individually may possibly be met by working from aggregate to detail, by accepting the village, or other such area, as the unit for calculating the amount of reduction to be given, and leaving it to subordinate officials of approved character merely to distribute this amount according to the degree of the loss sustained by individuals. Where a landlord is interposed between the ryots and the Government, his assistance will often be of value in making this distribution, as it is in the interest of his rental collections that it should be fair. Such a system will no doubt offer difficulties of its own, and careful supervision would be indispensable. But the Government of India are not satisfied that, in certain well-known tracts of insecure land, where crops are liable to violent fluctuations in produce, some such plan is not required in the interests of the people, and the question of its introduction will receive fresh consideration. It would be essential that the working of the system should be under the supervision of European officers of experience, at all events during the first years following its introduction.

(3) Expediency of meeting local deterioration with prompt relief.

37. In a country of the size and diversity of India exceptions must occur to the general rule of agricultural progress, and localities are to be found where the conditions are those of actual deterioration. The Governor General in Council has in mind not only the losses of population and of produce which are the unavoidable consequences of severe famine, but the circumstances of tracts and villages which lose ground owing to such special causes

as the effect of decimating epidemics of malarial fever or other conditions, whether connected or not with vicissitudes of season. For some years past the Government of India have insisted upon the importance of the early detection of cases of local deterioration, and have committed to Provincial Departments of Land Records and Agri culture the conduct of systematic enquiries to this end. But the information thus collected has not always been fully utilized, and there have been cases in which a reduction of revenue was not granted till the troubles of the people had been aggravated by their efforts to provide the full fixed demand. It is no doubt true that any alteration of the assessment is in conflict with the terms of the original contract, by which the landholder has undertaken a liability for loss in return for an expectation of profit. But in this matter the interests of the Government are identical with the interests of the people, and it is unwise to exact from impoverished persons a revenue which they really cannot pay, merely because they are under an engagement to pay it. The Governor General in Council is convinced of the desirability of granting prompt relief in these cases, whether they involve tracts or single villages, even though such a course may involve a departure from the strict principles of settlement. The amount of revenue which the concession will cost to the State will be insignificant compared with the advantages obtained in assisting and encouraging an afflicted population. **INDIA.**

Summary of propositions established.

38. In the review of their land revenue policy which has now been brought to a close, the Government of India claim to have established the following propositions, which, for

INDIA. convenience sake, it may be desirable to summarise before concluding this Resolution :—

(1) That a Permanent Settlement, whether in Bengal or elsewhere, is no protection against the incidence and consequences of famine.

(2) That in areas where the State receives its land revenue from landlords, progessive moderation is the key-note of the policy of Government, and that the standard of ·50 per cent. of the assets is one which is almost uniformly observed in practice, and is more often departed from on the side of deficiency than of excess.

(3) That in the same areas the State has not objected, and does not hesitate, to interfere by legislation to protect the interests of the tenants against oppression at the hands of the landlords.

(4) That in areas where the State takes the land revenue from the cultivators, the proposal to fix the assessment at one-fifth of the gross produce would result in the imposition of a greatly increased burden upon the people.

(5) That the policy of long-term settlements is gradually being extended, the exceptions benig justified by conditions of local development.

(6) That a simplification and cheapening of the proceedings connected with new settlements, and an avoidance of the harassing invasion of an army of subordinate officials, are a part of the deliberate policy of Government.

(7) That the principle of exempting or allowing for improvements is one of general acceptance, but may be capable of further extension. INDIA.

(8) That assessments have ceased to be made upon prospective assets.

(9) That local taxation as a whole though susceptible of some redistribution is neither immoderate nor burdensome.

(10) That over-assessment is not, as alleged, a general or widespread source of poverty and indebtedness in India, and that it cannot fairly be regarded as a contributory cause of famine.

The Government of India have further laid down liberal principles for future guidance and will be prepared, where the necessity is established, to make further advance in respect of—

(11) the progressive and graduated imposition of large enhancements;

(12) greater elasticity in the revenue collection, facilitating its adjustment to the variations of the seasons, and the circumstances of the people;

(13) a more general resort to reduction of assessments in cases of local deterioration, where such reduction cannot be claimed under the terms of settlement.

Conclusion.

39. In thus defining their policy, the Government of India would not desire to claim for the land revenue system of British India an exactitude or a freedom from blemish to which it cannot pretend. Historically it owes its immediate origin to

INDIA practices inherited from the most decadent period of native rule, and its form to changes made slowly, and not without mistakes, by men who were aliens to the country, and could only with difficulty, and by slow degrees, assimilate the requirements or enter into the feelings of the people. Where habit and precedent count for more than wisdom, there has been need for caution in reform; and logical completeness or simplicity could not be expected of a system born amid such surroundings, applied to such manifold conditions and to so heterogeneous a population, and subject, in the various stages of its development, to considerations of practical expediency rather than of abstract symmetry or scientific perfection. Indeed the one claim which the Government of India would decline to make for the land revenue system of this country is that it can properly be regarded as a science at all. In no country can land valuation be so described; and India, in spite of records, estimates, and tables is no exception to the rule. A part of the weakness of the criticisms which have been directed against it, arises from the erroneous assumption that it can be regulated by fixed laws, or shaped by arithmetical standards. Assessments cannot be dictated by the theorist in his study; they elude dogmatic treatment, and can only be safely worked out by the Settlement Officer in the village and on the fields. While they may admit of statistical analysis, they are liable to be hampered by premature statistical definition. The true function of Government is to lay down broad and generous principles for the guidance of its officers, with becoming regard to the traditions of the province and the circumstances of the locality, and to prescribe moderation in enhancement, and sympathy in collection. Above all it is its duty to exercise discrimination in the choice of the agents whom it employs for this most critical and responsible of tasks. The Governor General in Council acknowledges with gratitude the services that have been rendered to Government in this respect by a long line of devoted and capable officers, and he believes that the existing system, if pursued upon the lines that have been indicated, is both well suited to the present conditions of the country, and compatible with its future development, and that the revenue which it provides, and which is more lenient in its incidence than at any previous stage of Indian history, is capable of being levied from the people with surprisingly little hardship and without discontent.

CHAPTER II.—SUMMARY OF REPLIES OF THE LOCAL GOVERNMENTS.

In succeeding chapters will be found the replies of the various Local Governments to the particular allegations made with regard to their land revenue system by Mr. Dutt. The Government of India in the Resolution which forms Chapter I have refrained from commenting upon these seriatim, preferring to leave to the local administrations the task of reply. The reproduction of their replies in connected form will, it is hoped, be of public service in resolving doubts which have their origin for the most part in an imperfect acquaintance with the history and development of the land revenue policy of Government. The charges brought by Mr. Dutt against the administration of each province and the rejoinders to them will be here briefly summarized, in sequel to the general exposition which has already been made.

THE CENTRAL PROVINCES.

2. (*a*) *That both in the settlements of 1863—68 and in recent re-settlements the rents of tenants were fixed too high ana much in excess of one-sixth of the gross produce.*—In these provinces rents as a general rule are low. The enhancements resulting from the settlements of 1863—68 were not authoritatively imposed by Government, but were obtained by agreement with the landlords and tenants; in more than half of the number of districts there was practically no rent enhancement, and such

enhancements as were secured were paid without difficulty and left rents at a very low level. During the 30 years' currency of these settlements, rents in some tracts rose largely, in the main as the result of landlords' demands. At the recent re-settlements Government intervened for the reduction of such as seemed oppressively high. The enhancements imposed upon tenants whose rents had not been raised by their landlords were moderate, exceeding 16 per cent. in no district but Sambalpur, where the ryots hold direct from Government, the previous assessment having been almost nominal, and the Settlement Officer's figures only raising the rate per cultivated acre to 5½ annas. The existing rents in no district reach a sixth of the gross produce and in most districts are nearer a tenth. To raise them to a sixth would impose a crushing addition, and the propriety of Mr. Dutt's standard has been publicly repudiated by a gentleman—himself a landholder—who lately represented these provinces in the Imperial Legislative Council.

SUMMARY OF PROVINCIAL REPORTS.

3. (*b*) *That at the settlements of 1863—68 and at recent re-settlements the assessment on the villa proprietors (malguzars) has been unduly severe.*—The settlements of 1863–68 reduced the land revenue of the Central Provinces: during their currency the provinces prospered exceedingly, and there is probably no part of India which showed greater progress in the ensuing 30 years. The value of land rose rapidly, and a large export trade developed. Of the nine districts, the re-settlement of which has recently been completed, in only two does the share of the landlord's income taken by Government exceed that

SUMMARY OF PROVINCIAL REPORTS.

formerly taken, and the increase is, respectively, only from 50 per cent. to 51 per cent. and from 49 per cent. to 50 per cent.; in the other seven districts the share was reduced and in some cases very substantially reduced. In districts which were re-settled before the commencement of the period of agricultural depression, such as Raipur and Bilaspur, the new revenue, though largely exceeding the former revenue, was collected without any difficulty. And, finally, even making allowance for the large proportionate area of poor soil, the incidence of the revenue on cultivation is now exceedingly moderate, in only one district approaching one rupee per acre and in four of the nine districts being less than 6 annas per acre.

4. (*c*) *That by the "half-assets" rule of 1855 the Government was bound to take no more than half of the existing rental as its revenue; and that the common disregard of this rule and its final abrogation by the Government of India in 1888 was a serious injustice to the people.*—The misapprehension on which this criticism is based has already been fully exposed, and a reference may be made to the Minute by the Honourable the Chief Commissioner for a refutation in detail of Mr. Dutt's contention.

5. (*d*) *That the method of land valuation employed for the increase of rents is too complicated to be understood by the people and leads to excessive enhancements.*—Land valuation extending to separate fields or holdings must always be a technical process; it is necessary to employ differential rates for the valuation of land of different qualities, and the arithmetical calculations used in

the Central Provinces merely serve the purpose of a sliding scale to facilitate the adoption of valuations which are not averages for a tract but are suitable to particular villages, and do not exceed present payments by a larger sum than can reasonably be imposed. Fixed scales of average rates are unsuitable for a country of very heterogeneous soils, and, where rents are low and uneven, frequently result in larger increments than the tenants can be asked to pay. The object of the system is to moderate enhancement, not to facilitate it, and it has proved of special service in the reduction of oppressive rents which has formed an important feature of several recent re-settlements. The classification of the land is effected in accordance with distinctions and is expressed in terms which are well known to the people, and their opinion has always been taken into careful account in fixing the relative values of the various soil classes. **SUMMARY OF PROVINCIAL REPORTS.**

6. (*e*) *That over and above the revenue the Government takes cesses amounting to 12½ per cent. on the assets.*—Mr. Dutt has erroneously imagined that cesses are calculated on the assets. They are calculated on the revenue, and under a half asset assessment they amonnt to only 6¼ per cent. on the assets. The addition of cesses to a 60 per cent. assessment raises it to 67½ per cent. and not to between 70 and 80 per cent. as supposed.

7. (*f*) *That the sufferings of the people during the past seven years have been largely the result of over-assessment.*—The districts which show the greatest deterioration—Saugor and Damoh—have during the past seven years not paid even as much revenue as was due from hem under the former settlement, and it has not bee n

SUMMARY OF PROVINCIAL REPORTS. possible to trace any connection between incidence of assessment and the amount of famine relief which has been required.

MADRAS.

8. (*a*) *That the principles accepted during the early years of the ryotwari settlement gave the ryots a right to a permanent settlement which has been unjustly confiscated within the past forty years.*—Save for an unauthorized proclamation issued by the Settlement Officer of the Salem district over 100 years ago, no declaration has been made to the people binding the Government to a permanent settlement. During the discussions which attended the introduction and gradual evolution of the ryotwari settlement, opinions were recorded—in some cases by highly-placed officers of Government—in favour of the eventual permanency of the assessment, and so late as 1862 a guarded adherence to this view was expressed by the Secretary of State. But whatever weight may at the time have attached to these views they remained mere expressions of opinion as to the future policy of Government, and were never given practical effect to or adopted as a principle for immediate application. A necessary preliminary to the introduction of a permanent settlement was the fair initial valuation of the land, and this, under the conditions of a ryotwari settlement, was a task of great difficulty which could only be successfully completed after years of experience and the correction of many unavoidable mistakes. Moreover, during the first-half of the last century, the revenue administration of the country was disturbed by the constant necessity of reducing the demand, and the

introduction of a permanent settlement was barred by the impossibility of stereotyping a revenue which was more than the people could pay. Meanwhile a change took place in the views and policy of the Government, and in 1868 the Secretary of State decided finally against making any declaration that the existing assessments should be permanent. The only claim that the ryots of Madras can urge to a permanent settlement rests on the fact that at one date the eventual making of such a settlement was in contemplation, and no rights were affected by the subsequent decision that the time had not come for limiting the maximum amount of the land revenue.

SUMMARY OF PROVINCIAL REPORTS.

9. (*b*) *That, accepting the principle that the revenue is to be liable to periodic revision, the people have been subjected to unjust enhancement by the decision of 1885 that revenue might be enhanced on other grounds than a demonstrable rise in prices.*—This contention has been considered in paragraph 22 of the Resolution. It is discussed very completely in paragraphs 24 to 33 of the letter from the Madras Board of Revenue (*vide* Chapter VII).

10. (*c*) *That in calculating "net produce" as the basis of assessment an insufficient deduction for cost of cultivation is made from the produce of inferior soils.*—It is extremely difficult to estimate a ryot's expenditure in the cultivation of land of different qualities, but the Madras Government has always safeguarded itself by liberal deductions from the gross produce on other grounds, and, further, by the general adoption of assumed rates which are below those indicated by its calculations. It is obvious that as a

SUMMARY OF PROVINCIAL REPORTS.

general rule, less money or trouble is spent on the cultivation of poor than of good land: it is impossible to frame a scale of charges which is more than approximately correct; but there is nothing to show that the minimum deduction employed to represent cost of cultivation is unduly small. When Mr. Dutt writes that R6 do not cover the cost of cultivation of any culturable soil in India, he must have omitted to consider, for instance, the large area of poor land which is sown after perfunctory ploughing with the smaller millets. It is shown, moreover, that the deductions made from the produce of poor soils, though low in themselves, are relatively higher than those allowed in the case of good soils, and their sufficiency is further illustrated by the fact that accepting the produce estimates as adequate, they would leave little or no margin of profit to a ryot cultivating on the half produce rent which is commonly exacted by sub-leases. But, as has been pointed out in paragraph 16 of the Resolution, these calculations of the produce and expenses of cultivation have never been pressed to their full conclusion, and the exact rates employed are much below those which the "half net produce" principle would justify. It may be remarked that there is no warrant for the statement referred to by Mr. Dutt that the severity of the rates used for assessing poor land has kept three million acres out of cultivation. Under the ryotwari settlement cultivation has increased very largely—by no less than 63 per cent. during the latter half of the past century—and the area now recorded as unoccupied consists in great part of land which is only nominally culturable.

11. (*d*) *That the adoption of 30 per cent. of the gross produce as a maximum limit of assessment has led to over-assessment.*—This proportion of the assumed gross produce was referred to by the Madras Government in 1856 as a measure of assessment. But its adoption as a guide was objected to by the Court of Directors and was finally negatived in 1864. A reversion, according to Mr. Dutt's advocacy, to the gross produce as the basis of assessment and the adoption of a fifth share as the portion of the Government would double the existing revenue, which is calculated to be equivalent to about one-eleventh of the produce of the land, excluding live stock from calculation and the value of such secondary products as straw. **SUMMARY OF PROVINCIAL REPORTS.**

12. (*e*) *That the ryots are unjustly treated by the compulsory levy under the Irrigation Act of 1900 of water-rate for land commanded by an irrigation work.*—Lands are not liable to water-rate unless they necessarily receive sufficient water to grow an irrigated crop and no charge is made when the effect of percolation from a Government irrigation work is merely to facilitate irrigation from wells. The Act was passed after the fullest consideration by both the Madras and the Supreme Governments subject to the condition, insisted upon by the latter, that the water-rate should only be levied in cases where a full and constant supply of water is assured; and its general effect is to relieve the tax-paying community of a share of the cost of State irrigation works by taking a small contribution from the individuals whose land they assist to enrich

SUMMARY OF PROVINCIAL REPORTS.

BOMBAY.

13. (*a*) *That since the country passed under British rule, the land revenue has been continuously raised and is now enormously in excess of its amount at the time of cession.*—A comparison made in the year 1880 showed that the land revenue demand of 1878-79 was very nearly the same as that paid by the country during the latter days of native rule. Enhancements imposed since 1878-79 have raised the demand by 15 per cent. only and the general result is that the re-assessments of the past 30 years have done little more than recover reductions made during the earlier portion of the last century.

14. (*b*) *That the assessments are made without reference to either produce or prices and are excessive, absorbing more than a fifth of the gross produce which is suggested as a maximum limit.*—The process of revenue assessment in Bombay works from aggregate to detail, as must indeed be almost always the case, whatever be the theoretical basis of assessment, when Government is dealing with the cultivators direct. An examination is made of the circumstances of each tract with special reference to those which indicate the increase in the value of land since the last preceding settlement. An estimate is framed of the revenue enhancement which may be fairly imposed on each tract—or group of villages—and this enhancement is distributed over the ryots' holdings according to a holding valuation based on a survey of the area and of the quality of the soil. The valuation is relative, not absolute, and is practically used for distribution only, the actual

amount of the assessment depending on the judgment formed of the aggregate assessment which can be fairly imposed on the tract or group of villages. The total enhancement is not framed with exclusive regard to prices, but prices are among the factors considered, and it can be shown that enhancements have commonly fallen short of the limit which the rise in prices would have justified,—a fact which is borne out by the rapid increase in the value of land, and the desire of the trading and money-lending classes to invest money in its acquisition. No attempt is made to reconcile the assessments with any theoretical share of the gross produce, but it can be shown that, taking the Presidency as a whole, the assessment falls much below a fifth of the gross produce, and is indeed nearer a tenth, even allowing for the chance that one year in every three should prove unfavourable. In the fertile country of Gujarat the assessments are much higher in proportion to produce than elsewhere, and reach their maximum in the Broach district, where they are equivalent to about a fifth of the gross produce *in grain*, but to less than this if allowance be made for the superior value of the cotton crop which covers a large portion of the land. The ryots commonly sublet at a rent of half the gross produce, and the assessment is on the average equivalent to about a fifth of the amount which such a rent would bring the revenue-payer.

SUMMARY OF PROVINCIAL REPORTS.

15. (*c*) *That enhancements on individuals should not exceed the limits imposed by law in Bengal on the judicial enhancements by landlords of tenants' rents, and that the proceedings of assessing officers should be liable to be*

SUMMARY OF PROVINCIAL REPORTS.

called in question in the Civil Courts.—This contention appears to rest on the assumption that the revenue of the State is of no more importance than the income of individuals, and that the State cannot safely be trusted with special powers for the assessment and collection of its taxes. Such powers are taken universally, and without them Government would be impossible. The limitations which the law of some provinces has placed on landlords' rent enhancements are specially directed to increasing the tenants' share of the profits left for division among private interests by the demands of the State, and could not reasonably be adopted to the detriment of the public revenue. Moreover, it is not the case that the Bengal Tenancy Act imposes definite limits to judicial rent enhancements which rest on the ground that the existing rent is below the prevailing rate or has been depreciated by a rise of prices. In the latter case enhancement is not permitted to the full extent of the rise; but under the Bombay settlement procedure such a margin is invariably left when the course of prices is used as a basis for enhancing the revenue. An instance in point is given in paragraph 10 of the Bombay Report.

16. (*d*) *That the land revenue assessment is generally excessive, and that it has impoverished the people and made them resourceless and helpless in years of bad harvests.*—It has already been remarked that the land revenue is much lighter than it would be under Mr. Dutt's proposal of one-fifth of the gross produce. It falls short of the rent at which most of the land is sublet with a profit of from 200 to 300 per cent. on the assessment. That the

rates employed for the assessment of unoccupied land have not checked its reclamation seems evident from the fact that the 40 years ending with 1895-96 witnessed an expansion of 60 per cent. in cultivation—double the rate at which population increased. There is nothing to show that the revenue demand is exorbitant. But its effect on the people has undoubtedly in recent years been seriously complicated by the great uncertainty of the seasons. The regulation of the assessment by an average which allows for this uncertainty assumes that the people will save in good years to meet the losses of bad years,—an assumption which experience has hardly justified. Nevertheless a comparison of the features of last year's famine with those of the famine of 1876-77 shows much that is encouraging. There was but little of the relinquishment of land in the Deccan which was so marked 25 years ago, and the proportion of cultivators who sought relief on famine work was much smaller. Indeed, save in Bijapur and Sholapur, where the failure of crops was complete, the cultivators were able to maintain themselves without State assistance, and in these two districts the proportion seeking relief never exceeded 12 per cent. of their number.

SUMMARY OF PROVINCIAL REPORTS.

THE PUNJAB, THE NORTH-WESTERN PROVINCES AND OUDH, AND BENGAL.

17. There is but little which remains for remark in Mr. Dutt's criticisms so far as they apply to the northern provinces. It is shown that the adoption of one-fifth of the gross produce as the standard of the Government

SUMMARY OF PROVINCIAL REPORTS.

revenue in the Punjab would lead to a very large enhancement in the demand—probably indeed a larger enhancement than in any other province, since the assessment is notoriously light and very much below the pitch justified by the half assets principle in its narrowest sense. The reports from the North-Western Provinces similarly indicate the care which Government has taken not to use this principle to enforce its rights to very large enhancements, the assessments of the eighteen districts which have been re-settled during the last 15 years falling at only 47 per cent. of the assets.

18. In regard to these provinces, Mr. Dutt has raised the expediency of further interference by the State to prevent the ejectment and rack-renting of tenants by their landlords. The relation of landlord and tenant is not of course peculiar to Upper India. Under the ryotwari systems of Bombay, Madras, and Burma a large and increasing proportion of the land is regularly sublet at a rent of half the produce, and the growth of a tenant class who find a means of livelihood between the land and its nominal cultivators is at once a consequence of a moderate land revenue assessment and a proof of its moderation. In the northern provinces of India, however, the employment of tenants for the cultivation of the land is not a comparatively recent outgrowth of our revenue system, but a practice of long standing, generally due to the grant or seizure by private individuals of rights intermediate between those of the actual cultivator and those of the State; and in these provinces the Government has interfered to protect by law, at all events, a section of the tenants from the pleasure of

their landlords. It is of the utmost economic importance that the man who actually cultivates the soil should have the energy and resources to cultivate it well, and it is a matter for regret that in recent settlements in the North-Western Provinces and Oudh it has not been found possible actually to reduce rents which were too exorbitant to be taken as a basis of assessment. But interference in the interest of the tenant-cultivator not uncommonly misses its object; and when, as frequently happens, its result is merely to secure to one class a surplus which is discounted by sub-letting to another, it serves no public end except in so far as it may tend to the general orderliness of the population. Within the last 15 years the Legislature has created a strong body of occupancy tenants in Bengal, has secured the tenantry of Oudh against enhancement at over-frequent intervals and in immoderate proportion, and has practically given to every tenant in the Central Provinces fixity of tenure at a fair rent. Nearly two-thirds of the tenant area in the North-Western Provinces and about a fifth in the Punjab are held by tenants with rights of occupancy. This is not the place to discuss the measure for extending tenant right in the North-Western Provinces which has recently passed the local Legislative Council. As regards the Punjab, the opening given to cultivators by the canal colonization schemes, which are among the most successful features of recent land administration, have probably obviated for some time to come any need of interference to protect the tenant class from the effects of competition for their holdings.

SUMMARY OF PROVINCIAL REPORTS.

CHAPTER III.—BENGAL.

From the Government of Bengal, to the Government of India. No. 838 T.—R., dated the 24th June 1901.

The Lieutenant-Governor directs me to express his regret that there has been so much delay in answering your letter No. 2045, dated the 13th October 1900, which enclosed a copy of Mr. Romesh Chunder Dutt's letter to His Excellency the Viceroy. He has been much engaged with other matters of greater urgency.

Original status of zemindars.

2. He consulted the Board of Revenue and some selected officers on the matter of the letter. Their replies are longer and more diffuse than he expected, and he thinks Mr. Dutt's letter does not require from the Bengal Government a very detailed answer. Mr. Dutt's description of the Bengal zemindars prior to the English conquest is an interesting picture. Its correctness is challenged in all the papers before the Lieutenant-Governor. The controversy as to whether the zemindars, confirmed at the Permanent Settlement, were landholders in the English sense or revenue collectors of varying length of standing is familiar to all the readers of the revenue discussions in Bengal. A somewhat authoritative opinion on it was delivered by the High Court in what is known to Provincial history as the great rent case of 1865, in a sense very different indeed from that presented by Mr. Dutt. But the truth probably lies between the position adopted by the advocates of the two sides of the question, and while there were large numbers of middlemen suddenly converted into landholders, there were also hereditary Chiefs, with all the attributes of proprietorship that were known in their time in India. The discussion was and always will be interesting, but its bearing

BENGAL. on the point which Mr. Dutt seeks to enforce is not very obvious. If the Permanent Settlement recognized as landlords persons who had no legitimate claim to that position the mistake was not greatly to the credit of that measure. If it recognized or endeavoured to recognise the right persons, it shared the aim of every temporary settlement that has been made in India.

3. Again, another of the preliminary assertions of Mr. Dutt, which has been strongly challenged in the papers before the Lieutenant-Governor, does not strike him as very apposite. Mr. Dutt says the revenue taken by Akbar from Bengal, Behar, and Orissa was two crores, whereas the Permanent Settlement imposed on the same area a burden of four crores. The design of his letter is to show that a permanent settlement is the panacea for all rural troubles and sorrows, and it is not very easy to see with what object the one Permanent Settlement of India is discredited as an oppressive and exhausting measure. Possibly Mr. Dutt wished it to be understood that the panacea itself must be applied with the care and caution suggested by the terrible experiences of the one experiment—a sentiment in which every one will join him. But if he wished to press his point, it might have been reasonably expected that he would develop it further. The revenues of Great Britain were in 1854 fifty-four millions; in 1900 they were a hundred and twenty-eight millions; but the mere statement of these figures does not prove that the taxation of Great Britain in 1900 was excessive, or the taxation of 1854 unduly light. Either suggestion requires the support of a careful enquiry. The huge militia of Akbar's time, of which Mr. Dutt reproduces such exact detail, was paid by the people in addition to their taxes, and Mr. Dutt forgets that if a revenue of four crores was the assessment of the Permanent Settlement, it was only the confirmation by the English Government of the assessment by the native rulers which they found in force. Mr. Dutt would have found a far more useful argument for the conclusions he wishes us to draw, if he had referred to figures

Revenue take at Permanent Settlement.

which are accessible in every official library. The land revenue of Bengal during the past year consisted of the following items:— **BENGAL.**

		R
Permanently-settled lands	. .	3,23,22,617
Temporarily ditto	. . . .	34,23,267
Government estates	. . . . .	41,04,753
	TOTAL .	3,98,50,637

After more than a hundred years the province still pays to the State less than four crores of land revenue. At the time of the Permanent Settlement the Government share of the rental was assumed to be 90 per cent. The gross rental of the province was, as far as could be judged by the administrators of the time, say, $4\frac{1}{2}$ crores. The annual value of the land in cultivation is now periodically assessed and revised, not for the purpose of enhancing the land revenue, but for the purpose of determining the local rates and cesses, from which is mainly met the cost of district roads, primary schools, and rural dispensaries. The rental of Bengal, Behar, and Orissa, according to the Board's Cess Report for 1899-1900, is $16\frac{1}{2}$ crores of rupees. If Mr. Dutt's argument is that a permanent settlement is under ordinary conditions an enormous concession to the payer of land revenue, the figures furnish the most ample proof of his contention.

Its incidence on present rental.

4. Whether the gain to the State is of equal value is a question on which opinions will differ to the end of time. The official controversies on the matter have lasted for a century. The official pendulum has swung backwards and forwards with the periodical oscillations which mark all the great problems of Indian politics, and the official libraries are filled with the literature on both sides. The Lieutenant-Governor does not propose to add to it. He is not aware that there is any present intention of seriously re-opening the discussion. His own opinions are in

BENGAL.

entire harmony with the decision that the system of permanent settlement shall not be further extended.

Arguments for and against settlements in perpetuity.

A moderate assessment on the unearned increments which reach the landlord in the continuous progress of the country is in accordance with the immemorial expectation and custom of the country. The country, as it progresses, requires increased revenue for the increased charges and the increased undertakings which progress compels; and the maintenance of an ancient and familiar and equitable form of taxation is incomparably better than the introduction of new and doubtful ones. The suggestion that revisions of the revenue assessment should be based exclusively on a rise of prices has been discussed in the temporarily-settled provinces at immense length. In the conclusions arrived at in that correspondence, the Lieutenant-Governor agrees, and he is pleased to find that the Board of Revenue in Bengal are of the same opinion :—

The last and most important proposal is that where districts have been once surveyed an increase in prices be made the sole ground of enhancement in future settlements. It may be presumed that if the revenue rose with prices it would also fall with them, as in the case of the rent of occupancy tenants. We would thus have a perpetual settlement of all India, the standard being in corn, not in silver. It is not suggested to extend this protection to the actual cultivators; the sole gainer is to be the middleman, the loser being the general taxpayer. As has been stated above, Mr. Nolan sees considerable advantages in a perpetual settlement, in developing a class of educated and loyal men. He also considers that for such a settlement a corn rent is better than one fixed in money. But on the whole, he prefers to maintain the present system of the periodical adjustment of revenue to the existing facts. This is done better, as experience accumulates, and has even at present some advantages besides the obvious one of providing for the needs of the State in the way most in accordance with the traditions of the country and the principles of political economy. In Bengal some estates cannot in any way pay the assessment and lapse to Government; others struggle on with difficulty under disproportionate burdens; while others again pay a mere quit-rent of 2 per cent. or less on the assets. This inequality is not the result of improvements effected by the owner on one estate and neglected on another, but of activity in enhancing customary rents, or of circumstances beyond the zemindar's control. It seems best that under such conditions the demands of Government should be, from time to time, adjusted to the circumstances of the day. It is in the course of such adjustment that Government can most effectively protect the interests of the cultivators. Even in Bengal it has been found necessary to make such a survey and settlement at the public expense, merely in the interest of the parties, though there could be no adaptation of the revenue demand to the results, and much of its utility was therefore lost. BENGAL.

Mr. Dutt speaks of the distinguished loyalty of the Bengal zemindars as a product of the Permanent Settlement. The Lieutenant-Governor acknowledges with the heartiest pleasure the loyal sentiments to which Mr. Dutt refers, sentiments which he believes were absolutely genuine; but it is not Sir John Woodburn's experience that the zemindars of the Upper Provinces are less loyal than their neighbours in Bengal. Mr. Dutt appeals to the munificient gifts of the Bengal zemindars to all public purposes. The Lieutenant-Governor again admits, gratefully, the princely generosity which has distinguished some of these gifts, but he cannot truthfully say that he has observed among the rank and file of the zemindars a greater disposition to execute improvements on their properties, or to subscribe to local needs and local charities, than among the zemindars of the Upper Provinces.

5. Then Mr. Dutt claims it, as a consequence of the Permanent Settlement, that rent laws have been passed which secure to the peasantry a happy and easy subsistence. The Lieutenant-Governor fears that this is a proposition which cannot be maintained. Rent laws have been passed in every province in India for the protection of the cultivator from the demand of an excessive rent and from unjustifiable disturbance in his holding. From the need of such protection the favoured province of Bengal was not free, and the end of a long and careful enquiry into the condition of the cultivating classes in India was the conclusion that nowhere did rents press with such severity on the peopleas in the permanently-settled districts of Behar.

6. Mr. Dutt concludes his letter with certain practical recommendations.

BENGAL.

His first suggestion is that where the cultivator pays direct to the State the impracticable rule of realising one-half of the net produce or a third of the gross produce be abandoned, and the rule of fixing one-fifth of the gross produce as a maximum of rent be adopted. An alleged existing practice is condemned, and a maximum is proposed for future use. In Bengal the assessment on the cultivation is not based on half the net produce or one-third of the gross produce. As for the one-fifth proposal, Mr. Dutt has taken figures from compilations made 20 years ago, and shows that the proportion of rent to produce was about 20 per cent. He takes seventeen Bengal districts, one Behar district, and one each from Chota Nagpur and Orissa. The Director of Land Records has given some interesting recent figures from eleven districts, which are reproduced below :—

Proportion of rent to produce.

In the table below some figures are given for comparison with Mr. Dutt's figures (reconverted for the purpose into rupees and annas) which have been taken from various settlement reports and recent compilations of the Agricultural Department, and which are in each case intended to exemplify the average value of the produce of an acre of land, and the average rent paid for it, in the tracts to which they refer :—

District.	Value of produce.		Rents.		Proportion of rent to produce.		Remarks.
	Mr. Dutt's figures.	Present figures.	Mr. Dutt's figures.	Present figures	Mr. Dutt's figures.	Present figures.	
1	2	3	4	5	6	7	8
	R a. p.	R	R a. p.	R a. p.	P. ct.	P. ct.	
24-Perganas	35 0 0	45	6 12 0	4 8 0	19	10	
Nadia	19 0 0	40	2 10 0	3 0 0	14	7	
Midnapur	37 8 0*	40	4 8 0*	3 4 0	12	8	
Hooghly	25 0 0	50	7 8 0	7 0 0	30	14	
Birbhum	30 0 0	30	6 12 0	4 8 0	22	15	
Backergunge	18 0 0†	55	2 12 0†	5 0 0	15	9	
Noakhali	32 8 0*	40	4 8 0*	3 8 0	14	9	
Tippera	27 8 0	45	6 12 0	4 0 0	24	9	
Rajshahi	16 8 0†	30	4 8 0†	4 0 0	27	13	
Gaya	30 8 0	30	6 12 0	4 4 0	22	14	
Balasore	8 0 0	18	2 4 0	2 0 0	28	11	
Muzaffarpur	...	24	...	4 0 0	...	16	
Cuttack	...	20	...	2 12 0	...	14	

* For superior lands only.

† For inferior lands only.

The figures in this table indicate the sufficient clearness that rents **BENGAL.** in Bengal amount, on the average to little more than 11 per. cent of the value of the gross produce of the land, as compared with an average of 20 per cent. disclosed by the statistics given by Mr. Dutt. But that this proportion can hardly be claimed as the result of the Permanent Settlement is shown by the figures for the districts of Balasore and Cuttack, which are temporarily settled, and the following table, which gives figures for some Government estates, temporarily settled, in juxtaposition with those for some permanently-settled Ward's estates, illustrate this point still more clearly :—

District.	Estates.	Value of produce per acre.	Rent per acre.	Proportion or rent to produce.
1	2	3	4	5
Government temporarily-settled estates.				
		R	R a. p.	P. ct.
Noakhali	Government estates	35	2 8 0	7
Backergunge	Ditto	55	4 10 0	8
Midnapur	Potashpur temporarily-settled estates	21	3 2 0	15
Puri	Khurda Government estates	18	1 10 0	9
Palamau	Government estates	15	1 2 0	7
Gaya	Ditto	30	4 2 0	14
Bogra	Jaipur Government estates	30	2 8 0	8
Wards' permanently-settled estates.				
Burdwan	Burdwan Rajkhas mahals	45	4 8 0	10
Hooghly	Ditto	50	8 0 0	16
Monghyr	Narhan Wards' estates	27	3 4 0	12
Gaya	Tikari ditto	30	4 12 0	16

These figures are the most careful and accurate that the Director can furnish, and they at least establish that as a matter of practice and general average, rents in Bengal over large areas are well below the standard which Mr. Dutt would fix. Nevertheless the Lieutenant-Governor strongly deprecates the recognition of any such hard-and-fast rule. Fifty per cent. on the gross produce can be paid, and is easily paid, on fields which are barely scratched for the seed. Twenty per cent. of the net produce would be an impossible rent for a field of sugarcane. The tests of the pressure of rent on the land must be other and better. The recommendation which Mr. Dutt makes was supported by the Bengal Government in the discussions on the Bengal Tenancy

BENGAL. Bill in 1885. It was rejected—and Sir John Woodburn thinks rightly rejected—by the Select Committee.

Limitation of Revenue demand to half assets in temporarily-settled areas.

7. The next recommendation is that where the revenue is paid by landlords in temporarily-settled areas, 50 per cent. of their assets may be fixed as the maximum Government revenue. The Lieutenant-Governor believes that this is now a very general rule, and he has no doubt that the variations from it will be fewer and fewer. It is a good general rule, but all rules have exceptions, and there are proper exceptions to this. Where the landlords have been paying more than 50 per cent. of their assets, where there is a sudden and large increase to these assets, and when an assessment above 50 per cent. will not unreasonably intrench on their income, the rule cannot in the interests of the general taxpayer be rigidly applied.

Term of settlement.

8. And similarly with the last recommendation which the Lieutenant-Governor is called upon to notice, that the minimum term of settlement in temporarily-settled areas shall be 30 years. When it is known that the conditions of an area about to be settled will be shortly changed to a material degree, as, for example, by the construction of a railway and the consequent opening of a wider and larger market, it is inconsistent with the whole theory of the revision of assessment that the revision should be postponed to a remote future. The exceptions to the general rule are, however, becoming fewer, and an important decision has recently been given by the Secretary of State in Orissa, which will materially assist Mr. Dutt's advocacy of this particular point.

CHAPTER IV.—THE NORTH-WESTERN PROVINCES AND OUDH.

From the Government of the North-Western Provinces and Oudh, to the Government of India, No. 4256, dated the 22nd December 1900.

I am directed to acknowledge the receipt of your letter No. 2046, dated the 13th October 1900, forwarding a copy of a letter from Mr. R. C. Dutt, concerning land settlements in Northern India, and requesting that the Government of India may be furnished with a statement of the case in reply to Mr. Dutt, after consultation with the chief revenue authorities of the province.

2. In reply, I am to forward, for the information of the Government of India, a copy of a letter from the Board of Revenue, who were consulted as requested in your letter; and to say that the Lieutenant-Governor agrees with the Board that there is little in Mr. Dutt's proposals that calls for remark in so far as these provinces are concerned.

Standard of assessment.

3. In the earlier paragraphs of his letter Mr. Dutt gives an account of the history of land settlements in these provinces, which does not call for any lengthy criticism. The pitch of the assessments in the early years of British rule in these provinces followed the standard which we inherited from the native rulers. After experience the British Government found that standard to be too high, and lowered it before the Mutiny to 50 per cent. of the assets. This proportion of the assets is now in force as the Gevernment share, though it is not often—indeed, it is rarely—taken. As Mr. Dutt himself accepts 50 per cent. of the assets as fair revenue, nothing more need be said on this part of his letter. The Government of the North-Western Provinces and Oudh is, as a matter of fact, more lenient than Mr. Dutt claims it should be.

N.-W. P. & OUDH.

Protection of tenants.

4. In paragraph 14 of his letter Mr. Dutt states that the first object of Government is the protection of the cultivators, and that this object is imperfectly secured under the present law. He expresses a hope that the Government will so modify the law as to extend occupancy rights to all settled tenants in Northern India. As the Government of India is aware, the Lieutenant-Governor has, throughout his administration, had under his consideration the necessity of securing a greater measure of protection to tenants in these provinces than the present law gives them. The subject is encompassed with more difficulties than Mr. Dutt appears to realize, and his proposal to give occupancy rights to all settled tenants involves a more drastic departure from the existing law than the circumstances of the provinces require. As a Rent Bill making such changes in the law as the Lieutenant-Governor, after much discussion and consideration, decided to submit for the approval of the Government of India and Her Majesty's Secretary of State, is now before the Legislative Council, His Honour will not further pursue this subject, except to remark that if Mr. Dutt's praiseworthy motives impel him to give special prominence to the interests of the tenants, the Lieutenant-Governor, while having the interest of the tenants at heart, is bound to act fairly by the landlords also.

5. In paragraph 18 of his letter Mr. Dutt summarizes the proposals which he has made in his various communications on this subject under seven heads, (*a*) to (*g*). Of these, it would appear, from Mr. Dutt's letter under reply, that the only heads which he considers applicable to these provinces are (*a*), (*d*), (*e*), and (*g*), as no reference is made to the other matters in his remarks upon the North-Western Provinces and Oudh.

Reductions effected in State's share of agricultural earnings.

6. In paragraph 18 (*a*) Mr. Dutt suggests that, where the State receives land revenue through landlords the "Saharanpur Rules" should be universally applied, and the State demand should be limited to one-half the rental. As is well known, this rule is of universal application in the North-Western Provinces

and Oudh. But it is necessary to point out that, while the rule itself has remained in force since 1855, its application has since then been greatly modified in the interests of the agricultural classes. When the half-assets rule was first of all substituted for the practice of assessing at 66 per cent. of the rental, considerable discretion was left to the assessing officers, who reduced assessments that were found to press too heavily, and retained or raised assessments that they found could easily be paid, without minute regard to arithmetical estimates of rent-rolls. When rules were afterwards laid down for the ascertainment of assets, the rental assessed on was not necessarily the actual rental, but an estimate of what the rental should be under proper management. If a Settlement Officer thought the rents too low, he assumed that the landlord could, and should, raise them, and assessed on the supposition that they were raised to his standard. This system of assessing on prospective assets has been in all recent settlements set aside, and the Government now aim at securing a revenue which is only one-half of the assets actually existing at the time of settlement, provided these have not been kept fraudulently or negligently at an excessively low level. In practice, the standard is further reduced by allowances made for improvements carried out by the landlord, for precariousness of cultivation, for indebtedness or poverty of the landlords and for severity of enhancements. Moreover, where the landlords cultivate themselves, a rebate of varying amount is generally allowed on their *sir*, and the arrangements now made, for the graduation of their assessments, when any substantial increase is made in the revenue demand, are extremely liberal. The ordinary rule is that for the first five years of a new settlement the revenue should not exceed by more than 25 per cent. the demand previously payable, and that if the enhancement exceeds 40 per cent. there should be two progressive steps of five years each. In calculating the assets also, rents which are believed to be excessive are excluded; while the enhancement of rents on which the enhancement of revenue must ultimately depend has been restrained—in the North-Western Provinces by the occupancy law, which has kept the rents of

N.-W. P. & OUDH.

N.-W. P. & OUDH. the majority of tenants well below the level to which they would have been raised by unrestricted competition, and in Oudh by the statutory limitations imposed by the present Rent Act. Thus, while the half-assets rule has remained unchanged, its application has been greatly modified in the proprietor's favour. The Settlement Officer of earlier days assessed frequently above the level of existing rents if he thought they could be raised by proper management. The Settlement Officer of the present day does not, except in case of gross fraud or negligence, go beyond the ascertainment of the rents actually paid; and he frequently declines to accept as true assets rents which are actually recorded, but which are, in his opinion, too high to be regularly paid.

Incidence of revenue on ascertained assets.

7. While the method of calculating assets has thus been modified in favour of the landlords, the percentage taken has also, in practice, been lowered below half assets for the reasons indicated in the foregoing paragraph. The following table gives the percentage of revenue to assets at the time of settlement in all districts in which settlements have been completed during the last fifteen years:—

Province.	District.	Term of settlement in years.	Assets.	Revenue.	Percentage of revenue to assets.
			R	R	
North-Western Provinces.	Jalaun tract, in Jalaun district.	16	15,72,752	7,54,229	47·9
	Dehra Dun (Eastern and Western Dun.)	20	1,68,627	82,476	48·9
	Gorakhpur . . .	30	52,53,160	24,38,112	46·40
	Basti	30	42,49,026	19,44,175	45·7
	Bulandshahr . .	30	41,61,348	19,76,659	47·5
	Saharanpur . . .	30	30,41,692	14,32,427	47·09
	Muzaffarnagar . .	30	33,07,223	15,91,246	48·11
	Jhansi (excluding Lalitpur.)	20	11,07,285	5,51,175	49·78
	Bijnor	30	22,98,980	10,66,927	46·41
	Lalitpur (Jhansi district)	30	4,02,479	1,97,308	49·05

N.-W. P. & OUDH.

Province.	District.	Term of settlement in years.	Assets.	Revenue.	Percentage of revenue to assets.
			R	R	
OUDH.	Unao	30	33,21,105	16,03,028	46·53
	Partabgarh . . .	30	29,68,676	13,46,522	45·36
	Bara Banki . . .	30	44,50,546	20,28,399	46·00
	Rae Bareli . . .	30	34,09,102	16,06,948	47·13
	Sultanpur . . .	30	32,10,876	14,99,705	46·7
	Lucknow . . .	30	21,03,530	9,86,569	46·9
	Sitapur . . .	30	34,94,273	16,15,760	46·3
	Fyzabad . . .	30	32,96,490	14,61,922	44·35

Term of settlement.

8. With reference to the term of settlement dealt with in paragraph 18 (*d*) of Mr. Dutt's letter, the ordinary rule in these provinces is that settlements should not be made more frequently than once in thirty years. In several cases this term has been extended, and at present no district is under twenty years' settlement, except Dehra Dun, Jhansi, and a part of the Jalaun and Naini Tal districts.

Cesses on land.

9. In paragraph 18 (*e*) of his letter Mr. Dutt suggests that no cesses should be imposed on the rental of the land except for purposes directly benefiting the land, and that the total of such cesses should not exceed 6¼ per cent. of the rental in any case. The reasons justifying the imposition of cesses have been discussed at the time of the passing of the different enactments on the subject, and it would open up a very wide question to consider now how far the various cesses imposed can be considered as benefiting the land within Mr. Dutt's meaning. As the Board of Revenue point out, the only cesses which Mr. Dutt specially objects to are those for schools and dispensaries, the amount of which is insignificant. The total amount of cesses levied in these provinces comes to 8 per cent. of the rental, and is thus 1¾ per cent. in excess of the scale proposed in Mr. Dutt's letter. This is the only point in which the adoption of Mr. Dutt's pro-

N.-W. P. & OUDH.

posals would mean any change in the direction of greater liberality in the arrangements in force in these provinces. The reduction of the proportion taken in cesses would involve alteration in the arrangements of Local, Provincial, and Imperial finance, and is not a matter which the Lieutenant-Governor feels called on to discuss; but I am to point out that, owing to the liberality shown in assessing the revenue, the total amount taken as revenue and cesses is, in the great majority of cases, actually less than the amount which, even according to Mr. Dutt's views, may be reasonably accepted as fair. The assessment of cesses is ordinarily made in practice, as is well known, on the revenue and not on the rent. In place of assessing 8 per cent. on the gross assets, the Settlement Officer calculates 16 per cent. on the revenue as being the cesses. If the assessment of revenue is made at 48·5 per cent. of the assets, the total payments on account of revenue and cesses will be almost exactly equal to the $56\frac{1}{4}$ per cent. of the assets which Mr. Dutt recognises as fair. If the revenue assessment is below 48·5 per cent. of the assets, the total payments will be below $56\frac{1}{4}$ per cent. Thus, if the assessment is made at 48 per cent. of assets, the total payments for revenue and cesses amount to —

$$\frac{48}{100}\left(1+\frac{16}{100}\right)=\frac{1}{100}\left(48+\frac{48\times 16}{100}\right)=\frac{1}{100}(48+7{\cdot}68)=55{\cdot}68 \text{ per cent.}$$

of the assets. On a consideration of the percentages given in paragraph 7 of this letter, it will be manifest that in almost all districts of these provinces the Government already shows greater liberality to the revenue-payers than is asked for in the memorial.

Adjudication of assessment disputes.

10. In paragraph 18 (*g*) Mr. Dutt requests that appeal be allowed to an independent tribunal in the case of any difference between cultivators and Settlement Officers in the matter of assessment. This proposal is not discussed in the body of Mr. Dutt's letter; no reasons are given for it; its acceptance might conceivably touch the financial solvency of the Government, and would certainly be altogether subversive of the principles hitherto followed in the assessment of land revenue in British India. From time immemorial the Government's right to a share in the

produce of the soil has been unquestioned, and the Government alone has decided what that share should be. The rule under which the Government takes only one-half of the assets is a rule which Government has imposed on itself, and it cannot allow any agency which it creates or maintains to judge between itself and the revenue-payer. No tribunals, except those in the Revenue Department, have the requisite knowledge to dispose of disputes relating to land assessment: nor can any authority, except the Government itself, mitigate the severity which the enforcement of a just claim (such as an assessment at 50 per cent. of the assets) might entail on the revenue-payers. It is on the Government that the responsibility must rest of determining how the rule should be applied in cases of a class or an individual. It would be an unfortunate day for the country if the Government were to divest itself of this responsibility, and place upon the Civil Courts the responsibility which it has hitherto exercised itself and which it alone can exercise with due regard to the public interests, and yet with the leniency which the circumstances of time or place may call for.

N.-W. P. & OUDH.

From the Board of Revenue, North-Western Provinces and Oudh, to the Government, North-Western Provinces and Oudh, No. $\frac{664}{I.-2934}$, dated the 21st November 1900.

Present:
Honourable Mr. H. F Evans, C.S.I., and Honourable Mr. D. T. Roberts.

With reference to G. O. No. $\frac{3539}{I.-962D.}$, dated 23rd October 1900, I am directed to submit the following remarks by the Board regarding the matters referred to by Mr. R. C. Dutt in his letter of the 12th May 1900 on land settlements in Northern India.

2. There is little in Mr. Dutt's letter that calls for remark with reference to the settlements of the North-Western Provinces and Oudh. To a critic who admits that "the principle on which the land revenue is fixed in Northern India, *viz.*, at one-half the rental is fair," it is perhaps unnecessary to reply. It is possible, however,

N.-W. P. & OUDH. that he is not aware to what extent Government has refrained from exacting in full that proportion of the assets which he considers to be a fair standard for the revenue, where the circumstances of the zemindari bodies called for and justified such moderation.

3. He quotes statistics showing the large increase in revenue due to revision of settlement in Oudh, Garhwal, and Budaun. Bearing in mind the fact that the revised demands have been generally below half assets, the conclusion is that the revenue of the expiring settlements had, from various causes, fallen considerably below what he accepts as a standard of the fair share of the assets to which the State is entitled, and that to this cause alone is due the fact that the revision of the demand involved a large increase.

The suggestion that the high rentals in Oudh, which have led to the enhancement of the demand, have been *caused* by the revision of settlement is not borne out by the facts ascertained at that revision and reported in full detail by the assessing officers.

4. In paragraph 16 of his letter Mr. Dutt criticises the system of cesses. He argues that the reduction of the revenue from 66 to 50 per cent. of the rental loses all point if the difference is again taken in the shape of cesses. Cesses were, however, not entirely unknown even when the demand was fixed at the higher percentage of the assets. He admits a cess for roads is open to no objection. He omits to express an opinion as to the patwari and *chaukidari* cess, and presumably cannot find reason to object to them. He takes exception only to the cesses for schools and dispensaries, the amount of which is insignificant.

5. As to Mr. Dutt's remark in paragraph 14 regarding fair rents and secure tenures for cultivators, the need for legislation in this direction has been fully recognised in these provinces, as Mr. Dutt will no doubt admit when the Rent Bill has passed into law.

CHAPTER V.—THE PUNJAB.

From the Government of the Punjab and its Dependencies to the Government of India,—No 243, dated 28th December 1900.

In accordance with the instructions contained in your letter No. 2047, dated 13th October 1900, I am directed to submit a copy of a letter, No. 953, dated 7th December 1900, from the Junior Secretary to Financial Commissioner, and its enclosure, being a Note by the Honourable Mr. J. Wilson, Settlement Commissioner of the Punjab, which contains a statement of the case in the Punjab in answer to the criticisms contained in Mr. R. C. Dutt's letter on land settlements in Northern India received with your letter under reply.

2. I am to say that the opinions expressed by the Financial Commissioner and Settlement Commissioner have the concurrence of His Honour the Lieutenant-Governor subject to the following remarks. Two controversial matters are touched on in Mr. Wilson's Note, *viz.*, the proposed amalgamation of land revenue and cesses and the tenancy question. The first of these has not yet reached a stage at which an authoritative opinion can be expressed by the Punjab Government. The second is happily at rest in the Punjab at present, and owing to the large areas of Crown waste which are being brought under cultivation with the aid of new perennial canals the demand for cultivators during the next 20 years is likely to be so great that ordinary agricultural tenants will to a large extent be able to make their own terms with their landlords.

3. In regard to the effect on cesses of the Saharanpur Rules, I am to say that, while the case is correctly stated in paragraph 8 of Mr. Wilson's note, the following additional observations appear to be required. The XXXVIIIth of these Rules expressly provided for the payment of three cesses aggregating 2½ per cent. on the land revenue, and the intention of taking cesses in addition to land

PUNJAB. revenue was clear, while at the same time there was no engagement on the part of Government that the number of cesses should not in course of time be increased. Rule XLII further provided that these three cesses and the pay of the village chaukidars should be assumed as payable from the net assets before the determination of the Government demand. If it be taken that one chaukidar on R3 per mensem is sufficient for a small village paying a land revenue demand of about R500, two chaukidars for a village paying R1,000, and so on, the pay of chaukidars would amount to about 7 per cent. on the land revenue. The total amount assumed as payable from the net assets would thus be 9¼ per cent. on the land revenue, or half that percentage of the net assets which would thus be reduced from 100 to 95·4. The limit to the land revenue demand would thus be 47·7 per cent. and not 50 per cent. of the net assets. In view of what is explained in paragraphs 7 and 9 of the Note this small correction does not, in Sir Mackworth Young's opinion, affect the conclusion arrived at by Mr. Wilson, that the aggregate of land revenue and cesses in the Punjab is a moderate and reasonable proportion of the net assets received by proprietors from their land.

From the Financial Commissioner of the Punjab to the Government of the Punjab,—No. 953, dated 7th December 1900.

In your letter No. 189 of 29th October 1900 you asked that a reply might be prepared to certain criticisms by Mr. R. C. Dutt on the system of land settlements in Northern India. In reply, I am directed to forward, in original, a Note by the Settlement Commissioner which makes, Mr. Tupper thinks, a very good reply to Mr. R. C. Dutt, and which has his general concurrence subject to the few remarks which follow.

2. As regards what is said in paragraph 6 of Mr. Wilson's Note, Mr. Tupper thinks that the disturbing effect of re-assessments is much less now than what it used to be 25 years ago. The people have got more accustomed to our methods and have

more confidence in the limitations of our demands. Moreover, it is thoroughly understood that re-assessment brings with it the often much-needed re-adjustments of demand and other measures of relief where the former assessment has in course of time become unsuitable. PUNJAB.

3. The Lieutenant-Governor is probably acquainted with Mr. Wilson's views on lump sum payments as expressed in paragraph 10 of the Note. The present is not a suitable opportunity for the discussion of this subject, nor is it necessary, for the purpose of answering Mr. Dutt, to give an opinion upon it. Accordingly Mr. Tupper will only say here that the question of principle involved has arisen separately in connection with Mr. Wilson's proposals for the assessment of the lands which will be irrigated by the Jhelum Canal and will in this way come before Government.

4. In paragraph 13 of the Note Mr. Wilson does not fully state the case as to the twelve years' rule in the Punjab. What he probably meant was that ever since 1868 it has been a rule of law laid down by the Tenancy Act that no tenant shall acquire a right of occupancy by mere lapse of time. In the early Punjab settlements made by officers who brought with them from the North-West the practice prevailing a twelve years' rule was frequently applied. It was not, however, authoritatively established; the nature as well as the length of the occupancy was considered; and in some places or with reference to some classes of tenants periods of 10 or even 20 years were substituted. There is sufficient information on the matter in paragraph 200 of the Settlement Manual. Of course it should not be forgotten that the ryot of Bengal is the peasant proprietor of the Punjab, and that the Bengal zemindar has no place here. The tenancy question is therefore in a different plane; and arguments draw from provinces where there are zemindars of the Bengal type have no application. Any re-opening of the tenancy question in the Punjab at the present time would, in Mr. Tupper's opinion, be not only quite unnecessary but extremely harmful.

PUNJAB. *Note by the Honourable Mr. J. Wilson, Settlement Commissioner, Punjab, dated 30th November 1900.*

1. I propose in this Note to confine myself to the discussion of those criticisms and suggestions, contained in Mr. Romesh Chundra Dutt's letter dated 12th May 1900, which relate to the land revenue system of administration in the Punjab. He summarises his proposals in paragraph 18 of his letter, and I take the suggestions there made in order.

2. (*a*) He recommends that where the State receives land revenue through landlords, and the revenue is not permanently settled, the State demand be limited to one-half the rental.* This rule is already in force in the Punjab. In paragraph vii of the Assessment Instructions of 1893, sanctioned by the Government of India, the rule is stated as follows :—

State's share of rental.

"The assessment of an estate will be fixed according to circumstances, but must not exceed half the value of the net assets;" and in Rule vi it is said—

"A full fair rent paid by a tenant-at-will, though sometimes falling short of the net assets, may generally, in practice and for purposes of assessment, be taken as a sufficiently near approximation to them on the land for which it is paid."

I understand that Mr. Dutt is satisfied with these instructions.

3. (*b*) He asks that where the State receives land revenue direct from cultivators, the rate be limited to a maximum of one-fifth of the gross produce of the soil. As a matter of fact, in the Punjab the land revenue nowhere exceeds one-fifth of the gross produce, and usually it equals a much smaller fraction. No particular fraction of the *gross* produce is, however, prescribed as the limit of the land revenue demand, the only limit being that already mentioned, *viz.*, half the value of the *net* assets. Almost exactly half† the cultivated area of the Punjab is cultivated by the owners themselves, *i.e.*, the State receives the land revenue of half the

Incidence of State's share on produce.

* Douie's Settlement Manual, Appendix I.

† Annual Revenue Report, Statement No. XII.

cultivated area of the province direct from the cultivators. In assessing the land revenue demand on such land, the rule above quoted is adhered to, *i.e.*, the assessment is limited to half the value of the "net assets," a term which is defined as meaning "the average* surplus which the estate may yield, after deduction of the expenses of cultivation including profits of stock and wages of labour"; and the best basis for an estimate of the net assets in such a case is taken to be the fair rents paid by tenants-at-will for similar land in the neighbourhood. Such rents are often, in the Punjab, paid in kind, the share of the gross produce taken by the landlord varying in different parts of the province from one-half to one-fourth or one-fifth, according to the quality of the soil, the rainfall, the facilities for irrigation, the density of the population, and so on. Where the prevalent rent is one-half the gross produce, the theory of half-net assets would make the limit of the State's demand one-fourth of the gross produce, but as a matter of fact, so many deductions are made by the Settlement Officer in calculating the net assets, and so well below the half-net assets brought out by his calculations, does he keep in his actual assessment, especially in assessing owners who cultivate the land themselves, that, as already said, the actual assessment nowhere exceeds one-fifth of the gross produce. It is more often equal to one-seventh, one-eighth or even a smaller fraction of the gross produce; and to introduce a rule limiting the revenue to one-fifth of the gross produce would be more likely to lead to an increase than a diminution of the assessments now made. Probably, if Mr. Dutt were acquainted with the circumstances of this province, he would prefer to retain the present 'half net-assets' rule, without the addition he advocates. **PUNJAB.**

4. In order to ensure that the poorer classes of peasants cultivating their own lands are not too highly assessed on the basis of rents paid on lands in their neighbourhood, it is proposed to introduce into the Punjab the system followed in the North-Western Provinces, under which such poor peasants are assessed on the lands they themselves cultivate at rates considerably lower

*Assessment Instructions, paragraph vi.

PUNJAB. than those charged on similar lands owned by rent-receiving landlords. This will ensure a lenient assessment to such cultivators much better than the rule proposed by Mr. Dutt.

Rise in prices as a sole basis of enhancement.

5. (*c*) He proposes that where the State receives land revenue direct from cultivators, an increase of prices should be the sole ground of enhancement at the time of re-settlement This rule would be very difficult to carry out in practice, and would be very unfair in its operation. It is extremely difficult, indeed impossible, to arrive at any certain conclusion as to the percentage by which prices have increased between one settlement or another. Are we to take the averages of periods of five years, of ten years or of fifteen years? Are we to compare present prices with those of a period of years before, or a period of years after, the last settlement? Are we to include or to exclude the prices of years of exceptional scarcity or of exceptional plenty? In the Punjab it is very usual for small landowners who cultivate part of their own lands to let part of it to tenants, and in such cases it is only fair to take into account a rise of rents due to an increase of population, which again may be due to the construction of a railway or canal at the expense of the State. Again, if an increase of prices were made the sole ground of enhancement, this would naturally lead to a fall of prices being made the sole ground or almost the sole ground of reduction of assessment; and this would end in a grossly unfair distribution of the total land revenue demand. At every re-settlement it is found that the distribution of the assessment, which may have been fair enough when the settlement was made, has become very uneven. In some holdings the net profits of the owner have increased owing to causes beyond his control; in others, they have diminished, as for instance, owing to the spread of sand or of salts in the soil, the falling-in of a well, the growth of weeds difficult to eradicate, the migration of population, and such like; and if in such cases the old assessment were enhanced proportionately all round merely with regard to an increase of prices, the result would be ruin to many, and a most unfair

distribution of the land revenue demand. In the Punjab very liberal remissions of land revenue are made in consideration of new improvements, *e.g.*, the land revenue on a new well is not enhanced for a period of twenty years, and these remissions are sufficient to ensure that improvements are not unduly taxed; witness the steady spread of cultivation and increase in the number of wells, embankments, and other permanent improvements in most districts of the Punjab, which show that the landowners have no fear that their improvements will lead to an unfair enhancement in the land revenue assessment, and that the present rules do not deter landowners from expending capital and labour on the improvement of their land. **PUNJAB.**

6. (*d*) He asks that settlements be made not oftener than once in thirty years. In the Punjab the settlements of most of the districts in the east of the province were made for thirty years, but the instructions* now are that "no re-assessment is to be fixed for more than twenty years except with the permission of the Government of India," and the usual practice now is to fix a term of twenty years for a new assessment. The history of the discussion regarding the term of settlements will be found in paragraphs 481—493 of Douie's Settlement Manual, and it will be seen that the term of twenty years was adopted as a sort of compromise between two sets of opinions. The orders† then passed contemplate the possibility of fixing a shorter term in backward tracts and under exceptiona circumstances, and it would certainly not be advisable to lay down any hard-and-fast rule that the term shall in no case be less than thirty years. In some parts of the Punjab the development of the resources of the country is likely to be so rapid, owing to the construction of railways and canals at the expense of the State the shifting and increase of the population and the rise of prices that it would not be fair to the rest of India to make the assessment for a longer term than twenty years and so leave to individuals

Term of settlement.

* Assessment Instructions, paragraph X.

† Government of India's Circular No. 27, dated 16th December 1895.

PUNJAB. too large a share of the unearned increment which is the due of the State. Moreover, as already said, it is desirable, especially in a country of small peasant proprietors, that at no long period of time there should be a re-adjustment of the land-revenue apart from the question of enhancement. The evils of re-settlement proceedings are apt to be exaggerated. In the Punjab the improvement in the system of record has been such that re-settlement proceedings last a much shorter time than they used to do, and cause little change in the ordinary course of district administration. The disturbance of men's minds due to re-settlement operations is of no great importance, and is caused much more by the revision of the record which generally accompanies re-assessment proceedings than by the re-assessment itself. There seems no good ground for re-opening the question in the Punjab, and the present orders, quoted above, should be allowed to stand.

Limitation of cesses.

7. (*e*) He prays that no cesses be imposed on the rental of the land except for purposes directly benefiting the land; and that the total of such cesses assessed on the rental may not exceed $6\frac{1}{4}$ per cent. in any province of India.

In the Punjab, besides the small cess which goes to pay the common expenses of the village, and which is not realised by the Government, the cesses realised on the land revenue are—

(1) The village officers' cess levied under section 29 of the Punjab Land Revenue Act, which may not exceed $6\frac{1}{4}$ per cent. on the "annual value," a term which is defined to mean double the land revenue. The cess has hitherto generally been assessed at something less than this rate. The proceeds do not go to Government, but go to pay the village headman, rural notables and village accountants, whose services are of great value to the land-owners, as well as to the Government.

(2) The local rate levied under section 5 of the Punjab District Boards Act, 1883. This also may not

PUNJAB.

exceed 6½ per cent. on the "annual value," and at present is almost everywhere R5-3-4 per cent on the "annual value." The proceeds of this rate are expended on local purposes, such as the provision of roads, schools, dispensaries, seráis, arboriculture and the other matters detailed in section 20 of the Act.

Percentage of annual value taken in revenue and cesses.

Thus the maximum percentage on the "annual value" at present allowed by law for cesses is 12½ per cent. The "annual value" is double the land revenue assessed on the land, and if the land revenue were assessed at the maximum allowed by the Assessment Instructions, *i.e.*, at the full half-net assets, the annual value would equal the rental, and the total maximum sum realisable by the State from the land would be 50 per cent. on the rental as land revenue, and 12½ per cent. on the rental as village officers' cess and local rate, *i.e.*, 62½ per cent. of the total rental or total net assets. Mr. Dutt would limit the State's demand on the land to 50 per cent. of the rental for land revenue and 6¼ per cent. for cesses, total 56¼ per cent.

8. Now, in the first place, it is misleading to write of the "Saharanpur Rules" as if they reduced the State's demand for land revenue *and cesses* to 50 per cent. of the rental. They were intended to reduce only the *land revenue proper* from 66⅔ to 50 per cent. of the rental, and it was never intended to abolish cesses over and above the 50 per cent. Cesses were realised to a very large amount over and above the land revenue by the native rulers who preceded us, and although they were greatly reduced and simplified, cesses still continued to be realised over and above the land revenue, when the State's demand for land revenue was theoretically 66⅔ per cent. of the rental, and it was all along intended, and understood by the people, that cesses would continue to be realised over and above the land revenue, after its reduction to 50 per cent. of the rental by the Saharanpur Rules.

9. Secondly, while the maximum demand fixed for the State at present for land revenue and cesses is 62½ per cent. of the net assets or rental, we nowhere in the Punjab realise this maximum,

PUNJAB. and in most districts the total land revenue and cesses actually realised falls very far short of it. The cesses imposed in most districts total up to less than 11 per cent. on double the land revenue, instead of the maximum of 12½ per cent.; and the land revenue itself in most districts is well below the allowable maximum of 50 per cent. of the net assets.

For instance, in the Shahpur* district, resettled in 1893, the assessment imposed amounted to only 39 per cent. of the estimated net assets. In Gurdaspur † it was a little more than 25 per cent. In Peshawar, ‡ settled in 1896, it works out to just over 25 per cent. In Hissar it was about 45 per cent. In Jhelum district, recently settled, it is about 35 per cent. of the estimated net assets. In the Mooltan and Muzaffargarh districts, now under settlement, the assessments proposed are generally about 45 per cent. of a very liberally estimated net asset. So that even in districts where the assessment most nearly equals the maximum allowable, the actual demand for land revenue and cesses is 45 per cent. + ($11 \times \frac{45}{50}$ =) 55 per cent. of the total rental against the 56¼ per cent. allowed by Mr. Dutt. For the Punjab generally the present assessment of land revenue and cesses together certainly does not exceed 45 per cent. of the net assets.

Advantages of a consolidated demand.

10. I am myself of opinion that our present system, under which we realise from the owners of agricultural land a large proportion of the net assets as land revenue to be expended on general administration, a smaller percentage for the payment of village officers and another smaller percentage for local improvements, although it has not led to over-assessment, is unnecessarily complicated and confusing, and is unsuited to the circumstances of the province. The individual land-owner has not, and cannot hope to have any power to alter the percentage of his net assets which is realised from him for any of those purposes. That is fixed, and must continue to be fixed, by the Government. It does not matter to

* Settlement Report, paragraph 70.

† Settlement Report, paragraphs 60 and 67.

‡ Settlement Report, paragraphs 23 and 78.

him personally how the different sums realised from him are credited. What concerns him is the total sum realised from him under all heads. The present system requires us to calculate out on each holding the amount of land revenue due from it, the amount of village officer's cess and the amount of local rate, and the elaborate calculations thus required for each of the three millions of owners' holdings in the Punjab entail an immense amount of unnecessary labour annually, confuse the peasant, the patwari and all account offices, and lead to the impression that the total demand from the land is higher than it really is. It would be much simpler and more satisfactory if the demand for land revenue and cesses were lumped together and assessed on the land in one sum, the total proceeds for each district being allotted in fixed proportions by one annual calculation at head-quarters to the different heads of expenditure. The objects on which the cesses are at present expended must continue to be maintained, but we need not work out the fraction required for such purposes on each holding. Whether the consolidated demand representing land revenue and cesses should be limited, as at present, to 62½ per cent. of the net assets, or, as Mr. Dutt proposes, to 56¼ per cent. or even to a smaller proportion, is a matter for decision with reference to the general finances of India. If it could be reduced to 50 per cent. of the net assets, the balance being made up by making the rich province of Bengal contribute its fair share to the Imperial finances, or by making the wealthy and prosperous classes whose income does not come directly from the land subscribe more than they at present do for Imperial purposes, I should be glad for the sake of the land-owners of the Punjab. But until the general state of the finances allows of this being done, it is no great hardship for the Punjab land-owners to be required to pay for general and local purposes up to 62½ per cent. of their net profits from the land. Little more than fifty years ago, the whole of the net profits of cultivation were taken from them by the State; and in the early days of our rule the land revenue demand absorbed nearly the whole of the net profits. The proportion of the net profits realised as land revenue and cesses has steadily diminished, until now the selling value of proprietary rights in the land is returned at 70 years' purchase of the land-revenue.* (The figures on which this calculation is based may be exaggerated, but it is certain that average land in the Punjab can be sold at fifty times the land revenue assessed upon it.) And of the total realisations from the land a much larger proportion than formerly is spent on local purposes directly benefitting the land-owner.

Water-rates.

11. (*f*) He prays that where the Government provides water for irrigation, the cultivator may be left the option of paying for the water if he chooses to use it, and that no compulsory water-rate be imposed. In the Punjab this is the universal rule so far as the occupiers' rate is concerned, *i.e.*, the cultivator need not take the water unless he likes, and pays for it only if he takes it. It is also generally the rule as regards the charge made as owners' rate on enhanced land-revenue on the land-owner of canal-irrigated land in regard to the increased value of his net profits or rental due to canal irrigation. In a few districts, however, the land-revenue on land irrigable by a canal has been enhanced on the ground that the land is rendered secure from drought by the presence of the canal, and that as the land-owner is therefore safe to get his rent in both good and bad years, he should pay a higher fixed land revenue whether he uses the water or not. I am myself in favour of making the owners' rate or enhancement of land revenue fluctuate with the area actually irrigated in each harvest, but the subject is at present under discussion and will shortly be considered by the Punjab Government and the Government of India in connection with the re-assessment of the Fazilka tahsil of the Ferozepore district.

Adjudication of assessment disputes.

12. (*g*) He prays that in the case of any difference between cultivators and Settlement Officers in the matters of assessment, an appeal be allowed to an independent tribunal not concerned with the fixing and levying of rents and rates. In the Punjab appeals in matters of

* Annual Revenue Report, paragraph 7 (*c*).

assessment lie from the Settlement Officer to the Settlement Commissioner and from him to the Financial Commissioner. None of these authorities have anything to do with the fixing of rents except those of occupancy tenants. More especially, they have no power to fix the rents of tenants-at-will on which the net assets estimate is calculated. I presume Mr. Dutt's objection under this head would not apply to the Punjab. PUNJAB.

Protection of tenants.

13. In paragraph 14 of his letter Mr. Dutt suggests that it should be considered whether a maximum limit of rents in proportion to the gross produce should not be laid down by law in the case of ordinary cultivated lands and that the law should be so modified as to extend occupancy rights to all settled tenants in Northern India. In the Punjab the relations of landlord and tenant have from time to time been very fully discussed and Tenancy Acts were passed in 1868, and again in 1887. A history of the controversy and the results attained will be found in Douie's Settlement Manual, paragraphs 197 to 222. In the Punjab, as already said, land-owners themselves cultivate about 50 per cent. of the total cultivated* area, some 10 per cent. is held by tenants with right of occupancy, and the remaining 40 per cent. by tenants-at-will. The tenants with right of occupancy are protected by law from arbitrary ejectment or enhancement of rent, and their position is a very secure one. The tenants-at-will may be ejected or may have their rents enhanced at the will of the landlord, the only protection given them by the law being that, if ejected, they can claim compensation for improvements, and if they broke up the land from waste, compensation for disturbance also. The rule that 12 years' continuous cultivation gives a tenant a right of occupancy has never been introduced into the Punjab. There will always be a difference of opinion as to whether protection from ejectment and from arbitrary enhancement of rent should not be extended to a larger body of tenants than those now protected, and if the question were re-opened, I myself, like Mr. Dutt, should be in favour of greatly extending it; but the landlord and tenant question is

* Annual Revenue Report, Statement XII.

PUNJAB. nowhere so acute in the Punjab as to justify us in re-opening the controversy which was closed by the Tenancy Act of 1887. That Act has on the whole worked well, and the tenants-at-will are generally in a prosperous condition. Rents will always depend largely on the pressure of the population on the soil, and in the south-west of the province at all events the demand for tenants is greater than the supply. The Hissar district mentioned by Mr. Dutt has always been exceptional in the matter of notices of ejectment, the average number of such notices issued in the last eight years having been 2,302 per annum, so that the figure quoted by Mr. Dutt, *viz.*, over 2,000 in 1898-99, was nothing unusual for that district. It was not due to any great extent to the approval of settlement operations, as the term of settlement has still a number of years to run except in one of the five tahsils into which the district is divided, and in that tahsil the number of notices issued in 1898-99 was only 540, or not much more than a fifth of the number issued in the whole district. The total number of holdings of tenants-at-will in the Hissar district is 109,660; so that even in this exceptional district, only about 2 per cent. of the total number of tenants-at-will receives a notice of ejectment every year. In the great majority of these cases ejectment does not actually take place; the landlord being content with a small enhancement of rent, and this, in ordinary times, the increase of population and rise of prices enable him to secure.

There are in the Punjab some three million tenants-at-will cultivating over ten million acres, and there is no grievance so great as to justify us in stirring up the excitement and bad feeling between the landlord and tenant classes which would certainly be caused by any attempt to alter the present relations between them.

14. I need say nothing about the Punjab Land Alienation Bill, which has now been passed into law after full discussion.

CHAPTER VI.—THE CENTRAL PROVINCES.

From the Chief Commissioner, Central Provinces, to the Government of India, No. 1862, dated the 11th April 1901.

I am directed to acknowledge receipt of Mr. Maconochie's letter No. 2048, dated the 13th October 1900, with which was forwarded, for the opinion of the Officiating Chief Commissioner, a copy of a letter from Mr. R. C. Dutt, late of the Indian Civil Service, concerning land settlements in the Central Provinces.

2. Before submitting his own views in the matter Mr. Fraser has consulted, as suggested in your letter, the chief revenue authorities of the province, Mr. J. B. Fuller, C.I.E., Commissioner of the Jubbulpore Division, and Mr. L. S. Carey, Commissioner of Settlements and Agriculture, who possess special experience both of the settlement problems and of the agricultural circumstances of the province. Copies of the replies of these officers to Mr. R. C. Dutt's criticisms are herewith forwarded.

3. I am also to forward copy of a Note recorded by the Officiating Chief Commissioner, setting forth his own views on the matters referred to in Mr. Dutt's letter. I am to express regret that Mr. Fraser has found it impossible to do this by the 31st of December. But the Government of India are aware how great has been the burden of public business of late in the Central Provinces.

Note by the Honourable Mr. A. H. L. Fraser, C.S.I., Officiating Chief Commissioner of the Central Provinces, on Land Settlements.

I have been requested by the Government of India (in letter No. 2048, dated the 13th October, from the Department of Revenue and Agriculture) to submit to them my views on the matters referred to in Mr. R. C. Dutt's letter of the 12th February 1900 concerning land settlements in this province. I have

CENTRAL PROVS.

obtained (as desired by the Government of India) the opinion of Mr. Fuller and Mr. Carey and shall submit them also. I am sorry that I have not been able to dispose of this reference sooner. But I have been fully occupied with very urgent work connected with the recent famine, and have not had leisure to turn aside to the consideration of Mr. Dutt's letter.

2. I am sure that Mr. Dutt has been actuated by a desire to benefit his fellow-countrymen, and to assist the Government in remedying or avoiding harsh and injudicious action in respect of land assessments; and, after the courteous manner in which he has referred to me personally in his letter, I need not pause to say that I sympathise with him in that desire. But I am bound to say that Mr. Dutt seems to have rushed into this discussion without adequate preparation. He held the high office of Commissioner of Division under the Bengal Government before he retired from the Indian Civil Service. It is only to be expected, therefore, that very considerable weight will be attached to his views on questions of Indian administration. I know, of course, that an officer trained in Bengal may be utterly ignorant of the revenue system of another province. But I felt that I might reasonably expect from Mr. Dutt great care in the study of a subject on which he proposed to speak as an authority, and some hesitation in accepting views which seem to involve harshness, severity, and blundering on the part of the Government, whose motives he ought not to have so lightly misunderstood and misjudged. It is disappointing to find how inaccurate his statements are, and how readily he seems to have been persuaded to condemn the action of the Government he has served.

3. Briefly stated, Mr. Dutt's allegations are—

(*i*) That at the old settlements, made in 1863 to 1867, the rents were too high, inasmuch as the Settlement Officers fixed rents equal to one-third of the gross produce.

(*ii*) That too much revenue was taken from the malguzars, because in defiance of orders the

Settlement Officers took more than half the actual assets. **CENTRAL PROVS.**

(*iii*) That at the recent re-settlements these mistakes were continued and intensified under the sanction of Government.

Tenants' rents.

4. The first allegation, *i.e.*, that rents were too high because the Settlement Officer fixed one-third of the gross produce as rent in the settlements of 1863 and the following years, is inaccurate. In the first place, the Settlement Officer did not fix rents at that settlement, the matter being arranged, after the announcement of the revenue, by agreement between landlord and tenant with the assistance of a subordinate Revenue Officer. In fixing his assets the Settlement Officer took account of such immediate enhancement of rents as he deemed to be reasonably possible. He estimated the real letting value of the land by such tests and comparison as were possible to him. He then fixed his revenue on the assets so estimated. He communicated the assessment to the malguzars, and left the fixation of rents to them. He had no authority to fix the rents. That was done by the landlords and tenants, sometimes assisted by a subordinate Government officer, in the manner described by Mr. Fuller.

5. In the second place, the rents were not one-third of the gross produce. In this connection I would draw attention to paragraph 3 of Mr. Fuller's letter and paragraph 15 of Mr. Carey's letter. The actual facts are about as far removed as they could possibly be from the allegations of Mr. R. C. Dutt, who does not appear to have been at any pains to ascertain the truth. As Mr. Carey points out, had the rents been as high as Mr. Dutt asserts, the people, after paying other taxation and the price of imported commodities would have had exactly 9 annas per head per annum to live upon.

Position of tenants under native rule.

6. The truth is that Mr. Dutt has entirely misapprehended, if he has ever tried to ascertain, the history of tenancy legislation in this province. Under native rule, a system of short leases prevailed which left

CENTRAL PROVS.

to the patel or revenue-farmer the duty of apportioning the revenue demand among the ryots of the village. He could in a few of the most fertile tracts force up rents by competition, but his demands were limited by the fact that it was more difficult to secure ryots than land. Excessive demands made by the State resulted in the ruin of particular lessees, but this again had the effect of bringing down the revenue demand of the village, and under these short settlements the abuse tended to rectify itself. Such conditions could not, of course, conduce to general prosperity, but they prevented any large and permanent excess of rents. The great bulk of the rental thus assumed a customary character, and tradition protected the ryot from enhancement so long as the State did not increase the revenue demand.

The figures given in paragraphs 3 and 4 of Mr. Carey's letter show that constant efforts were made under British management to reduce the revenue exacted by the Native Government both in the Saugor-Nerbudda territories and in the Nagpur province, and in this indulgence the ryots protected by tradition of course shared. Only in Chhattisgarh did the revenue rise, but it was throughout ridiculously low, and, as Mr. Fuller shows (paragraph 5 of his letter), the revised revenue imposed at the first regular settlement only fell at 5 annas per each cultivated acre.

Growth of landlordism.

The tradition in favour of the ryots only began to weaken when the conferral of proprietary rights, accompanied by a long-termed settlement with the village farmers, and the growing demand for land caused by the greater security ensured by British rule, enabled the newly-created landlords to increase rents without fear of the Revenue Officer's demands upon them being increased, and without risk of themselves being evicted. The growth of landlordism as opposed to mere village management was more rapid in the north of the province longest under British rule, where the conferral of proprietary rights had been preceded by their virtual recognition by the twenty years' settlements made in 1835 to 1838. It was, therefore, found necessary to protect some of the oldest ryots, and to secure to others the chance of earning occupancy right. The remainder, constituting the majority of the tenant body, continued tenants-at-will, whom it was later on found necessary to protect from the landlords by the tenancy legislation of 1883, 1889, and 1898. CENTRAL PROVS.

Comparison of old and present rents.

7. Mr. Carey has clearly shown that the allegation of Mr. Dutt that the rents of tenants were fixed by the Settlement Officers in 1863-67 at a third of the gross produce ends in a *reductio ad absurdum*. The inaccuracy of his statement can also be established by comparing the rates of ordinary tenants' rents as they stood at the beginning and end of the thirty years' settlement respectively in the highest rented tracts of the province, the rise having been due to the action of the landlords. A column is added showing what the Settlement Officers at revision did with these rents :—

District.	Tahsil.	Tract or Group.	Rate of rent paid by Ordinary Tenants.		
			Paid at beginning of 30 years' settlement.	Paid at end of 30 years' settlement.	As revised by the Settlement Officer.
			R a p.	R a. p.	R a. p.
Hoshangabad	Harda . .	Timarni .	1 0 1	3 4 2	2 4 10
Do. .	Do. . .	Fokarni .	0 14 1	3 7 7	2 4 4
Do. .	Seoni . .	Seoni . .	1 3 0	3 5 1	2 1 3
Do. .	Sohagpur .	Sobhapur .	1 1 3	2 9 10	2 2 11
Jubbulpore .	Jubbulpore .	Patan . .	2 3 5	4 8 7	4 2 1
Do.	Do. .	Mangela .	2 13 3	4 5 5	4 5 5
Do. .	Do. .	Singaldip .	2 10 2	4 6 11	4 2 1
Do. .	Sehora .	Lamkana .	2 14 1	4 7 4	3 12 0
Narsinghpur .	Narsinghpur .	Chhindwara .	1 13 8	3 7 10	3 4 6
Do. .	Do. .	Supla-Themi	1 8 5	2 13 0	2 8 0
Do. .	Gadarwara .	Bohan	1 10 9	2 13 11	2 8 3

If rents generally were as high as Mr. Dutt contends it would obviously have been impossible for the landlords to have enhanced them as they did.

8. As the Government of India are aware, the province was formed in 1862 of districts widely different in history and agricultural circumstances, which it would take much time and space to discuss in detail. But the province possessed one feature common to all its districts, *i.e.*, that until the opening up of the country by the railway it was a landlocked place, where prices were low, population sparse, and surplus grain could not find a market. It was hence perfectly impossible that Government or the landlords could demand from the cultivators a share of produce which (according to Mr. Dutt) was double that rendered in more advanced regions where population pressed on land, and produce could be readily exported. That the rents paid at the old settlements were high has never been alleged by anyone, and it is left to Mr. Dutt to discover the fact 35 years later. Where Mr. Dutt obtained his information I do not profess to determine; but that he should not have been able to discover such an obvious and patent absurdity before he launched into this discussion, is surely deplorable. As is pointed out by Mr. Fuller (paragraph 8 of his letter), the standard of one-sixth of the produce which Mr. Dutt assumes as a fair rental would, if followed in these provinces, result in a large enhancement of the rental fixed at the revised settlements. This is not a statement made to rebut the charge brought by Mr. R. C. Dutt. It is the estimate made by experienced Settlement Officers in the course of their business with no thesis to justify and no object in stating anything but the truth on this point. That it is also plain to anyone acquainted with the subject is shown by the evidence of Mr. Gangadhar Rao Chitnavis, C.I.E., late an Additional Member of the Viceroy's Legislative Council, and a large landlord in this province. In a letter to the *Pioneer* of the 16th November 1900 Mr. Chitnavis says: "While deeply grateful to Mr. R. C. Dutt for his able and disinterested advocacy, I am not prepared to go with him when he says that our tenants'

Present incidence on gross produce.

CENTRAL PROVS.

rents are above the standard he lays down, *viz*, one-sixth of the produce. Even after revision they are lower than what that standard would allow."

The Government demand on landlords.

9. The second allegation made by Mr. Dutt is that the Settlement Officers departed from the half-assets rule in assessing revenue in spite of the orders of Government requiring them to follow it. Here Mr. Dutt stands on firmer ground, for he is not hampered by his ignorance of village conditions; but a very short examination of the subject will show that he is again wrong in his facts. On this point, Mr. Dutt states, "the principle that one-half of the malguzar's assets should be demanded as revenue was repeatedly laid down and insisted upon in the orders of the Government of India, and I have failed to discover under what authority this principle was departed from in practice." In a subsequent letter to the *Times of India* (Wednesday, December 21st, 1900) he has further enlarged on the same subject.

History of the half-assets rule.

10. In the first place, the authority quoted by him for the half-assets rule applies only to the Saugor-Nerbudda territories. In the second place, the assets referred to were not the actual assets at the day of the enquiry, but the average assets which the village might be expected to yield, having regard to both the cultivated and culturable land. The instructions on the subject contained in Rule XXXVI of the Saharanpur Rules run as follows:—

The assets of an estate can seldom be minutely ascertained, but more certain information as to the average net assets can be obtained now than was formerly the case. This may lead to over-assessment; for there is little doubt that two-thirds, or 66 per cent. is a larger proportion of the *real* average assets than can ordinarily be paid by proprietors or communities in a long course of years. For this reason the Government have determined so far to modify the rule laid down in paragraph 52 of the "Directions to Settlement Officers" as to limit the demand of the State to 50 per cent, or one-half of the average net assets. By this it is not meant that the jama of each estate is to be fixed at one-half of the net average assets, but that in

CENTRAL PROVS. taking these assets with other data into consideration, the Collector will bear in mind that about one-half, and not two-thirds as heretofore, of the well-ascertained net assets should be the Government demand. The Collector should observe the cautions given in paragraphs 47 to 51 of the Treatise quoted, and not waste time in minute and probably fruitless attempts to ascertain exactly the average net assets of the estates under settlement.

11. It is on these instructions that Mr. Dutt bases his interpretation that the rules require the assessment not to exceed half the actual assets at the time of the enquiry. If the whole rule be carefully read, it is clear that it does not admit of this interpretation. The terms used are of necessity vague, because the matter referred to is itself undefined. Such expressions as "real average assets" and "net average assets" cannot be taken to mean actual assets at the time of enquiry. Paragraph 52 of the "Directions" was not abrogated, the standard proportion was merely changed from 66 to 50 per cent. That paragraph runs—

It is desirable that the Government should not demand more than two-thirds of what may be expected to be the net produce to the proprietor during the period of settlement, leaving to the proprietor one-third as his profits, and to cover expenses of cultivation. By net produce is meant the surplus which the estate may yield, after deducting the expenses of cultivation, including the profits of stock and wages of labour; and this is an estate held entirely by cultivating proprietors will be the profit on their *sir* cultivation, but, in an estate held by a non-cultivating proprietor and leased out to cultivators or *assamis* paying at a known rate, will be the gross rental.

12. Rule XXXVI of the Saharanpur Rules specially directs attention to the cautions conveyed in paragraphs 47 to 51 of the same treatise. Paragraph 49 for example runs—

If the net produce of any one year, or any given number of past years, could be determined, it would afford no certain guide to the produce of years to come. The future produce may be more if there is waste land to come into cultivation; if the former system of cultivation were faulty and expensive; if the products of the land are likely to come into demand in the market; or if the opening out of new channels of commercial intercourse is likely to improve the local market. The future produce may be less if the reverse of all these be the case.

Paragraph 50 then goes on to say— CENTRAL PROVS.

Not only would the actual ascertainment of the net produce of an estate be a fallacious basis, on which alone to found any certain determination of the demand, but it is in itself often more difficult to accomplish, and the attempt to effect it is likely to produce many serious evils. In villages where the collections are in kind, or where the proprietors cultivate themselves and pay the jama by a rate upon their *sir* land, it is almost impossible to ascertain either the net or gross produce with any certainty. When once it is known that the Government demand is to be limitted to a fixed portion of the proved produce, there is a general combination to deceive and mislead the Settlement Officer.

13. Every one of these instructions goes to show that the "net average assets" were the rough valuation of the assets which the estate was likely to yield during the currency of the settlement, and it was because the Settlement Officer's estimate of the assets, as thus understood, was likely to be below the mark that the Government of the North-Western Provinces thought it better to lower the fraction to be assessed on this estimate. It is also the case that these instructions justify the iuclusion of farming profits in the Settlement Officer's estimate of the "average assets"—a course which was not adopted in the first regular settlement of this province, and which has been directly negatived in the present Settlement Code. In replying in the public press to the Government of India's orders on the Nagpur Settlement, Mr. Dutt lays special stress on the fact that the assets referred to in the Saharanpur Rules were the actual assets of the time. It is reasonable to suppose that he has not read these directions, in which case he can hardly be said to have exercised that due diligence to discover the truth which should precede an argument of the kind which he has advanced.

14. In the Nagpur province there was never any order to adopt even nominally a half-asset rule. In paragraph 16 of the Government of India's letter No. 2279, dated the 28th June 1860, which issued in the Foreign Department to the address of the Commissioner of the Nagpur province in the reply to the proposal of the Commissioner "to leave the malguzars from 35 to 55 per

CENTRAL PROVS.

cent." of the gross rental and in some cases 40 per cent., it was written as follows:—

> The true gross rental of each estate having been ascertained by a careful enquiry, the Governor General in Council would be disposed to leave the malguzars in all cases 40 per cent. for expenses of management and proprietory profits, and to extend the limit in special cases even to 50 per cent.

The expression "true gross rental" is of course not defined, but it is quite clear that if the Government of India had meant the actual present rental. it would have been very easy to have said so. As in the case of the term "average net assets" the expression was clearly intended to convey the ascertained rental value of the land, irrespective of the rental at the time borne on the rent-roll, which the malguzars might reasonably be expected to increase.

It is, however, quite inconceiveable that even had the expressions "average net assets" or "true gross rental" been used in these orders as a clumsy and unnecessary periphrases for the actual existing rental, that the Chief Commissioner who initiated the settlement proceedings, the Settlement Commissioner who supervised them, and the Settlement Officers who carried them out should all alike have conspired to disobey their instructions, and that the Government of India who criticised and confirmed these settlements when reported to them should have allowed their positive orders to be ignored. That the Settlement Officers assessed on what they thought the rental should be or would become, not on what it was, is patent to everyone who studies their reports and the methods to which they openly resorted to arrive at the fair rental figure. There was no concealment and no evasion. It is futile now to assert that one knows better what the Government of India meant than the Government itself when it confirmed the settlements more than thirty years ago.

Incidence of revenue in old settlements.

15. As Mr. Fuller has said (paragraph 5 of his letter), "that the settlements were light and that the province prospered under them is a matter of notoriety." Mr. Dutt will no doubt be relieved to

CENTRAL PROVS.

learn, however, that after excluding the farming profits of proprietors, of which the orders admitted the inclusion, in the eight districts to which the Saharanpur Rules applied, the fraction of revenue assessed on *actual* assets was actually below half-assets in three (Seoni, Narsinghpur, and Hoshangabad), that it was exactly half-assets in Jubbulpore, and that it exceeded half-assets only by a little in Saugor (51 per cent.), Damoh (54 per cent.) and Mandla (56 per cent.) and that only in Nimar was it apparently very high (64 per cent.) The reason for this excess in the case of that district is that the district having been practically a ryotwari country, a large number of ryots were made proprietors of their plots, and that the malguzars were only entitled to, and allowed, a small commission on the revenue payments of these ryots. The actual fraction assessed on the malguzari assets was only 32 per cent.

16. In the Nagpur province where the Settlement Officer's orders were to leave the malguzars 40 or in exceptional cases 50 per cent. of the "true gross rental," the fraction taken was high only in Nagpur (78 per cent.), Wardha (79 per cent.), Chhindwara (66 per cent)., and Betul (64 per cent.). In these districts the malguzars were afraid to raise rents after announcement for fear of further enhancement of their revenue. The revenue was enhanced only in Betul of these four districts, while in Chhindwara it was actually reduced by 13 per cent. In Bhandara and Chanda the assessment was at 60 per cent.; in Bilaspur it was 57; and in Raipur only 53. Sambalpur, where the tenure is *quasi*-ryotwari, may be left out of account. The district pays one of the lightest revenues in India.

Increase in rents during term of settlement.

17. Lest it might be supposed, however, that the rental as revised upon agreement by landlord and tenant after the announcement of revenue was not realised and was excessive, it is right to show how it rose by the action of the landlords and the progress of the country during the currency of the thirty-years'

CENTRAL PROVS.

settlement. The districts for which these returns are available are sufficiently typical of the several tracts :—

DISTRICT.	Rental of tenant at the end of the 30 years' settlement.	Rental of tenants at the beginning of the 30 years' settlement.
	R	R
Damoh	4,03,000	5,47,000
Jubbulpore	9,77,000	14,47,000
Narsinghpur	6,72,000	9,19,000
Hoshangabad	7,42,000	11,29,000
Wardha	5,24,000	7,13,000
Nagpur	8,74,000	10,58,000
Raipur	7,13,000	10,84,000
Bilaspur	3,20,000	6,00,000

I trust that the facts and figures which I have advanced will show convincingly to the Government of India, if they ever had any doubt on the subject, that the settlements of 1862 to 1867 were fair, that they did not contravene the orders, that the rental was not fixed by the Settlement Officers, and that it did not absorb such an unheard of fraction as a third of the gross produce.

Present system of settlement.

18. I now turn to the third point raised by Mr. Dutt—the unfairness of the revised settlements. It seems hardly necessary for me to enter on a disquisition upon the system of settlement which was sanctioned by the Government of India for the revision of settlements in the Central Provinces. The facts and rules are well known to the Government of India. So far as the assets are concerned the rules fulfil the conditions advocated by Mr. R. C. Dutt that assessment should be based on actual assets. The actual assets are ascertained and consist of the following :—

(*a*) The present rents *minus* any reduction made by the Settlement Officer.

(*b*) The rental enhancement, if any, imposed by the Settlement Officer, and brought into immediate force.

(*c*) The rental valuation at present rates of home-farm and service land. **CENTRAL PROVS.**

(*d*) A moderate estimate of siwai or miscellaneous income based on the ascertained actuals of the past, with a drawback for fluctuations.

On these assets 60 per cent. is the maximum assessable unless the existing revenue already exceeds that proportion and has been paid without difficulty, in which case it may be maintained subject to a further maximum of 65 per cent.

19. Upon the settlements concluded under these rules Mr. Dutt makes *inter alia* the following remarks :—

The settlement which has been effected in the Central Provinces since 1890 has been felt as more harsh and severe, and has caused more actual suffering and distress than any previous settlement in any part of India. My information is that the rents now fixed can with difficulty be paid even in years of good harvest, that they leave no fair margin for saving for bad years, and that they can never be realized by malguzars from year to year. Large tracts of country which were previously under cultivation have gone out of cultivation owing to over-assessment, and instances have occurred in which malguzars have applied to surrender their estates in order to be relieved of their liability to pay a Government revenue which they cannot pay, and their application has not been granted.

After making a brief allusion to the soil-unit system, he writes :—

These complicated calculations were unintelligible to the cultivator and were, moreover, made in the dark. What the cultivator did understand was that a general enhancement had been effected over the high rental of the old settlement, and there was alarm and consternation in the country when the new enhanced rents were proclaimed. * * * * If after the experience of nearly a century of administration it has been found in Northern India that the wisest, safest and most considerate policy is to let landlords make their own arrangements with cultivators as regards rents, subject to salutary checks imposed by the Government, is it a wise policy in the Central Provinces for the Government to fix after calculations which are unintelligible alike to landlord and tenant, what rent each cultivator should pay for his holding? If private landlords in Northern India consider one-fifth of the gross produce a fair rent for the lands held

CENTRAL PROVS. by their tenants, is it considerate of the British Government to impose on the poorer peasantry of the Central Provinces a rent of one-third or more of the gross produce?

20. Such are his allegations regarding rents. As regards the revenue he says :—

> The authorities of the Central Provinces asked the sanction of the Indian Government to demand 50 to 65 per cent. of the malguzari assets as revenue. The Government of India had some hesitation in allowing in any case so high a percentage as 65 per cent. to be taken, but nevertheless did grant the permission in some cases and made 60 per cent. the maximum rate in other cases. If we add to these high rates another 12½ per cent. which has been added as rates, it will be easy to see that between 70 and 80 per cent. of the landlord's *supposed* assets, *i.e.*, nearly 100 per cent. of his real assets are now demanded by the Government as revenue.

21. Any one would gather from a perusal of this that the Government have made a large enhancement of rents forcing them up to a third and over of the gross produce, that they had exacted the uttermost revenue which the rules allowed from the malguzars, and had in fact taken all their assets, and that the country in consequence was becoming a wilderness, while the cultivator, being compelled to pay 6 annas in the rupee of his gross produce, is impoverished in good years and driven to relief works in bad years.

22. The picture drawn is a gross travesty of the true facts, and would, if true, be an indictment of the Administration for gross misgovernment. Not a single one of the *propositions* contained in the extract has been, or can be, substantiated. To take the case of rents first, Mr. Dutt impugns both the method of the enhancement and its amount. As regards the extent of the enhancement the figures set forth by Mr. Carey in paragraph 29 of his letter, show what the rent rates are as revised by the Settlement Officer in a number of districts. They also show that except in the case of Sambalpur, where rent was fixed for the first time on new cultivation and is singularly low, the largest enhancement imposed has been 16 per cent. in Nagpur, of which district the revised settlement was recently sanctioned by the Government of India, and in which district also there has probably

been less deterioration owing to famine than in almost any part of the province. The great bulk of the enhancement imposed by the Settlement Officer was placed on the holdings of protected tenants of which the rents had hardly risen during the currency of the settlement, although the prices of produce had doubled. So far as ordinary rents were concerned, it was only in the Mahratta country, in which the landlords are still to some extent influenced by the old tradition condemning rent enhancement, without revenue enhancement, that these rents admitted of an increase except in a few individual cases. In the northern districts, where the landlords have been more powerful, the rents which they had demanded of the ordinary tenants were much higher than any which the Settlement Officer could have imposed. CENTRAL PROVS.

Soil-unit system.

23. The soil-unit system upon which Mr. Dutt attributes so much obscurity merely consists of a method by which differential soil-rates may be thrown into a common denominator by reducing the value of each soil to terms of the value of the poorest soil in cultivation. It enables the existing rental incidence of an area of mixed land to be ascertained with accuracy, and the enhancement which is justified either by prevailing rates or rise in prices to be distributed appropriately over the various holdings of a village. The amount of the enhancement is determined precisely on the same considerations which have influenced Settlement Officers in all parts of India, and which are the accepted economic principles of rent revision. The soil-unit system does not, as seems to be supposed, enable the Settlement Officer to fixed rents by a mere arithmetical calculation. It rather supplies him with a convenient test by which to direct his enquiries in respect of the comparison between the incidence of rents in different villages, and to check the exercise of his judgment in the fixation of individual rents. The enquiries have to be made, and judgment has to be exercised, all the same. The system also enables a more complete check to be exercised over a Settlement Officer's proposals than any system yet devised, because the precise amount of the deduced rents which the Settlement Officer's rate will involve in any village

CENTRAL PROVS. can be foreseen beforehand. This enables higher authority to check immediately any tendency to undue enhancement. This is a matter of ordinary experience in settlement work.

Comparison of actual and deduced rents.

24. Mr. Dutt seems to imagine that, while the rents settled by agreements between the landlords and tenants are bound to be moderate, those evolved or deduced by the Settlement Officer with the aid of the system which he regards as so dangerous are grossly excessive. The following statement compares the ordinary rental in a number of districts as demanded by the landlords before revision with the rental value of the same land deduced by the Settlement Officer from his rates:—

DISTRICT.	Rental of ordinary tenants before revision.	Deduced rental of the same land.
	Rs.	Rs.
Damoh	2,83,026	2,44,226
Jubbulpore—Jubbulpore Tahsil	3,66,712	2,80,420
Do. Sehora Tahsil	1,85,859	1,62,447
Hoshángabad	5,12,914	3,02,103
Narsinghpur	4,08,339	2,60,569
Wardha	2,36,950	1,68,742
Nagpur	2,97,502	2,78,401
Raipur	4,49,046	4,30,937
Bilaspur	3,04,223	2,90,143

These figures show the excess over large tracts in which the effect of a number of low-rented holdings obscures the results. Many villages could be found in which the present rents of ordinary tenants as fixed by the landlords exceeded much more largely the Settlement Officer's deduced rental; and a reference to the village rent fixation volumes would show hundreds of cases in which the tenant's rent was double, treble, or quadruple of the deduced rental. It is noteworthy that in Hoshangabad the rental demanded from ordinary tenants by the landlords is almost 70 per cent. higher than the Settlement Officer's deduced rental.

CENTRAL PROVS.

Incidence of Government rent rates on gross produce.

25. The allegation that the revised rental exceeds a third of the gross produce is again completely exposed by Mr. Carey in paragraph 28 of his letter. If any further exposure is needed, it is proved by the fact that, if the revised rental of the land really exceeded a third of its gross produce, the gross produce in some districts would barely suffice for seed. In Bilaspur, for instance, a district which is always cited by agitators as a flagrant example of over-assessment, the rental rate per acre as revised at the settlement was 6 annas 9 pies per acre. Three times this is R1-13-3; when the rent is deducted, there remains only R1-3-6 per acre. The average price of the coarsest rice is 17 seers the rupee in Bilaspur, equivalent to 34 seers of seed rice. It takes 90 lbs. at least to sow an acre, and costs R1-5-0 at normal rates. According to Mr. Dutt's contention, the land in Bilaspur would yield less than 1½ times the seed, or about 125 lbs. an acre. The normal produce of the various districts has been carefully estimated by the Settlement Officers, who assuredly have better means of ascertaining it than outside critics with no experience of the province. At the prices of some ten years ago (which have since risen) the rental of no district exceeds 15 per cent. of the normal produce. The highest fraction reached is one-seventh, while in some districts the proportion does not exceed one-fourteenth.

Present incidence of revenue rates.

26. Next as regards revenue, the arguments adduced to show that the rental generally, so far from exceeding a third of the produce as alleged by Mr. Dutt, is not even as large (sometimes less than half as large) as the sixth, which Mr. Dutt states that every ryot in India recognizes as a fair and equitable rent, effectually cut away the ground from his contention that the assets on which the revenue is fixed are *supposed*, and not real or realisable. There remains only to be dealt with his statement that including cesses the assessment absorbs between 70 and 80

CENTRAL PROVS. per cent. of the malguzari assets. He has made the extraordinary mistake of supposing that cesses are calculated on assets, whereas they are calculated on the revenue and range between 6 to 7½ per cent. of the assets (*vide* paragraph 19 of Mr. Carey's letter). His strictures as to the fraction assessed are similarly inaccurate, or, although the rules may permit the assessment of 60 per cent., they never enjoined that that fraction should be invariably taken; and, as a matter of fact, outside Nagpur and Wardha the highest fraction assessed on a district has been 55, and in two districts—Seoni (47 per cent.) and Hoshangabad (49 per cent.)—the revised assessment is less than half the assets. The highest fraction 5·88 per cent. (or including the revenue of plot proprietors 61 per cent.) was taken in Nagpur, in which district the proprietory body have gained by resettlement. The fractions in this district and Wardha were lowered from 79 and 78 per cent. respectively, which, in respect of the assets existing at the former settlement, involved the reduction of revenue paid for thirty years. Over the province as a whole the revised revenue falls on the revised assets at 53 per cent.

27. One by one the fallacies with which Mr. Dutt's letter teems have been exposed, but I do not desire on that account to underrate the depressed condition of agriculture in some parts of the province, nor to forget the areas in which, owing to the continuous losses of the past few years, including two famines, revision or abatement has been found necessary. The Government of India share fully in the sympathetic anxiety with which I view the condition of parts of this province, and the desire I have to do all I can for its amelioration. The effect of the losses and failures which have been entirely caused by unfavourable climatic conditions cannot well be exaggerated, and it is to them, and not to the settlements, that the deteriorated condition of certain districts is now due.

Losses by famine and drought.

28. The question how far the famine conditions which have prevailed can be attributed to assessments has been examined and reported in paragraphs 341-345 of the Report on the famine of 1899-1900 recently

submitted to the Government of India with Mr. Craddock's letter No. 892-A, dated the 27th February last, and it is hardly necessary to repeat the arguments here. Suffice it to say that the people of the province have during the last seven years lost produce to the value of 40 crores. During the whole period the increase in their revenue demand has not exceeded a crore of rupees, of which a portion has been suspended or remitted. Only perverse blindness could attribute agricultural depression to the assessment, and not to the losses, particularly as the people have received in unrecovered takavi and charitable loans much more than the crore taken from them in increased revenue, not to mention 6½ crores spent on famine relief. Nor is it out of place to mention that it is the districts which have not paid their revised assessments which have suffered the most. The Khurai tashil of Saugor, the Damoh district, Hoshangabad, and Balaghat, are all tracts in which the present agricultural depression is most severe. None of them have paid their enhanced revenue; because crop failures prevented their being levied, and necessitated suspension or remission even of the old demand which had been regularly rendered for thirty years in seasons of only normal fluctuations. Most of the Chanda district, which has suffered so severely in the recent famine, is still paying a revenue fixed 35 years ago.

CENTRAL PROVS.

29. The facts which I have stated should show that the allegations of Mr. R. C. Dutt have no foundation in fact, and must have been unsupported by even the most superficial enquiries. It is the irony of fate that the one point upon which he lays so much stress should have been proved by experience the weak point in the recent settlements. Abatement on account of loss of cropping is necessary wherever successive failures have caused a deterioration which is not merely temporary. Where owing to repeated losses of his crops the cultivator has exhausted his credit and lost his cattle, he has been unable to cultivate his holding. Where there is no crop to reap, not even the most moderate rent can be paid. In those places abatements in proportion to loss of cropping are

Abatements due to loss of cropping.

CENTRAL PROVS.

necessary. Such abatements may become expedient anywhere, irrespective of the assessment, when cultivators lose their all; though it may surprise critics like Mr. Dutt to learn that the only large areas over which such deterioration has occurred are situated in districts in which half-assets settlements have been made. In two tracts only has it been found advisable to make a permanent revision of the rents fixed at settlement—the Hoshangabad district and the rich *haveli* of Jubbulpore, and in them this has been necessary not because the Settlement Officer followed his statistical conclusions and neglected the rental fixed by agreement between landlord and tenant, but because he followed the landlords and neglected his statistical conclusions. When these settlements were made, the Settlement Officer had not the legal power to lower the rents of ordinary tenants. And the propriety of bringing pressure to bear on landlords to reduce such rents when shown by the deduced rents to be excessive, was only partially recognized. The result has been the necessity for a revision of these rents, with the consent of malguzars and tenants alike, on the basis of the very system which Mr. Dutt condemns. The law now also empowers the Settlement Officer to reduce excessive rents.

Benefits of the fixation of rent by Government.

30. When the revised settlements were made, the Settlement Officer had no power to reduce the rents of ordinary tenants, the only rents which are fixed by agreement between landlord and tenant in this province. Rents, which his statistical conclusions under the soil-unit system showed him to be unduly high, he could only reduce by putting pressure on the landlords. Some considerable reductions were made in the cases where actual areas had accrued; but much opposition was encountered, and it was asserted by the landlords that the rent which the Settlement Officer wished to reduce was realisable. Acting on these assurances the Settlement Officer allowed rents of this kind to stand, and it is these rents (on which revenue was naturally fixed) that have now been proved unpayable and have brought confusion on the landlords who refused to reduce them. The law now gives the power

to the Settlement Officers to reduce rents of this kind, and I am arranging for their reduction. The landlords themselves now bitterly lament their obduracy. One of the largest landlords in the Jubbulpore district, Rai Bahadur Ballabhdass,* admitted the fact publicly before the Famine Commission of 1898; and the malguzars in Hoshangabad are now clamouring for that reduction of ordinary rents which five years ago they successfully resisted. It speaks volumes for the moderation of our Settlement Officers in fixing the statutory rents of protected tenants that, even after the inclusion of these excessive rents in the rent-roll, the general rental incidence in these districts does not even reach that magic sixth which Mr. R. C. Dutt declares that "every ryot in India recognizes as fair and equitable." **CENTRAL PROVS.**

General conclusions.

31. It has been shown that the rents of the country generally are much below the standard which Mr. Dutt has laid down; it has been shown that a half-assets assessment has not saved from deterioration and abatement districts which have been overwhelmed by calamities of the seasons; it has been shown that rental fixed by the landlords is not that example of moderation which Mr. Dutt would have us believe. It only remains to say a word on the question of the fraction of assets which Government may take as revenue. There is no real virtue in the half-assets rule. The fairness of an assessment depends upon the means of subsistence which it leaves to the payer. The man who pays 60 per cent. in a village with

* In reply to the question of the Famine Commission of 1898 this gentleman stated that the revised assessments were too high.

He was further interrogated (page 189, Appendix IV, to the Report of the Indian Famine Commission, 1898)—

Q. Do you not know that no enhancement on cultivators' holdings was made?

A. It is true no enhancement has been made on the holdings of ordinary tenants, but the malguzars themselves had raised their rents so high as to render recovery impossible; hence the enhancement was merely a nominal one.

Q. Were remissions (reductions) allowed to cultivators?

A. Very little and not sufficient.

Q. Malguzars expressed their dissatisfaction on occasions of remissions (reductions) being granted to their tenants, was it not so?

CENTRAL PROVS.

assets of R5,000 is surely better off than his neighbour who pays 50 per cent. in a village with assets of R400. The suitability of a revised assessment depends less upon the fraction of assets which it takes, than on the reduction of income which it involves. It has been found possible to take 60 per cent. in Nagpur without reducing the incomes of the proprietors, while the half-assets assessments in Jubbulpore and Hoshangabad have proved most burdensome to them. The reason was that in these districts the landlords had themselves so immoderately increased their incomes that a half-assets assessment entailed on them a corresponding sudden loss. This they might have borne had seasons been propitious; but with the crop failures which followed in quick succession this became impossible. For the calamities of the seasons neither the landlords nor the Government are responsible; but for the increase in their assessments the landlords have only their own folly to thank. They have now learnt their lesson; their powers have been fettered by the law as contained in the legislation of 1898; and the measures which are now being adopted for abatement in deteriorated tracts, and for revision in the districts concerned, should go far, with other assistance, towards the restoration of the people to prosperity.

32. It may not be amiss to state in conclusion that the provisional census figures recently obtained fully bear out all that has been said above. The districts taken are those in which the new assessments have been longest in force or have actually been realized:—

District.	Fraction of assets taken as revenue.		Increase or decrease per cent. in population.
	At old settlement.	At revised settlement.	
Nimar	64	62	+14·3
Sambalpur	75	75	+4·2
Chhindwara	66	55	+0·2
Nagpur	78	61	−0·8
Wardha	79	59	−3·8
Raipur	53	53	−8·9
Bilaspur	57	54	−13·1
Narsinghpur	49	50	−14·5
Seoni	48	47	−11·7

By citing these figures I do not intend to imply that a high fraction can avert deterioration, but merely that deterioration has been independent of assessment, and that a high fraction, when otherwise justified, is not incompatible with prosperity. The highest assessed districts, so far as the fraction goes, have not been so continuously and severely afflicted as some of their neighbours, but they too have suffered very heavy losses. **CENTRAL PROVS.**

33. As I have already indicated, I am far from attributing any motive other than the best to Mr. R. C. Dutt. But I cannot but regret the course which he has adopted. He has attacked the Settlement Department in England and in India on what seems to me wholly inadequate information and without any apparent effort to ascertain the truth. I have no direct concern in the honour of the Settlement Department; for I have never been directly responsible for settlement work. But I have had excellent opportunities for judging of the work of the department in this province I know that there are no officers in India who do harder work, who know more about the people, or who have shown deeper sympathy with them in their troubles than the Settlement Officers. I know also the value of the information which their toil has placed at the disposal of Government. I regret, therefore, to find this attack made on them on the inadequate grounds which I have examined. Ignorant and prejudiced criticism coming from irresponsible persons does little harm; but more care might have been expected from a retired member of the Indian Civil Service, whose late position gives to his statement what is in this case a wholly specious value. Action in the direction of granting abatement and revision had been commenced by the Administration long before Mr. R. C. Dutt's letter saw the light and will be steadily continued where required; but the end in view is not to be reached by attempting to upset the system of settlement, which rests on too solid a foundation of experience to

CENTRAL PROVS.

be shaken by the statements which I have examined. I have written at some length; but that has seemed necessary for the sake of dealing fully and clearly with the matters on which an expression of my opinions was invited by the Government of India.

A. H. L. FRASER,

Offg. Chief Commissioner,

The 9th April 1901. *Central Provinces.*

From J. B. Fuller, Esq., C.I.E., Commissioner, Jubbulpore Division, to the Honourable the Chief Commissioner, Central Provinces No. C.-290, dated Camp Sehora, the 1st December 1900.

I have the honour to offer the following observations on Mr. Romesh Chandra Dutt's open letter to His Excellency the Viceroy regarding the Land Revenue Settlements of these provinces, a copy of which was forwarded under your endorsement No. 4320, dated the 27th ultimo.

2. Mr. Dutt includes in his strictures the settlements of 1863—68 as well as those made during the past 12 years, urging that under both of them the rents payable by cultivators to landlords were fixed too high, and an unduly—and unwarrantably—large share of the landlord's assets taken as revenue.

Results of settlements of 1863–68.

3. Turning in the first place to the settlements of 1863—68, it is to be observed that the Settlement Reports of that time do not always state very clearly or definitely the financial results of the Settlement Officer's action which has sometimes to be gathered from a comparison of statistics given in various passages of the report. In 1886 I compiled a note examining in some detail the results of these settlements, and those which preceded them, and from this note I extract the following figures showing the effect on tenants

and on landlords of the revision of the demand in the years 1863—68 :— CENTRAL PROVS.

District.	Percentage by which the payments were enhanced.		Percentage of the proprietary assets absorbed by the Government Revenue.	
	Of tenants.	Of landlords.	Before revision.	After revision.
	Saugor-Nerbudda Territories.			
Saugor . . .	6	(—14)	74	54
Damoh . . .	5	(—5)	68	54
Jubbulpore . .	3	7	46	51
Mandla . . .	Not stated. but considerable.	48	45	Not stated.
Seoni . . .	About 30	56	39	48
Narsinghpur . .	6·5	27	42	49
Hoshangabad . .	32	43	42	46
Nimar . . .	31	15	66	64
Betul . .	5	32	51	64(?)
	Nagpur Territory.			
Chhindwara . .	4	(—13)	75	66
Wardha . . .	Trifling.	(—0·1)	?	79
Nagpur . . .	Trifling.	(—6)	83	78
Chanda . . .	5·6	2	69	71
Bhandara, including Balaghat.	25	12	66	64 (59 for revenue actually payable.)
Raipur . . .	Large.	64	Not stated.	54
Bilaspur . . .	Large.	61	75	56

Footnote.—I have omitted the Sambalpur District as this is settled *ryotwar* and not with proprietors.

Taking tenants first of all, it will be observed that in nine of the sixteen districts rents were enhanced in a quite trifling degree or not at all. In the remaining seven districts enhancements were considerable. It must be realized that in those days the authoritative fixation of rents was no part of a Settlement Officer's duties. In estimating the assets on which his revenue was to be based he allowed for such rent enhancement as seemed to him reasonable, but he did not give practical effect to his judgment in this matter. At the time the revised revenue assessment was

CENTRAL PROVS.

announced, an officer, usually a native Deputy Collector, was deputed to endeavour to bring landlords and tenants to agree to and distribute such enhancement of rents as would be in accord with the new revenue assessment, and the extent of the enhancement actually accepted depended less on the Settlement Officer's forecast than on the strength of the landlords, the custom of the country and the trouble taken over the business by the Officer-in-charge of the adjustment. From what I have been able to gather, this part of the Settlement proceedings often received most inadequate attention, as it was not taken up till after the reassessment had been sanctioned and (in many cases) the Settlement Officer had left the district. In Mandla and Seoni rentals were before the revision exceedingly low, and a large area is held by talukdars of position. Rents rose largely, but that they were still light is shown by the large further rise in the rentals of these districts during the currency of the settlements. The lightness of the revenue demand is shown by its incidence on the cultivated area, 2·8 annas per acre in Mandla and 5·8 annas in Seoni. These remarks also apply to Hoshangabad, where the landlord's rental rose enormously during currency of settlement. In the case of these three districts it is, moreover, believed that the rentals as recorded previously to settlement were much understated, and that much of what is classed as enhancement was in reality merely disclosure. In Nimar a very large proportion of the ryots are plot proprietors paying revenue not rent, and in their case enhancement was effected authoritatively and left them paying less than a full rent. In the Nagpur country the Bhandara District alone shows any considerable rent enchancement due, I believe, to special care taken by the native officer who was deputed to adjust rents. In the Chhattisgarh districts of Rajpur and Bilaspur rent enhancement was large. But it left the tenants paying on the average only 9 annas per cultivated acre, and the lightness of their rents is evidenced by the very great further enhancements which occurred during the currency of the settlement. Having regard to the facts that in more than half the number of districts rents were left practically untouched, and that where they rose, they rose by consent and were still exceedingly low, it is quite preposterous to tax the Government of that day with harshness in fixing the payments of cultivators.

CENTRAL PROVS.

The half-asset principle.

4. Turning now to the interests of the landlords, exception must be taken to the representation made by Mr. Dutt of the "half-asset" principle. It is true that the Settlements of the Saugor-Nerbudda Districts were effected under a ruling of the North-Western Provinces Board of Revenue that the demand of the State, which had previously been a nominal two-thirds, was to be limited to "one-half to the average net assets." But the terms "assets" had a more comprehensive meaning than that of "actual revenue." It meant the income which a proprietor would enjoy if the whole of his land was fairly rented, and it threw on him and not on the State the cost of the special rental privileges enjoyed by protected ryots. As the assets were to be an "average," it was open to the Settlement Officer to take into consideration probable increases during the currency of his Settlement. Moreover, as under the procedure of those days the assets were settled before rents were re-adjusted, their amount included the Settlement Officer's estimates for rent enhancement. If a village contained protected or privileged holdings, or if the Settlement Officer's estimates were not fulfilled, an assessment which was nominally fixed at the half-assets might absorb a very much larger proportion of the actual income. Procedure has been changed, and the assets on which the revenue is calculated now correspond with actual income. The "assets" we now follow are at once less comprehensive and more definite than the "assets" of former days, and in both respects form a basis of calculation which favours the interests of proprietors. A serious inaccuracy on Mr. Dutt's part is his assumption that the "half assets" rule applied to the Nagpur and Chhattisgarh districts, the Settlements of which were made under orders "allowing malguzars in all cases 40 per cent. of the true gross rental and in certain cases 50 per cent." . (Paragraph 25 of my note.)

CENTRAL PROVS.

Incidence of revenue in earlier settlements.

5. The figures given in my paragraph 3 above show that in two of the Saugor-Nerbudda districts (Saugor and Damoh) the previous assessment was much above *actual* half-assets, and in both cases it was reduced. In Jubbulpore the revenue enhancement was small and the assessment was but a trifle over *actual* half-assets, and would be much below a prospective *average* half-assets. In the other districts of this part of the Provinces, excepting Nimar and Betul, the landlords were left with half actual assets or more. In Nimar the assessment exceeded half-assets because of the large number of plot proprietors who paid revenue not rent. In Betul a considerable excess was due to rents not having risen to the extent anticipated by the Settlement Officer. In three districts of the Nagpur country (Chhindwara, Wardha and Nagpur) the existing assessment was reduced, and in a fourth district (Chanda) it was left practically untouched. The percentage of the revenue to the assets remained high, but it was not understood that the orders of Government contemplated the reduction of assessments which were found to be paid without difficulty. A large revenue enhancement was imposed on the Chhattisgarh districts of Raipur and Bilaspur. The existing assessment was extraordinarily light, and the revised demand was not more than 5 annas per each cultivated acre. A rapid rise in the proprietor's rental very soon raised their profits to much more than the equivalent of the Government revenue. The general result of this examination is to show that where the revenue was heavy, it was reduced; that where it was enhanced it was fixed at a figure which, taking into consideration increases of rents in the near future, was not inconsistent with the standard prescribed. That the Settlements were light and that the Provinces prospered under them are matters of notoriety.

Recent settlements.

6. I come now to the Settlements of the past 12 years. In two statements appended some figures are given showing, for ten districts, the Settlement Reports of which have been prepared, the financial effect of re-settlement on tenants and on landlords, respectively. State-

ment A is concerned with tenants, and the first point I would note is the lightness of the revised rental as shown by its incidence on the cultivated area (column 3). In Sambalpur this incidence is less than 6 annas per acre. In four other districts it is below one rupee. I next invite attention to the figures of column 5 showing the percentage by which rents were enhanced by the Settlement Officer. In only the Sambalpur District was the enhancement large, and the Sambalpur ryots hold on ryotwari terms under Government and had suffered no enhancement during the currency of the preceding Settlement, although they had extended their holdings so largely that the incidence per acre of the revised assessment was no higher than that of the previous assessment. In no other district did the Settlement Officer's rental enhancements exceed one anna in the rupee. In Jubbulpore and Narsinghpur they were quite inconsiderable. **CENTRAL PROVS.**

Rental enhancements.

7. The figures in column 4 give the percentage rise in rent-rate from the time of the previous Settlement, and include the enhancements made by landlords during the currency of Settlement as well as those made by the Settlement Officer. The rise is largest in Wardha and Bilaspur, but in both districts the rental of the previous Settlement was found to have been much understated. The enhancements in rent-rate have, no doubt, been considerable but they are due in the main to pressure gradually applied by the landlords and not to the action of Government. Nor, when it is considered that since the days of the previous Settlements, the country has been opened out by railways and the value of produce almost doubled, can increases of 30 or even 40 per cent. in very low rent-rates be held to impose an unreasonable demand on the cultivators. In some tracts where the rise in rent-rate had been unusually large, an endeavour was made to reduce very high rents by consent of the landlords, and substantial reductions were made in this way in Jubbulpore, Narsinghpur and Hoshangabad. We might have gone further in this direction with advantage. But we had at the time no legal powers of interference, and proprietors would not very willingly consent to a reduction of their rent-rolls.

CENTRAL PROVS.

It will of course be understood that the rental enhancements effected by the Settlement Officer in districts which showed a substantial rise in rent-rate at the time of his enquiries, only touched the privileged classes of ryots whose payments had been stereotyped by law.

Share of produce.

8. Mr. Dutt adopts a sixth of the produce of land as a measure of a fair rental for it. It is presumed that he does not mean this standard for application in particular cases. Much land is let in these and other Provinces at half-produce, and it is obvious that the share of the produce which land can pay depends largely on the cost of cultivation and that, for instance, sugarcane cannot render nearly as large a proportion as wheat. A fraction of the produce may be taken as a guide to what land can pay on the average, though I am unaware of any substantial reason for the adoption of a sixth. Average gross produce is of course extremely difficult to ascertain and deductions based on its amount have little practical value. But it is quite certain that in the majority of our districts, the rental is far below a sixth of the produce, and that the adoption of Mr. Dutt's rule would warrant a very large further enhancement. For eight of the ten districts used as illustrations estimates of the amount and value of the gross produce were framed at Settlement. They are compared with the rental in columns 10 and 11 of the statement. In four districts the rental is less than 10 per cent. of the produce: in one it is 10 per cent. and in the three others it is respectively 14, 15 and 16 per cent. Rents had in these three districts been largely enhanced during currency of Settlement. It may be objected that the Settlement Officer's calculations cannot be relied upon. But the Settlement Officer in making his estimates had no particular thesis to justify, and if he is not capable of estimating the produce, I do not know whom else we are to turn to.

Revenue enhancements.

9. Passing now to the effect of the re-settlements on landlords' interests, it must be noted that the Settlement Officers in fixing the share of the proprietor's income to be taken as

CENTRAL PROVS.

revenue acted not under the indefinite guidance of the old "half-assets" rule, but under the orders specially issued for them by the Government of India laying down that in view of the narrower meaning now attached to the term "assets," a higher proportion than 50 per cent. might be taken, but no higher proportion (in enhancing) than 60 per cent. The "assets" thus to be shared between Government and the landlords did not include the payments of plot proprietors on which the landlords were to receive a commission only. Column 6 of Statement B shows the effect given to these orders in each of* nine districts, and taken with column 5 compares the percentage of revenue to *actual present assets* at the new Settlements and at those preceding them. The percentage exceeds 60 in Nagpur and approximates to it in Wardha, because it is calculated on assets which include the payments of plot proprietors. In both districts the share of Government has been largely reduced. In no other district does the share exceed 55 per cent. The share was raised in Jubbulpore and Narsinghpur, but in one of these districts is under 50 per cent. and in the other only just above it.

10. The precentage enhancements shown in column 2 are in some cases undoubtedly high. But so are the percentage increases in cultivation, and it is obvious that the greater the profits made by landlords during the currency of a Settlement, the greater must be their losses when the Settlement is revised. The rent enhancements effected by the Settlement Officer put money into their pockets, and the real measure of enhancement is to be found by deducting the amount of these enhancements from the increase in revenue assessment. The results of this calculation are shown in column 13. From this point of view the pressure of the new assessment is much less than it would appear at first sight. And it must be remembered that the larger is the increase in the demands of Government the more profitable is the Settlement to the landlords compared with that which preceded it.

* I have omitted Sambalpur as this district is not settled with proprietors.

CENTRAL PROVS.

11. Writing from experience I believe that had the introduction of the new assessments been accompanied and followed by seasons of even moderate productiveness, we should have heard very little of their heaviness. It has unfortunately happened that the imposition of an enchanced revenue demand in many districts synchronized with the commencement of a chain of disasters. Seven lean years, two of which were years of famine, have inflicted tremendous losses on the agricultural classes, and the wonder is not that the Settlements excite complaint, but that they have not broken down altogether.

Cesses.

12. Mr. Dutt in his paragraph 11 writes of "another 12½ per cent. which has been added as rates." This is incorrect. Cesses were levied under the old Settlement. The increases in them have been (1) the 2 per cent. imposed by the Additional Rates Act, (2) the raising of the road-cess from 2 to 3 per cent., and (3) the imposition of a patwari cess at rates varying from 4½ to 6 per cent. The latter cess was not new. Over the greater part of the Provinces the proprietors have all along maintained patwaris, but paid them direct instead of through the Government Treasury. In the Jubbulpore District, for instance, patwari cess was payable under the old Settlement, at 3 per cent. on the rental which is a higher rate than that now charged. But no doubt the maintenance of the Land Record Staff costs landlords more than it did, and we may fairly assume that the patwari rate is generally 2 or 3 per cent. on the revenue higher than its equivalents under the former Settlements.

13. I will add in regard to Mr. Dutt's paragraph 10 that I personally took a part in announcing the revised rents in a number of districts, and in no district but Sambalpur did the people manifest any dissatisfaction nor was any dissatisfaction to be expected. The enhancements imposed by the Settlement Officer were light, and in some cases the tenants had a reason for gratitude in reductions effected.

CENTRAL PROVS.

STATEMENT A.

Statistics indicating the Pressure on Tenants of the new Settlements in the Central Provinces.

District.	Tenants' rent-rate per acre at old Settlement.	Tenants' enhanced rent-rate per acre at new Settlement	Enhancement per cent. in rate.	Enhancement per cent effected in tenants' payment by Settlement Officer.	Rental Valuation Adopted. Malik-makbuzas' payments.	Tenants' rents.	Sir khud-kasht and privileged holdings.	Total.	Gross produce as calculated by Settlement Officer.	Percentage of Column 9 on Column 10.	Remarks.
1	2	3	4	5	6	7	8	9	10	11	12
	R a. p.	R a. p.			R	R	R	R	R		
Damoh	0 13 10	1 1 10	29	11	22,098	6,05,559	1,73,901	8,01,558	54,25,484	14	
Jubbulpore	1 1 4	1 3 8	13	4	56,937	13,59,828	5,11,005	19,27,770	1,26,14,085	15	
For open country only.	2 1 0	2 12 8	35	...	...	..	...		.		
Seoni	0 9 8	0 10 10	12	9	4,507	4,22,586	1,75,474	6,02,567	82,41,394	7	
Narsinghpur	1 5 1	1 11 7	31	6	21,758	9,62,620	2,93,168	12,77,486	80,61,912	16	
Chhindwara	0 9 11	0 9 9	..	12	3,462	4,07,585	1,17,860	5,28,907	1,00,61,740	5	
Wardha	0 10 7	0 15 0	42	14	51,076	8,18,172	2,13,813	10,83,061	1,47,16,115	7	(a) For regularly settled area only.
Nagpur	0 12 10	1 0 3	25	16	1,36,481	12,24,054	3,15,677	16,76,212	(c) 1,88,05,833	.9	(b) For district as whole
Raipur	(a) 0 8 11	(a) 0 10 6	18	12	(b) 4,619	(b) 11,77,152	(b) 3,27,659	(b) 15,09,430	.	10	(c) Excluding bye products.
Bilaspur	0 7 3	0 9 9	34	11	15,819	6,65,321	1,71,774	8,52,414	.	..	

CENTRAL PROVS.

STATEMENT B.

Statistics indicating the Pressure on Malguzars of the new Settlements in the Central Provinces.

District.	Increase per cent.		Percentage increase in rate of revenue per cultivated acre.	Fraction of assessment.		Malguzar's actual profit and loss by re-settlement.				Remarks.
	In Government revenue.	In cultivated area.		Old	New.	Gained by rent enhancement.	Lost by revenue enhancement.	Net loss.	Percentage of loss on former revenue.	
1	2	3	4	5	6	7	8	9	10	11
						R	R	R		
Damoh . .	58	31	22	54	54	81,506	1,63,243	81,737	29	
Jubbulpore . .	65	44	15	50	51	85,616	3,92,789	3,07,173	50	
Seoni . . .	79	50	21	48	47	40,308	1,29,628	89,320	54	
Narsinghpur . .	49	17	27	49	50	57,301	2,12,324	1,55,023	36	
Chhindwara . .	37	60	[—14]	66	55	44,207	79,728	35,521	16	
Wardha . .	25	18	6	79	59	1,10,713	1,32,283	21,570	4	
Nagpur . .	18	13	4	78	61	1,86,884	1,62,251	24,633	3	
Raipur . . .	70	42	18	54	54	82,625	2,15,777	1,33,152	43	Regularly settled area only.
Bilaspur . .	80	40	34	56	54	70,698	2,22,941	1,52,243	60	

From L. S. Carey, Esq., Commissioner of Settlements and Agriculture, Central Provinces, to the Chief Commissioner, Central Provinces, No. 50—147, dated the 8th January 1901. CENTRAL PROVS.

I have the honour to acknowledge the receipt of your endorsement No. 4321, dated the 27th October 1900, forwarding for opinion a letter from Mr. R. C. Dutt, late of the Indian Civil Service, to His Excellency the Viceroy, on the subject of land settlements in the Central Provinces, and in reply to state as follows.

2. Mr. Dutt, at the outset, impugns the 30 years' settlement of these provinces, alleging that the intentions of Lord Canning's Government were not carried into effect, with the result that rents were fixed too high and too large a percentage of assets was taken as revenue from the malguzars. And he goes so far as to lay down that the rent fixed in those settlements was one-third of the gross produce. He next proceeds to complain that the mistakes of the past have been repeated in aggravated form at the recent revision, the rental approximating to six annas in the rupee of the gross produce and the revenue absorbing nearly 100 per cent. of the real assets of the malguzars.

3. It will, I think, be profitable to glance momentarily at the previous revenue history of the—

(I) Saugor-Nerbudda Territory,

(II) Nagpur country,

(III) The Chhattisgarh districts of Raipur and Bilaspur,

from the time that the British Government first became connected with these territories. This history is ably summarised in Mr. Fuller's note of 1886 on Land Revenue Settlements of the Central Provinces, from which I cull the following information: first as to the Saugor-Nerbudda Territory which was ceded by Apaji Bhonsla in 1818, a tract which had been harassed by constant war and ground down by exceedingly heavy taxation. A system of short leases ruled, and villages were given to the highest bidders. The patels had to content themselves with one-tenth of the whole profits,

Early revenue history of the province.

CENTRAL PROVS.

and the majority had to make way for a race of speculating farmers who agreed to any conditions the revenue authorities might make in the hopes of securing a footing in the village for better times to come. At the outset short-term settlements were made under British rule, and an abortive attempt was made to maintain and even improve upon the revenue handed over to us by the Bhonsla Government. The policy is characterized as one of those tremendous mistakes the effects of which many years of subsequent moderation and justice have hardly been able to wipe away. After about 10 or 15 years during which two-thirds of the English correspondence of those times related solely to revenue reductions, the necessity of substantial abatements in the land revenue demand was fully recognized. Then came a 20 years' settlement in 1836-37 which, allowing for dislocation caused by the Mutiny, brings us up to the time when preparations were made for the revision that resulted in the 30 years' settlement. The following figures are instructive :—

DISTRICT.	Annual demand after cession.	Annual demand 20 years after cession.	Annual demand 20 years after cession.	Demand of 20 years' settlement made in 1836-37.
1	2	3	4	5
	R	R	R	R
Saugor	5,88,100	6,27,900	6,09,600	6,27,900
Damoh	3,53,500	3,24,400	2,43,300	30,5,100
Jubbulpore	4,48,200	6,41,000	6,05,000	4,75,700
Mandla	65,900	46,300	34,100	36,200
Seoni	1,76,000	1,74,100	1,67,900	1,24,500
Narsinghpur	6,67,700	5,27,700	4,00,000	3,47,000
Hoshangabad (excluding Harda)	2,56,700	2,70,000	1,88,000	1,68,600
Betul	2,86,600	2,03,500	1,61,200	1,40,000
TOTAL	28,42,700	28,14,900	24,09,100	22,25,000

They indicate the steady reduction and adjustment of the demand to the paying capacity of the people, and it is noticeable that the tract comprising these districts or portions of districts paid only 23½ lakhs in 1886, as the demand of the 30 years' settlement. This represents a fall of five lakhs below the revenue realized at the time of cession. CENTRAL PROVS.

4. The history of the Nagpur country is somewhat different. Sovereignty was only acquired in 1854, but owing to the minority of the Raja the districts were under British management between 1818 and 1830. During this period of 12 years changes of far-reaching importance were made. The native rule during the period of 1830 to 1854 was very lax and the land revenue demand declined. On the escheat in 1854 a further considerable reduction took place when summary settlements were concluded. The latter were ultimately abandoned in favour of a 30 years' settlement coupled with the grant of proprietary rights under the orders of the Government of India issued in June 1860. The following figures show the decline in the demand between 1830—1854:—

DISTRICT.	Payable in 1830.	Payable in 1854.	After the summary settlement effected in 1854	Prior to 30 years' settlement.	Rendered payable in 30 years' settlement.
1	2	3	4	5	6
	R	R	R	R	R
Wardha and Nagpur	16,64,000	15,70,000	13,87,000	...	...
Chanda	4,85,000	3,26,200	2,65,200	...	...
Bhandara	3,81,000	3,45,500	3,05,500	...	...
TOTAL	25,30,000	22.41,700	19,57,700	19,81,288	19,72,084

The net demand on these districts, as fixed in the 30 years' settlement, is then about six lakhs less than the taxation of 1830, *i.e.*, some 30 years previously. The British occupation brought them some pecuniary relief to the patels apart from the greater fixity of tenure which culminated in the conferment of proprietary right.

CENTRAL PROVS.

5. The Raipur and Bilaspur districts of Chhattisgarh were ruled by the Hai Hai Bansis, a Hindu dynasty, for 1,000 years and the lowness of the revenue demand is attributed, partly to the readiness of those Chiefs to accept services in lieu of a portion of their revenue, partly to the comparative immunity of Chhattisgarh from foreign invasions and imposts. But from 1741 to 1818 this tract was under Mahratta rule, and during the latter years of that period it is stated to have presented "an uniform scene of plunder and oppression uninfluenced by any consideration but that of collecting by whatever means the largest amount possible." For all that the revenue did not run up very high. Possibly the agents who were far away and out of control of their Bhonsla masters pillaged the villages for themselves and not for the reigning dynasty, and the revenue accounts were shaped accordingly. Moreover, the revenue of the tract was apparently more elastic than in the northern and southern districts of the Central Provinces, and there was abundance of land awaiting cultivation at the hands of new tenants. The revenue demand did not then recede as was the case in the other tracts alluded to in the previous paragraphs, but as shown below advanced slowly though steadily in spite of scarcities in 1835 and 1844, which ruined a large number of villages:—

Year.	Demand. R	
1818 .	3,63,200	
1830 .	3,85,800	after 12 years of British management
1854 .	4,00,000	after 24 years of Mahratta rule.
1862 .	4,61,000	after the escheat in 1854.

6. So much for the previous revenue history of the principal tracts comprising the Provinces. In 1860 Lord Canning's Government issued its letter No. 2279, dated the 28th June, to the Commissioner of the Nagpur Division, which sanctioned the grant of proprietary right in the soil,—whereby at a stroke of the pen the patels who had hitherto held as *mere* lessees and had enjoyed no rights of proprietorship acquired a fee simple in their estates, subject only to the payment of revenue to the

Conferment of proprietary rights.

Government. In the same letter it was laid down that the *true gross rental* of each estate having been ascertained by careful enquiry, the Governor-General in Council would be disposed to allow the malguzars in all cases at least 40 per cent. for expenses of management and proprietary profits and to extend the limit in special cases even to 50 per cent. These orders related merely to the districts of the Nagpur and Chhattisgarh Divisions (less Sambalpur).

Page 19 of the old Settlement Code.

7. The corresponding orders for the Saugor-Nerbudda territories are to be found in the proclamation of the North-Western Provinces Government, dated the 24th June 1854. In paragraph 2 thereof the intention to confer proprietary right is stated, and in paragraph 10 will be found the origin of our malik-makbuzas or plot-holders, who in certain contingencies were to be recorded proprietors and to pay their *jama* direct to Government, or through a party engaging for the whole mahal in which the land is situate. Thirdly, it is laid down in paragraph 6 that the Settlement Officer will fix what he believes to be a fair *jama* with reference to the cultivated and culturable land. I would invite particular attention to the word *culturable,* for it has a very important connection with the interpretation to be placed on the term "assessable assets." Shortly after proprietary right had been granted apprehensions began to be felt that we had gone too far in the interests of the landlords and that something should be done to protect the ryots. The pendulum began to swing in the opposite direction and in 1865 orders issued for the recognition of the absolute-occupancy tenants. Thus commenced the limitation of proprietary right, which was originally intended to be well nigh unconditional, and the practical admission of the privileged ryots to a share in the proprietorship of villages, in so far as their rents fell short of the true market rate.

First 30 years' settlement. Determination of assets and Government share.

8. I would now invite a perusal of paragraphs 25 and 28 of Mr. Fuller's note which contain a disquisition as to what was really understood by the Settlement Officers of those days by assets. Our system of settlement was derived from the North-Western Provinces

CENTRAL PROVS.

and appears to have been based on the Saharanpur rules which are embodied in the old Settlement Code of the Central Provinces which bears date 1863. No. XXXVI of these instructions runs: "The assets of an estate can seldom be minutely ascertained but more certain information as to the average net assets can be obtained now than was formerly the case. This may lead to over-assessment, for there is little doubt that two-thirds, or 66 per cent., is a larger proportion of the real average assets than can ordinarily be paid by proprietors or communities *in a long course of years*. For this reason the Government have determined so far to modify the rule laid down in paragraph 52 of the "directions to Settlement Officers as to limit the demand of the State to 50 per cent. or one-half of the average net assets." Here we have the half-assets rule. Mr. Fuller, in paragraph 28 of his note, draws a distinction between *existing* assets and *real* assets, the latter representing what the malguzars ought to receive in the way of rent if the tenants paid up to the full letting value of their land. A re-adjustment of rents on announcement of the settlement was contemplated. Government was to afford facilities for the same, but the rental enhancements were to be settled by the malguzars and ryots amongst themselves. The rents so fixed were recorded by the Settlement Officer. On the other hand an authoritative enhancement of rents by the Settlement Department was not permitted. From Statement A appended it will be gathered that in many districts very little in the way of rent enhancement resulted from this procedure. Mr. Fuller explains this to be due to these operations being left to subordinates at the close of the settlement when the Settlement Officer had usually left the district, also to the fact that as in many districts revision resulted in a loss of revenue, no great reasons existed for assisting the malguzars to increase their rental. The advocates of the malguzars had their day when proprietary right was awarded. Now was the time for the ryots' friends to assert their rights.

9. In paragraph 7 above I have invited special attention to the use of the word "*culturable*" in the instruction to Settlement

Officer to fix a fair *jama* not only with reference to cultivated but also culturable lands. Here again we have a further clue to the procedure of the past, and I have not infrequently, during the course of my long connection with the Department, consulted old Settlement officials, such as Rao Bahadur Bhargao Rao, as to what was meant by the Settlement Officers of the past by the term "*prospective*" assets. I have gathered that what the Settlement Officer aimed at was to fix a revenue that would approximate to half-assets midway through the Settlement. Assets might increase directly after announcement of the revised revenue by the adjustment of rents in the manner above described. With a rise of prices there would be likewise appreciation of the produce of the home-farm. The rent-roll would also increase as new land was brought under the plough. In villages then where there was a large area of culturable land and owing to the pressure of population in the vicinity the probability existed of much new land being brought under the plough in the approximate future, a higher percentage of assets could be taken than where no such scope existed. Similarly where rents appeared low to the Settlement Officer, and he expected a considerable accession of income to the malguzars on the adjustment of rents which followed revenue announcement, he would take a higher fraction. There is another reason which accounts for high percentages of revenue in certain tracts, and that is the concealment of the rental by the malguzars. This was specially the case in Wardha, where according to paragraph 48 of Rai Bahadur Parshotam Das' Settlement Report of 1896, the tenants-at-will held 43 per cent. of the occupied and 55 per cent of the total rent-paying area at the old settlement, and there was good reason for supposing that their payments to the malguzars had been greatly understated in the *lagwans*. Mr. Chisholm also alludes to a widespread conspiracy to conceal rents in the Bilaspur District. The scope for discretion in fixing the fraction was therefore very large,—much larger indeed than our presen system, under which the assessments are based on the actually ealisable assets of the day, permits of.

CENTRAL PROVS.

CENTRAL PROVS.

10. I reproduce below paragraph 10 of a note recorded on 30th June 1883 by Mr. Chisholm, who had years before settled the Bilaspur District :—

> After all, the fairest system of assessment both for the Government and the people is an assessment based strictly on "ascertained assets" and much of the discontent and dissatisfaction on occasions of re-settlement arise from the assessments being based not on ascertained assets, *but on the rental value of the estates calculated* on assumed rent-rates. These assumed rent-rates are the outcome of elaborate enquiries into the value of different soils and they are supposed to represent with fair accuracy the rental value of individual estates. But when applied to estates the rents realised in which are on an altogether different valuation of soils, they cease to represent facts as to rent, on which alone an assessment should be based, and represent only a *theory of rental value* prepared from the best available data.

I would also in this connection invite a perusal of paragraph 334 of Mr. Craddock's report of 1899 on the revision of the Nagpur Settlement.

11. It will be gathered from the previous paragraphs how it came about that high percentages of the malguzari assets (as recorded by the Settlement Officer at last settlement) were taken as revenue. A further very important consideration is that over a large tract of country the revision resulting in the 30 years' settlement amounted to a re-distribution rather than an enhancement of the revenue payable, while in four districts there was an actual reduction of the demand. The statistics tabulated in Statement A throw light on this point. The operations in Wardha, Chanda and Nagpur represented a mere re-distribution of the existing demand with some reduction in the latter district. In Saugor, Damoh and Chhindwara the demand was reduced appreciably. In the other districts enhancements were obtained, but the total revised demand of the Provinces amounted to something under 60 lakhs of rupees with an incidence of only 8 annas per cropped acre.

12. Where the percentage of the revenue on total assets after revision of settlement is high, this is generally due, as in Nagpur, Wardha and Chanda, to the reluctance of the Settlement Officer to reduce a land revenue demand which had been paid over a long series of years with ease. At the close of paragraph 4 of

letter No. 1994-2552, dated the 5th October 1900, from the Government of India in the Revenue and Agriculture Department, to the Honourable to the Chief Commissioner, on the subject of the revision of the Nagpur Settlement, it is stated that "to have reduced the revenue demand in such circumstances with the object of increasing the gains of persons already benefited beyond their legal deserts would have been a wanton sacrifice of public revenue." Apart from this it is manifest that the Settlement Officers considered the rent-rates paid by the ryots very low and expected a substantial accession of income on the adjustment of rents, which, however, rarely accrued. The position of the tenants had become so strong in the Nagpur country under British rule that they actually shared in the profits that were supposed to appertain to the proprietary status. Again, in view of the remarks of Mr. Chisholm quoted above, it is not unreasonable to suppose that Settlement Officers shrunk from following to their logical conclusion their so-called theories of rental value. The same remarks apply to the case of Chhindwara, where, however, the revenue was substantially reduced. **CENTRAL PROVS.**

The high percentage in Nimar is due entirely to the very large number of malik-makbuzas in that district, on whose payments the malguzar was only entitled to *hakut* tahsil at rates varying between 10 to 20 per cent., *vide* paragraph 10 of the Proclamation of the North-Western Provinces Government, dated 24th June 1854. The actual fraction of true malguzari assets taken in this district was only 32 per cent.

In Bhandara the high fraction shown in column 5 of Statement A is due to the fact that the *siwai* income, which is of considerable importance in this district, is not included in the assets. Were this source of income taken account of, as it should be, the percentage would probably fall to 55 per cent.

In Betul rents were very low and the Settlement Officer expected considerable increase; but as a matter of fact the adjustment of rents only raised them 5 per cent., "the cultivators for the past 25 years having been used to exceedingly light rents which they had come to consider as stereotyped."

CENTRAL PROVS.

13. As I read the correspondence and interpret the Saharanpur rules, the intention of Lord Canning's Government was that the malguzars should on an average during the currency of the settlement of long duration that was then being introduced get at least 40 per cent. to 50 per cent. of the gross rental. On the system of assessment on prospective assets they might at the outset get less than this share, in the middle of the term their profits were supposed to approximate to this fraction of the whole, and in the last half of the term they stood to make good for the deficiency that accrued to them during the first few years that the revised settlement was in force. In disticts such as Saugor, Jubbulpore, Seoni, Narsinghpur, Hoshangabad and Raipur their share was practically half-assets at the start of the settlement. In other districts, such as Damoh, Mandla and Bilaspur, the accrual of unearned increments rapidly raised their proportion to 50 per cent. or over.

In Nimar, as previously stated, they were left more than they were really entitled to at the commencement of the settlement period.

In Nagpur, at the time of the recent revision it was found that the malguzars were enjoying 42 per cent. of total assets, and excluding malik-makbuzas 44 per cent. of true malguzari assets. Similar figures follow for other districts :—

	Percentage of total assets.	Percentage of true malguzari assets.
Chhindwara	57	57
Wardha	47	48
Bilaspur	69	69
Raipur	63	63

I am not at present in a position to give statistics for Betul, Bhandara and Chanda, but the malguzari profits have expanded there in like fashion.

14. My conclusion then is that paragraphs 2 and 3 of Mr. Dutt's letter are based on a misconception of the term *assets* as understood by Government in those days, and I can detect

no deviation by the Settlement Officers from the orders of the Supreme Government. **CENTRAL PROVS.**

15. I have already shown that Mr. Dutt is inaccurate when he states that the Settlement Officers *fixed* the rents of the ryots. This was done by agreement between the malguzars and tenants, doubtless under the stimulus of a revised revenue demand. Still, the authoritative fixation of rents was not permitted by the orders then in force. The allegation that the rental demand on the tenants absorbed one-third of their gross produce is manifestly absurd. In those days the total rental value did not exceed one crore of rupees. Thus the gross produce, according to Mr. Dutt, must have been three crores or 30 millions of rupees. The population of the surveyed tract to which our figures relate was 7½ millions in 1866. Thus Mr. Dutt's scale would allow exactly 4 rupees a head for each person to live on during the year. But during the five years 1863 to 1867-68 the average value of our imports was 186 lakhs of rupees, while the total demands of the State in the form of land revenue, cesses, excise, stamps, etc., aggregated 73 lakhs. It is not clear how the people of so relatively unproductive a Province could afford to spend more than half of their gross income on comparative luxuries, nor is it manifest how even in the good old days a population of 7½ million souls could exist on 41 lakhs of rupees at exactly nine annas per head per annum. And in the above calculation no allowance has been made for seed-grain, which has to be provided out of the gross produce at a cost not far short of one crore of rupees.

Relation of old rents to gross produce.

16. The incidence of the rental on the gross produce has been calculated from time to time by many Settlement and Revenue Officers who can lay claim to a local experience which Mr. Dutt does not possess.

In reporting on his settlement of Bilaspur in 1868, Mr. Chisholm states that the rental absorbed 10 per cent. of the gross produce. In Hoshangabad, where much better prices were realisable by tenants for their produce, Sir Charles Elliott estimated that the revised revenue was about $\frac{1}{16}$th of the gross

CENTRAL PROVS. produce of the day. The rental then absorbed* $\frac{1}{12}$th of the gross produce. I have no doubt I could multiply evidence on this head by reference to other settlement reports, but the summarised conclusions of these two distinguished Revenue Officers suffice.

17. Mr. Dutt would have us believe that the rents fixed at the old settlement were fixed at a pitch unexampled elsewhere in India. Such certainly would have been the case had the rent absorbed one-third of the gross produce. Indeed it may be safely asserted that the proportion of inferior soil in cultivation in the Central Provinces is so large and its outturn so relatively inconsiderable that a rental fixed at $\frac{1}{8}$th of the gross Provincial outturn would be unrealisable. It is only in the richest portions of our most fertile and highly cultivated districts that such a proportion of the gross produce could be paid from year to year, the reason being that the balance left to the ryot out of a small outturn would not suffice for the support of himself and his family. This was recognized by the able Settlement Officers who came from the North-Western Provinces to effect the settlements which Mr. Dutt deems fit to impugn after the lapse of 35 years. I quote from Mr. Charles Grant's report on the Narsinghpur Settlement, paragraph 146 :—

> It may be as well to add a few words on the lowness of the absolute rate of assessment. Why should the sandy plains of the Ganges and Jumna Doab pay their two, three and four rupees per cultivated acre, while one of the richest valleys in India contributes at most one rupee per acre to the Imperial Treasury. The question is one of the highest importance and it may well be imagined that it has not failed to command the closest attention and the most earnest care from those entrusted with the charge of the State interest. In my own case, a previous employment in the Settlements of the North-West has perhaps served to put the contrast in an even stronger light than usual, but it may be shown, I think, that the difference is essential and therefore that the contrast is inevitable.

Mr. Grant then goes on to explain the lightness of the rent-rate as due partly to the operation of an obstructive revenue law and to the absence of demand for produce, but principally owing to the

* Rental to revenue in proportion of R1-4-5 to R0-9-6.

CENTRAL PROVS.

meagreness of the produce itself. He states that the average wheat produce of the Nerbudda valley is 6 maunds per acre where the Doab produces at least 18.

Increase in prosperity under old settlements.

It is clear then that in spite of the criticisms of Mr. Dutt who, as far as I can ascertain, has never visited these Provinces, infinite care was taken by the Settlement Officers of the past to make their assessments fair and suitable to the conditions of the districts with the welfare of which they were charged. I have shown above how substantially the revenue demand of various tracts in the provinces was reduced since they came under British management, and the assessments made after 1860 were not by any means universally directed towards securing an enhancement of revenue. Gauged by statistical consideration the various settlements passed the tests imposed by the Supreme Government and were confirmed, but the best criterion of their reasonable and equitable character is undoubtedly the manner in which they have since worked. The progress made by the Provinces during their currency is succinctly stated in Mr. Fuller's Review of the progress of the Central Provinces during the past 30 years, which was written in 1892. Moreover, a scrutiny of the annual reports on Land Revenue Administration during the eighties indicates how easily and with what a small amount of coercive processes the revenue was collected from year to year.

Mr. Fuller's report indicates a wonderful degree of progress and a steady rise in the standard of comfort which was maintained for some 30 years during which, with one exception, seasons were fairly favourable. The onlyreally unsatisfactory feature is the extent to which the malguzars of aboriginal castes became indebted and lost their villages to members of the money-lending classes. Reckless extravagance has in the main led to this unfortunate result; and enquiries made in the course of settlement operations have shown that the very rapid increase of profits during the 30 years' settlement, which was largely due to the improvement of communications effected by the opening of the railway, dazzled the proprietary body, and led them to launch out into wild

CENTRAL PROVS.

expenditure. This was recently very clearly brought out in the Betul District, where the increased demand for and rise in the price of myrabolam (harra) placed undreamt of wealth in the hands of a class which was not sufficiently educated to appreciate the gift of proprietary right.

18. I pass on now to more recent history and deal with that portion of Mr. Dutt's letter which relates to settlements effected on the present round of assessments, *i.e.*, since 1890. The final settlement reports of all districts are not as yet available, but there are some representative of all portions of the Provinces.

New settlements: comparative incidence on assets and cultivation.

Our assessments are now based on real existing assets, and there is now-a-days nothing of a prospective character about them. This in itself is a distinct gain to the malguzars, who will now appropriate the whole of the *ad interim* profits accruing from increase of cultivation and the rise in the value of home-farm and *siwai* produce during the currency of the settlement. I contrast below the percentages taken on revision with the corresponding figures of last settlement. I also add figures contrasting the incidence per acre in cultivation of the old and revised revenue :—

District.	Percentage of old revenue on assets of last Settlement.	Percentage of revised revenue on the revised assets.	Per cent. increase in cultivation since last Settlement.	Incidence per acre in cultivation.	
				Old Settlement.	New Settlement.
				R a. p.	R a. p.
Damoh . .	54	54	+31	0 9 6	0 11 7
Jubbulpore . .	50	51	+44	0 10 4	0 11 11
Seoni . . .	48	47	+50	0 4 6	0 5 9
Narsingpur .	49	50	+17	0 12 0	0 15 3
Chhindwara .	66	55	+60	0 6 11	0 5 11
Wardha . .	79	59	+28	0 9 7	0 10 2
Nagpur . .	78	61	+13	0 12 2	0 12 8
Raipur . .	53	53	+33	0 4 10	0 5 8
Bilaspur . .	57	54	+40	0 4 1	0 5 6

In Nagpur and Wardha malik-makbuzas are of importance, and the proportion of true malguzari assets absorbed on revision is only 58·8 and 58·1 per cent., respectively. Thus in most districts on revision 50 per cent. to 55 per cent. of assets has been taken, and in no case has 60 per cent. of true malguzari assets been absorbed. In Seoni, owing to the large increment of revenue obtainable and the relatively insecure character of cultivation in the Lakhnadon Tahsil, where part of the area cropped with millets is little better than street-rock, only 47 per cent. of assets has been demanded. In the districts * forming part of the old Nagpur country the percentage has been very appreciably reduced. This is a very substantial concession to malguzars and one that they could hardly have claimed as a right. The Chhindwara District has been treated with singular indulgence. As to individual villages, the rule has been throughout the provinces to accept 60 per cent. as a maximun in fixing and enhancing *jamas* and 65 per cent. has only been taken in reducing assessments, *i.e.*, where the revenue was previously in excess of this figure, it has been lowered down to this limit in accordance with the orders of the Supreme Government. **CENTRAL PROVS.**

Cesses.

19. I would now take the opportunity of correcting another of Mr. Dutt's somewhat numerous inaccuracies. He states that cesses are taken at 12½ per cent. of the assets. This is not the case. They are based on the kamil *jama*, and as 13½† per cent. is the highest rate at which they are taken in any district, 8 per cent. (13½ per cent. × 60 per cent. the maximum rate of assessment) is the highest rate at which they fall on the assets. The usual rate may be accepted as some figure between 6 and 7 per cent. of assets. In Seoni the incidence is 6 per cent. of the assets and in Nagpur 6½. Thus the percentage of malguzari assets absorbed by revenue and cesses ranges between 53 in Seoni and 66 in Nagpur. This disposes of Mr. Dutt's assertion that our assessments absorb 100 per cent. of malguzari assets. If he means to imply that in seasons of scarcity and famine rents are to a certain extent irrecoverable, this is not, I presume, a state of affairs peculiar to the

* Nagpur, Chhindwara, Wardha.

† In the lightly assessed districts of Raipur and Bilaspur.

CENTRAL PROVS.

Central Provinces, and the Government meet such cases by the grant of liberal suspensions which, should occasion demand, are ultimately converted into remissions. But what I presume we are now concerned with is the pressure of the revenue and rental demands on the people in periods of normal meteorological season.

Increase in prices.

20. The prices of agricultural produce have been found in the course of recent settlement enquiries to have risen 150 per cent. in Jubbulpore and Wardha, 100 per cent. in Hoshangabad, from 75 to 100 per cent. in Nagpur and Saugor, and from 60 to 70 per cent. in Narsinghpur and Chhindwara. As to Chhattisgarh, prices had in 1888 more than doubled and have since that year risen still further. Having regard to the appreciation of the silver value of agricultural produce, the rise in the incidence of the revenue per acre in cultivation is very moderate, even after full allowance is made for the relative inferiority of some of the land subjugated during the past 30 years. The incidences in Nagpur and Wardha are almost stationary, which is of course due to the reduction of the fraction of assessment. But for this, one would have expected a rise of incidence in districts where the increase of cultivation has not been so very large, for the mere maintenance of the rent-rate in tracts where much poor soil has been broken up is tantamount to an advance in the incidence of the payments. The fall in Chhindwara, a hilly district, is due to allowance being made for the fact that much of the newly broken soil is red gravel, very inferior to the rich pockets of black soil which formed the bulk of cultivation in the old days. We owe this desirable result doubtless to the soil-unit system which Mr. Dutt includes in his denunciations. Acreage rates are singularly deceptive, and it is the boast of our new system that it enables us to differentiate in our valuation of the different grades of soil.

Against Narsinghpur we find the highest percentage rise of incidence, *viz.*, 27 per cent. Here cultivation has only increased 17 per cent. and the fraction of assessment at last Settlement was very moderate. The district used to pay a much heavier assessment in the old days when the Bhonsla troops were quartered in the Nerbudda valley. In 1816 the Marathas drew ₨6,67,000 from the Narsinghpur District, but their Military expenditure in that district amounted in that year to ₨6,37,000, so that the greater part of the revenue was spent in the district. Prior to the 30 years' settlement the revenue had fallen to ₨3,31,392. This was raised by Mr. Grant to ₨4,21,700, which has been paid with ease. Since that time Narsinghpur has been linked to Calcutta and Bombay an has now ample facilities for the disposal of its surplus produce. The gross revenue fixed on recent revision is ₨6,42,615, and in spite of a prolonged series of most untoward seasons, the bulk of the revenue has been realised from year to year without an excessive number of coercive processes. **CENTRAL PROVS.**

Increase in cultivation.

21. Taking the Provinces as a whole the cropped area has increased from 12½ to 16 millions of acres since 1867-68, *i.e.*, by 27 per cent., and during that period the revenue on the roll has advanced from 60 to 86 lakhs of rupees, or 43 per cent. A large proportion then of the increment is mere assessment of newly-broken lands, and the increase of the revenue demand attributable to the enhanced value of agricultural produce is very small compared with the very great rise that has taken place in prices.

Rents and produce.

22. There remains the question of the effect of the recent revision on the tenants, who, Mr. Dutt asserts, are being ground down by a taxation which absorbs 5 or 6 annas in the rupee of the gross produce. The rental value of the malguzari area of the provinces may be stated as follows:—

	₨
Cash rents	1,23,00,000
Payments by malik-makbuzas . . .	5,85,000
Valuation of land held by revenue-free grantees	45,000
Value of home-farm at ₨0-12-2 the ryoti . .	33,00,00
TOTAL .	1,62,30,000

CENTRAL PROVS. Some three years ago, in a note on the crop statistics of the year 1896-97, I estimated the normal outturn of food-grains of the Central Provinces. The outturn of standard areas at standard rates worked out to 3,528,932 tons. I concluded then that 3,000,000 tons could safely be accepted. This, however, was deemed an under-estimate by the Local Administration.

A very moderate value rate would be R50 per ton, which corresponds to R1-12-0 per maund or 25 seers per rupee.

Valued at this rate the gross produce of food-grains would be R15,00,00,000. Ignoring all minor crops, such as hemp, castor, sugarcane, tobacco and miscellaneous garden crops, we have still to consider the value of the cotton, til and linseed crops.

23. The normal area devoted to til is 600,000 acres, and the normal produce per acre may be taken at 200lb, value R10 at 20lb per rupee. Thus the value of a normal outturn is 60 lakhs of rupees. Last year, when owing to the drought the crop was returned as only two-thirds of normal, *i.e.*, 133lb per acre, the export from the Central Provinces (after duly excluding 10,000 tons produced in our Feudatory States) amounted to 137lb for every acre in cultivation. A normal crop would at this rate exceed 205lb, and it is well known that there is considerable local consumption for which no margin is left by that year's estimate of outturn. The value of the exports in 1899-1900 reached 83¼ lakhs, but the area under the crop was abnormally large. In 1898-99 the value of til exports was 48½ lakhs, but the average does not exceed 35 lakhs.

24. The area under cotton has latterly increased to 1,000,000 acres, but 650,000 acres is our decennial average. Our standard outturn for cleaned cotton is 75lb to the acre, the value of which at 5lb to the rupee is R15. Thus the value of a normal cotton crop works out to R97,50,000. That our standard outturn is too low or that we very frequently nder-estimate the character of

this crop is proved by paragraph 23 of Mr. Craddock's report on the rail-borne traffic of the Central Provinces for the year ending 31st March 1900. It is there stated that for two years in succession the recorded exports have exceeded the total estimated yield of the crop. Our exports in— **CENTRAL PROVS.**

1898-99 amounted to (*a*) 787,875 maunds, value R120 lakhs.
1899-1900 „ (*b*) 592,351 „ „ 90 „

And in the latter year (*c*) 155,000 maunds were consumed by the local mills. Adding (*b*) and (*c*) we get 747,351 maunds, which valued at R15 per maund is worth R1,12,10,265. Here again there is no allowance for village consumption, if this be accepted as the value of the *whole* crop. However, the area under the crop in 1899 was somewhat above normal. It may then be accepted that the normal value of the crop does not fall short of one crore of rupees.

25. Linseed is a precarious crop and the area devoted to this oil-seed varies greatly. Our decennial average just exceeds one million acres. Our standard outturn is 200℔ per acre worth R10 or R11. Thus the value of a normal crop on an average area would exceed one crore of rupees. The largest export in any one year was 2,726,766 maunds, valued at about 108 lakhs of rupees. But our average exports for the past 15 years amount to only half this figure, the value of which would be 54 lakhs of rupees.

The three crops, *viz.*, linseed, cotton and til, should then bring in annually 260 lakhs of rupees, but to be on the safe side I reduce this estimate to two crores of rupees. This may be added to the value of food-grains estimated at 15 crores of rupees. This result is 17 crores of rupees, of which the rental value stated above at 162 lakhs absorbs less than one-tenth.

The normal cropped area is 16 millions of acres and the gross outturn falls therefore at R10-10-0 per acre, whereas the present all-round incidence per acre of the rental throughout the Provinces is R0-12-2.

CENTRAL PROVS.

26. These estimates of crop outturn are admittedly difficult to frame, but we have now a long series of crop experiments to guide us and our area statistics are reliable. The standard outturns have been subjected to check in the light of results obtained on the Nagpur Experimental Farm. We have, moreover, ascertained at that institution the amount of seed of each variety of crop that falls to the acre and how the outturn contrasts with the amount sown. Cultivators generally estimate their crops at so many fold of the seed sown, and this has enabled us to apply a further test to our standard outturns.

It is not claimed for the estimates that they have an exact quantitative accuracy; but they assuredly rest on a sufficient basis of fact to be considered a fairly trustworthy index to the amount of the gross outturn. Apart from this, I would not wish it to be understood that during the last five or six years of recurring crop failures, scarcities and famines the yield of the Provinces has approximated to these figures. Indeed my estimate of the food production of 1896-97 fell below half the normal and the loss has been still greater during the famine of 1899-1900. It has to be recognized that we have been passing through quite abnormal times such as have never been known even by tradition to the oldest inhabitants of these Provinces. But for this the revised Settlements would have worked as smoothly as their predecessors. It may be added that the term of the settlements made after 1860 in the Chhattisgarh districts was 20 and not 30 years, and revision took place in 1886-1891. No difficulty was experienced in realizing the revised demand until the famine of 1896-97 brought many tenants to ruin. In 1893-94, only 10 attachments of moveable property were effected with no sales, in 1894-95 the number was 23 with one sale and in addition 21 defaulters were brought to District Head-quarters. This represents the very minimum of coercion.

27. To return from this digression I would now quote from the reports of various Settlement Officers the proportion of the gross produce absorbed by the rental as calculated by them :— **CENTRAL PROVS.**

DISTRICT.	Gross produce.	Rental value.	Per cent. of 3 on 2.	
1	2	3	4	5
	R	R	R	
Damoh . .	54,26,484	8,01,558	14	$\frac{1}{7}$th.
Seoni . . .	82,41,394	6,02,567	7	$\frac{1}{14}$th.
Nagpur . .	1,88,06,823	16,76,212	9	$\frac{1}{11}$th.
Narsinghpur .	80,61,942	12,77,486	15·8	Somewhat less than $\frac{1}{6}$th.
Chhindwara . .	1,00,61,740	5,28,907	5	$\frac{1}{19}$th.
Wardha . .	1,47,16,115	10,83,061	7	$\frac{1}{14}$th.
Jubbulpore . .	1,26,14,985	19,27,770	15·2	Somewhat over $\frac{1}{7}$th.

The Settlement Officer, Raipur, does not give similar figures, but calculating in a different manner arrives at the conclusion that rent absorbs 8 to 10 per cent. of the gross produce (*vide* paragraph 31 of his report).

In none of the districts shown above does the proportion of the gross produce absorbed by the rental attain to three annas in the rupee. In Jubbulpore and Narsingpur the percentage absorbed is relatively high, but as shown in paragraph 29 most of the enhancement imposed on these districts has been effected by the malguzars. The Chhindwara Settlement is doubtless lenient, but I think the Settlement Officer has somewhat overvalued the produce, and it would probably be safer to substitute a percentage of 7 or 8 for 5 in column 4 above.

Proportion of gross produce absorbed by rent.

28. Mr. Dutt's contention is that our revised present rental value absorbs 5 or 6 annas in the rupee of the gross produce, and he asserts that every tenant in India understands and recognizes three annas in the rupee out of the gross produce of his holding as a fair and equitable rent. The rental value of our malguzari area now stands at 162 lakhs, and on the assumption

CENTRAL PROVS that the rental amounts to 6 annas in the rupee of the gross produce, the value of the latter would be only 432 lakhs. But the total revenue of the Provinces levied on the land, as cesses, excise, assessed taxes and stamps, amounts to 114 lakhs. Moreover, the average value of our imports of cotton goods, metals, salt and sugar approximates to 2 crores of rupees. This would leave 118 lakhs for a population of nearly ten million souls to exist upon annually, *i.e.*, little over a rupee per head. In this calculation no allowance has been made for the absolutely essential seed-grain. The cost of the same probably exceeds a crore and a half, for it costs 80 lakhs to sow our normal wheat area = 4 million acres. Again, the average value of our exports of food-grains, oilseeds and cotton amounts to 365 lakhs of rupees. In normal years there is very little import of food-grains into the Central Provinces the average of the eleven years 1883-84 to 1893-94 being the equivalent of 10 lakhs of rupees. In face of these figures it is not clear whence the people of these Provinces get their food supplies if the value of the gross products does not exceed 432 lakhs of rupees. Further, during the recent famine operations Government has expended 4¾ crores on affording bare subsistence to a portion of the population. The number on relief did not at any time greatly exceed 2¼ million souls, and if an average be struck for the year, it comes to 1½ millions.* Assuming that the prices that ruled during the famine were double the normal and making due allowance for the cost of establishments, plant, contractor's profits, etc., it may fairly be argued that the expenditure incurred by the State would not suffice for the bare maintenance of 4 millions in ordinary times for the period of one year, whereas if Mr. Dutt is to be believed the 10 millions inhabiting our surveyed areas exist from year to year on 432 lakh of rupees. These facts demonstrate, I think, very clearly the absurdity of Mr. Dutt's allegation that the revised rental absorbs 6 annas of the gross produce. If we took even half of that proportion, *viz.*, 3 annas in the rupee, as rental that would only leave an all-round average of

* Exact figure 1,506,222.

R5-8-0* per head for each person to support himself on throughout the year. These figures then tend to bear out the conclusions stated above, that over the Provinces taken as a whole the rental value absorbs little if anything over $\frac{1}{10}$th of the gross produce. However much the malguzars of the Central Provinces may desire the reduction of the fraction of assessment, few would be found to advocate any radical interference with rents in the way of reduction. Such a step would arouse a storm of opposition. The malguzars know full well that the rents are not excessive and that they can be and are for the most part collected in normal times. I quote from a recent letter of Mr. G. M. Chitnavis, dated the 26th November 1900, to the *Pioneer*, who may be regarded as the spokesman of the proprietary body :— **CENTRAL PROVS.**

In connection with this, I may remark that while deeply grateful to Mr. R. C. Dutt for his able and disinterested advocacy, I am not prepared to go with him when he says that our tenants' rents are above the standard he lays down, *viz.*, one-sixth of the produce. Even after revision they are lower than what that standard would allow.

Results of settlement officer's revision of rents.

29. The following statement shows the action of the rent-rates since last settlement :—

DISTRICT.	Tenants' rent-rate recorded at last Settlement.	Rent-rate as enhanced by Settlement Officer on revision.	Enhancement per cent. in rent-rate.	Enhancement in tenants' payments effected by Settlement Officer.
1	2	3	4	5
	R a. p.	*R a. p.*		
Damoh	0 13 10	1 1 10	+29	+11
Jubbulpore	1 1 4	1 3 8	+13	+4
Seoni	0 9 8	0 10 10	+12	+9
Mandla	0 5 8	0 6 3	+10	+3
Narsinghpur . . .	1 5 1	1 11 7	+31	+6
Chhindwara . .	0 9 11	0 9 9	−2	+12
Wardha	0 10 7	0 15 0	+42	+14
Nagpur	0 12 10	1 0 3	+26	+16
Raipur	0 8 11	0 10 6	+18	+12
Bilaspur	0 7 3	0 9 9	+34	+11
Sambalpur . . .	0 5 10	0 5 7	−4	+42

* 864 lakhs less $\left\{\begin{matrix}114\\300\end{matrix}\right\}$ lakhs.
450

CENTRAL PROVS.

There is nothing in these figures to bear out Mr. Dutt's assertion that harshness has been displayed by the Settlement Officers in revising the payments of tenants. In only one district, *viz.*, Sambalpur, has the action of the Settlement Officer resulted in a large enhancement, and here we find that the rate has actually declined 4 per cent. below the level of last Settlement. The reason for this is that the enhancements of ryoti payments in this district were all covered by an increase of cultivation on which nothing had been paid during the currency of the preceding settlement. In no other district has the Settlement Officer enhanced rents more than 16 per cent. The leniency with which the relatively poor plateau district of Seoni, Mandla and Chhindwara have been treated is conspicuous. In the latter district the Settlement Officer found that the all-round rent-rate had fallen with the extension of cultivation to poor soils from R0-9-11 to R0-8-8 per acre. He raised it to R0-9-9, which is below the level recorded in the 30 years' settlement. The bulk of the rent enhancement that has been effected in most districts is due to the action of the malguzars and not to that of the Government. But in no case does the rise in the rent-rate during the past 30 years appear excessive when compared with the great advance in prices during the same period.

30. To appreciate exactly the action that has been taken by the Settlement Officer, it would be necessary to analyse the incidences of the various classes of tenants from group to group in the eighteen districts of the Provinces. This would be a very lengthy undertaking, and it suffices to state that the bulk of the enhancement imposed on revision has fallen on the privileged classes of tenants belonging to the malik-makbuza, absolute-occupancy and occupancy classes. Their payments have been levelled up towards the pitch paid by tenants-at-will in the same village or in neighbouring villages of similar characteristics. The payments of ordinary tenants have, speaking generally, been little enhanced except in the Nagpur country, where they had become stereotyped by custom. On the other hand, in a few tracts where rack-renting had been practised substantial relief has been

accorded to this class. In the Jubbulpore District R37,698 were struck off the rental of 6,433 holdings and at the same time arrears aggregating R18,479 were remitted. In Seoni the rents of 734 holdings were reduced by R3,155. In Narsinghpur the Settlement Officer lowered ordinary rents by R43,261 and in the Harda Tahsil of Hoshangabad this beneficent action extended to the reduction of rents by R30,694, while arrears amounting to R92,082 were remitted. **CENTRAL PROVS.**

31. It is stated in Mr. Dutt's communication that there was alarm and consternation in the country when the new enhanced rents were proclaimed. This statement is not in accordance with the facts of the case. As a general rule the ryots accepted their revised payments readily enough and cheerfully acquiesced in the fairness of their enhancements. They infinitely prefer that their rents should be fixed by the State to being left to the mercies of their malguzars, and the number of appeals against rental enhancements has been very small indeed.

The only district which furnishes an exception to these remarks is Sambalpur, where the ryots and gaontias of a considerable number of villages combined to resist the revised assessment. It is in this district that rents were most enhanced by the Settlement Officer, the ryots having incorporated large areas of waste in their holdings free of payment. The effect of the Settlement Officer's action was to reduce considerably the proportion of the profits hitherto enjoyed by the ryots, but as to the fairness of the assessment there can be no question, for the incidence of the rental in Sambalpur is lighter than in any other district of the Central Provinces and, if the experience of recent years counts for anything, agriculture is more secure than in any other district of the Central Provinces. The character of this agitation is described in paragraph 83 of Mr. Fuller's Settlement Report, to which reference may be made.

32. While traversing then the various statements made by Mr. Dutt, I would not have it understood that I fail to sympathize with the malguzars and ryots in their recent losses. Where these are of merely temporary character I am sanguine that a few good

CENTRAL PROVS.

seasons will set matters right, but in other tracts, especially the rice and rabi tracts, where there has been serious deterioration since the revised assessments were framed, I am conscious that relief in the shape of temporary abatements will have to be granted. I have in the past brought at least one tract, *viz.*, that of the Hinganghat Tahsil of Wardha, to the notice of the Honourable the Chief Commissioner. For the rest, the matter is engaging the attention of the Administration and steps are being taken by means of abatements extending over a series of years to render the demand suitable to the altered condition of deteriorated regions. It remains but to add that the recent famine has been equally severe in districts such as (1) Chanda, where the old assessment is still in force; or (2) Betul, Balaghat, Bhandara and Nimar, where the revised assessments have been barely in force for a year, as in other districts of the Provinces which have paid the revised assessments for a number of years.

STATEMENT A.

Name of District.		Revenue at settlement.	Revenue after revision.	Percentage of Revenue on Assets. At assessment.	Percentage of Revenue on Assets. After adjustment of rents.	Percentage by which rents adjusted.	Percentage by which revenue enhanced or reduced.
1		2	3	4	5	6	7
		R	R				
Saugor	Gross	6,09,615	4,49,624	54	51	+6	−17
	Net	5,20,895	4,20,672				
Damoh	Gross	3,05,142	2,69,487	60	54	+5	−5
	Net	2,66,460	2,52,974				
Jubbulpore	Gross	4,75,760	6,06,928	53	50	+3	+18
	Net	4,75,145	5,59,443				
Mandla	Gross	42,819	61,841	65	56	+23	+48
	Net	41,684	60,001				

STATEMENT A—*contd.*

CENTRAL PROVS.

Name of District.		Revenue at settlement.	Revenue after revision.	Percentage of Revenue on Assets.		Percentage by which rents adjusted.	Percentage by which revenue enhanced or reduced.
				At assessment.	After adjustment of rents.		
1		2	3	4	5	6	7
		R	R				
Seoni . .	Gross	Old Seoni	2,23,921	65	48	Largely in parts, but Powars withstood it.	Net +56
	Net	1,32,449	2,07,679				
Narsinghpur .	Gross	...	...	54	49	+7	+27
	Net	3,31,392	4,21,700				
Hoshangabad .	Gross	...	4,45,458	61	46	+32 Rate R1-4-5.	+43
	Net	3,09,904	4,23,851				
Nimar . .	Gross	...	2,15,495	75	64	+31	+15
	Net	1,56,825	1,81,180				
Chhindwara .	Gross	...	2,26,208	65	66	+4	−13
	Net	2,45,322	2,13,486				
Betul . .	Gross	...	1,84,514	67	64	+5	+32
	Net	1,38,153	1,83,764				
Wardha . .	Gross	...	4,16,345	79 per cent.	79 per cent.	Inappreciable.	+0·1
	Net	4,11,930	4,12,411				
Nagpur . .	Gross	9,75,591	9,81,798	84 do.	78 do.	Not much.	+0·6
	Net	8,76,661	8,30,232				−6
Chanda . .	Gross	2,57,916	2,64,556	...	60 do.	+5 per cent. Only par rent.	+2
	Net	...	2,42,990				
Bhandara .	Gross	...	...	...	64 per cent. 59 do. regardless of siwai.	+20	+1
	Net	4,34,781	4,86,451				
Raipur . .	Gross	...	...	...	53 per cent.	Large.	+64
	Net	3,17,819	5,31,469				
Bilaspur . .	Gross	...	2,51,934	...	57 do.	Do.	+61
	Net	1,51,170	2,43,734				

CHAPTER VII.—MADRAS.

Resolution by the Board of Revenue, Madras, No. 542, dated 6th December 1900.

The Board has been called upon to express an opinion on the points discussed by Mr. Dutt in his letter, dated 20th February 1900, addressed to His Excellency the Viceroy. For a full comprehension of Mr. Dutt's views and for the purposes of reply, it is necessary to consider remarks in a book in which the letter has since appeared, and the Board will therefore occasionally travel outside the mere words of the letter under consideration.

2. The experience and the position of Mr. Dutt and his sympathy with the ryot entitle his remarks to every consideration, while a full discussion will help to elucidate several debated matters; the Board will therefore deal with the subject at some length.

3. Mr. Dutt's three definite suggestions are contained in paragraph 13 of his letter, but the preliminary paragraphs with their connected remarks elsewhere, necessarily call for criticism prior to the consideration of his formulated proposals; his main points are as follows:—

(1) that by the early ryotwari settlement the Madras ryot had a declared and indefeasible right to an unalterable and perpetual assessment, and that this right subsisted for the first half of the century (paragraphs 2 and 3); that this right has been confiscated by the British Government within the last forty years, when they established the new Settlement Department and introduced at that time permanency only for a period, whereby the assessment is subjected to possible revision after each such period (paragraphs 4 and 5);

(2) that subsequently to the introduction of this new principle it was laid down by Lord Ripon and accepted by the

MADRAS.

Madras Government, that the periodical settlement should be confined to revision "on the sole ground of the rise in prices," but that this result of long "years of mature deliberation" was subsequently rejected in the Secretary of State's despatch of 1885 which has thrown the Madras cultivators back into another era of uncertainty and "unjust enhancement" (paragraphs 6 and 7);

(3) that the present method of settlement is based on the principle of taking half the net produce for Government which involves calculations liable to error with, in such cases, results fatal to successful agriculture (paragraph 8);

(4) that a further rule is that the assessments should not exceed one-third of the gross produce on land not irrigated at Government cost, and that this rule being taken as a guide, leads to unduly high assessments, and that these unduly high assessments will or do necessarily impoverish the ryot (paragraph 9);

(5) that the recent Act to amend the irrigation law of the Presidency is contrary to custom, injurious in effect, and unjust in its provisions (paragraphs 10 to 12).

In his discussion of these points Mr. Dutt makes various remarks which will be alluded to in their place.

4. Mr. Dutt therefore suggests—

(*a*) that the proposals of Lord Ripon in 1882 be adopted as a necessary principle in the present and future settlements or re-settlements;

(*b*) that one-fifth of the gross and not half of the net produce be adopted as the future maximum;

(*c*) that the water-rate be not made compulsory.

Reasons for periodicity of present settlement.

5. *Point 1 in paragraph 3, supra.*—For about forty-five years the periodicity of settlements, in money at least, has been an accepted principle. From the date of the well-known order of Government, No. 951,

(Rev.) dated 14th August 1855, which originated the survey of the Presidency and the revision of the assessment, this has been the invariable and accepted practice notwithstanding that, in the early part of this period, remarks may be found, as quoted by Mr. Dutt, which seem to indicate an opinion that the original assessments were or were intended to be permanent. This survey and revision of the assessment have been expressly sanctioned by the Secretary of State, who, in the well-known despatch of 1862, in which the eventual introduction of permanency in the assessment was accepted, at the same time laid down the necessity, as a preliminary step, for the revision of the then assessment, observing that "the existing settlement records which determine the supposed extent of each holding and, by consequence, the actual rate of assessment, are in many cases untrustworthy," that "there is ample evidence that the actual incidence of the assessments as regards particular fields or estates requires careful readjustment," and that Her Majesty's Government considered that the Presidency was not then "in the condition which would warrant them in authorising a permanent settlement of the land-revenue on the assessed lands at the existing rates." The discussion of points (1) and (2) would therefore be of mere academic interest, but that the grave charge is made that Government has confiscated rights and has *thereby* been enabled to enhance assessments which were perpetual; moreover, the Board believes that the history and object of the present survey and settlement have been misunderstood and that they should be exhibited in a dry light. **MADRAS.**

6. Mr. Dutt bases the charges contained in point 1 in paragraph 3, *supra*, on a few sentences quoted from Sir Thomas Munro in 1812, from the Government in 1855-56, from the Board in 1857, and from Government in 1862. His exact words are as follows:—

The *first* point to which I desire to invite . . . . attention is that this right of the Madras cultivator to a fixed, perpetual and unalterable assessment, recognized by the British Government during

MADRAS. half a century, has been virtually confiscated by the British Government within the last forty years.

I cannot believe that the British Government deliberately desired on this or on any other occasion to violate a right which it had deliberately affirmed and recognized before. I am inclined to believe that in the Settlement and Survey operations which were introduced after 1857, the real position of the Madras cultivator was lost sight of, and rules were introduced to secure an increase of the land-revenue without an adequate consideration of the rights of the cultivator. So far as the Madras cultivators are concerned, there can be little doubt that the rights previously assured to them have in effect been withdrawn, and the pledges previously given to them have in effect been violated. And, at the present time, the Madras cultivator, instead of holding "his land in perpetuity without any increase of assessment," is subject to enhancement at each recurring settlement, and has been reduced to a state of poverty and indebtedness which makes him an easy prey to famines in years of bad harvests.

7. That the founders of the ryotwari system originally purposed the permanency of the assessment is beyond doubt; Colonel Read's proclamation in Salem in 1796 is clear on this point, and the writings of Sir Thomas Munro distinctly show that one of the leading ideas of the early system was that of a permanent assessment whether immediate or in the near future. Assuming, however, for the moment—which is incorrect—that Munro used the words "fixed" or "permanent" in the sense of perpetual or unalterable, it must be noted that this was merely a principle of the ideal or purposed ryotwari system; it was "his idea" to make the assessment permanent *when the time should arrive*, but the whole of his and other men's writings and the whole of the land revenue history of the Presidency show that this principle was, for a variety of reasons, never brought into practice; much less was it a declared right; and still less was such policy secured to the ryots as a right. "The history of the different districts, as given in the Manuals, is one of a series of new 'hukumnamas' or assessment orders by which rates were experimentally lowered, raised, and lowered again till, in 1855-58, a general and systematic resurvey and revision was ordered and the modern order of things began" (Baden-Powell, Volume III, page 38). Not merely

did the enormous assessments—especially enormous at the then prices—of both the original and revised (1818) systems, utterly preclude the fixing of the assessment in perpetuity and necessitate a continual series of reductions, remissions, and evasions, but the system itself, as an organised and declared system, was never fully introduced even in those districts where the system was most in vogue, whilst in others it was, as regards the existence of the permanent field survey and field assessment which were the declared basis of Munro's system, practically non-existent. Those who assert the right claimed must prove that the right ever existed, that it was defined and ascertained and was ascertainable in the middle of the century, and that if ascertainable it was practicable. Though such proof is absent the Board will adduce proof to the contrary on all the above points. MADRAS.

8. The Board will establish the following points :—

(*a*) that the words "fixity" and "permanency" as applied to the assessment did not, when used regarding the ryotwari system, connote the idea of perpetual immutability;

(*b*) that the right claimed was never made a "right" either by formal authoritative declaration or by enactment;

(*c*) that in the intentions of the founders of the system the idea of permanency was absolutely reciprocal; if Government could not demand more, neither was it ever to receive less;

(*d*) that if permanency had been established it would have ruined the ryot owing to the weight and inequality of the assessment;

(*e*) that, partly owing to the weight of the assessment at the then prices and conditions, partly to the absence of a proper survey, permanency was never established as a fact, but remained a mere intention or guiding purpose which was not binding in perpetuity but is alterable according to circumstances.

MADRAS.

True significance of "fixity" and "permanency" as used in old records.

9. *Point (a)—The words "fixity" and "permanency" as applied to the assessment did not, when used regarding the ryotwari system, connote the idea of perpetual immutability.* In the old papers on the ryotwari system, neither the word "fixed" nor "permanent," as applied to the ryotwari assessment, necessarily or usually means perpetual and unalterable as supposed by Mr. Dutt. The founder of the system, Sir Thomas Munro, used the word "fixed" as the opposite of variable, fluctuating, uncertain, or provisional; as he incessantly pointed out, one chief merit of the system was that a fixed assessment was, in theory at least, laid upon the field, not upon the produce or upon the man, whereas in former years, the assessment was wholly uncertain, without any standard, and varied according to season, produce, the health, wealth or capacity of the ryot, the whims of the officials, etc. Munro, in fact, used the word "fixed" or "permanent" assessment only in a qualified sense, as meaning a standard or maximum assessment which should be stable and not be liable to frequent alteration; he did not mean an unalterable assessment; the lands were to belong to the ryots in perpetuity, but the assessment though "permanent" and even a "maximum," might be raised or lowered according to the exigencies of the State. In 1820 when, as Governor, he was commenting on the settlement of Bellary, a district settled by himself and then considered a model of the ryotwari settlement, he observed as follows:—

> The survey rates having, under the lease, become unequal, in some places too high, in some too low, and in many been abandoned, it has become a question whether they ought not to be again corrected. I am decidedly of opinion that they ought not to be touched, and that they ought to stand as the foundation of *every future settlement*. By having such a standard, *Government may in every future period raise or lower the revenue*, according to the necessities of the State, by simply increasing or diminishing this standard by a certain rate.

Again, on the same district, he said:

> The last point for consideration is whether the reduction of 25 per cent. should be *permanent* or not. I think that it ought to be so. I do not by this mean that it is never to be altered, but that it is not

to be altered frequently, but only at distant intervals, when the exigencies or the prosperity of the State may *demand an increase* or admit of a reduction of revenue. **MADRAS.**

In 1824 in his well-known Minute on the condition of the people, he observed as follows of the survey assessment: "I trust that we shall never have to go beyond the original assessment," and in almost the last sentence of that Minute, in speaking of the district surveys (a term which then included settlement), he says "when completed they will furnish a groundwork on which the land revenue of the country may with safety . . . . be lowered or *raised* according to circumstances."

It is clear then that Munro himself, though hoping and preparing for a "permanent" assessment, had no intention, even by such settlement, of precluding Government from raising the assessment when necessary. Indeed no such idea was possible in the mind of the man who wrote in the same Minute as follows:—

> We are now masters of a very extensive empire, and we should endeavour to secure and improve it by a good internal administration. Our experience is too short to judge what rules are best calculated for this purpose It is only within the last thirty years that we have here begun to acquire any practical knowledge; *a longer period must probably elapse before we can ascertain what is best* Such a period is as nothing in the existence of a people; but we act as if this were as limited as the life of an individual. We proceed, in a country of which we know little or nothing, as if we knew everything, and as if everything must be done now and nothing could be done hereafter. We feel our ignorance of Indian revenue, and the difficulties arising from it; and instead of seeking to remedy it by acquiring more knowledge, we endeavour to get rid of the difficulty *by precipitately making permanent settlements* which relieve us from the troublesome task of minute or accurate investigation, and which are better adapted to perpetuate our ignorance than to protect the people."

Permanency not recognized by authoritative declaration or enactment.

10. *Point* (*b*).—*The right claimed was never made a "right" either by formal authoritative declaration or by enactment.* While "the principles" of the ryotwari system have been frequently mentioned in the writings of Munro, of other officers, of the Board, and of Government at various times,

MADRAS. those principles have never been authoritatively formulated and publicly notified, still less have they been legislatively established, as principles binding the Government and the ryot in a mutual contract as in the case of landholders under a "permanent settlement" (see Regulation XXV of 1802); the principles have been stated either unauthoritatively as the opinions or as the results of the settlements of individual officers, or, when authoritative, as general principles which should be the guides to uniformity and continuity in action; there has been no public declaration binding Government to future action or abstention from action, but only "instructions" to officers and explanations to authorities. In fact, the contrast between the action of Government in regard to the two systems is so remarkable as to be obviously intentional: in the case of the permanent (zamindari) settlement Government has bound itself for ever by legislative enactment and, as compelled by that law, has given to every such landholder a *sanad* declaring the perpetuity both of tenure and assessment; there is no such statute with regard to the ryotwari system nor has any such document ever been issued to ryots. In this connection it may be pointed out that in Regulation II of 1806 the non-zamindari districts are expressly spoken of as "districts of which the assessment of the land revenue is not permanently fixed." Regulation XXIX of 1802 appoints karnams to each village of a district "where the land revenue may have been permanently assessed on the lands;" this regulation applies only to zamindari areas, so that Regulation VI of 1831, in appointing the village officers in general, enacts that it shall not affect the office of karnam instituted by XXIX of 1802 in districts of which the land revenue has been "permanently" fixed, thus clearly differentiating, so late as 1831, between the permanently and non-permanently assessed areas. So also in Regulation IV of 1822, enacted after the introduction of the revised ryotwari system, the "permanent" and "temporary" settlements are again absolutely distinguished.

The case of Canara, originally consisting of the north and south divisions, is a crucial instance, for in that district the right of private property was always particularly clear, it was settled by Munro himself, and it was considered an especially good example of the ryotwari tenure and system. In that district (North Canara) the question of permanency has been judicially raised and decided in favour of Government by the High Court of Bombay (High Court Reports, Volume XII, 1875), the Court finding "that the assessment had not become unalterably fixed in law since the British acquisition." The reasoning applies with even greater force to the other districts, where rates were higher and more fluctuating, and system less distinct. **MADRAS.**

With the conclusive facts of the land revenue history before it, the Board does not desire to lay undue stress on this point since formal public announcements and long-established custom following thereon would, if found, warrant especially careful consideration in altering the principles of settlement; but the fact remains that Government is nowhere and in no way bound by any law, public notification or declaration as to permanency; on the contrary, in the laws up to so late as 1831, the settlement of lands other than those under the zamindari settlement was declared to be "temporary" and non-permanent. It will presently be shown that there has been no custom of permanency in the rates of assessment.

Moreover, if as Mr. Dutt claims (page 95 of his book), "the land revenue is a *tax*" it is difficult to see how, being a tax, it could be made permanent even by enactment.

Disadvantages to ryots of irreducibility of Government demand.

11. *Point (c)—In the intentions of the founders of the system the idea of permanency was absolutely reciprocal; if Government could not demand more, neither was it ever to receive less.* It is well to note the conditions of the "permanency" intended by Read and Munro, and which is represented as the leading characteristic of the ryotwari system and as a right of the ryot confiscated by Government. Colonel Read stated the case distinctly, and if the words implying perpetuity were excised, his proclamation would in that matter suit Munro's views: "the assessment of every individual field (in the holding) *when*

MADRAS. *at the full rate* is fixed for ever, that is to say, *the Government is never to require more or receive less nor you to pay less or more* than the present rate." In other words, there is a reciprocal contract that if on the one hand there shall be no increase, on the other, there shall be no reduction or remission. But in now claiming permanency it has been forgotten that the permanency extends to both parties; if the assessment could not be raised neither could it be reduced. Yet the whole history of land revenue from 1818 to 1855, and later, was an incessant clamour—and a rightful clamour—for heavy reductions of the "standard" assessment and for remissions, while every sort of evasion or artifice was resorted to, both by ryots and by officials, in order to lighten the assessment. This was necessitated by the enormous standard assessments based upon those found in existence at the assumption of the country, and by the continual fall in prices up to 1855; from that period prices so rapidly rose that further reductions no longer became necessary, and consequently the claim advanced, now that the original assessment is moderate in comparison with prices, is for permanency. But of two things one : either permanency or non-permanency, but not the one or the other according to circumstances and prices. In paragraphs 28 to 30 of its despatch No. 6 of 1868 to the Secretary of State, the Madras Government recognizes that the permanency had "hitherto been entirely one sided," and points out that if reductions and remissions were just in the case of a continued fall in prices or of bad seasons, the ryot could not claim to enjoy the sole benefit of a rise in prices. It must be added that had the principle of reciprocal permanency been more than a mere intention and idea, had it not in fact been abandoned as a working principle, every ryot in the country would have been ruined by the impossibility, at the prices of the second quarter of the century, of paying not merely the standard or maximum, but in many districts the reduced assessment. In fact, the standard or maximum was but tentative, it was erroneous and excessive, and it was never adopted as a permanency.

MADRAS.

12. *Point (d).—If permanency had been established, it would have ruined the ryot owing to the weight and inequality of the assessments.*—The Board does not propose to dwell on the other incidents attached by Munro and other officers to the ideal ryotwari system or belonging thereto as part of the then revenue methods, such as the liability of all the ryots of a village up to 10 per cent. of their individual dues for the default of any of their body, the compulsory nature of the contracts at the annual settlements, the custom of levying heavy assessments upon gardens (dry lands in which the owners had dug wells at their own expense); the history of the system as separately worked or varied in each district may be read, at least in outline, in the printed records available to every student. But since the permanency of the original ryotwari assessment has been claimed as a right of the ryot, it may be well to mention that the rates imposed by that assessment—based, as stated above, on the assessments of the previous rulers of the country—were, in many districts, far higher per acre than those now generally obtaining: the higher rates were so unbearable that the best wet lands were not cultivated, the average rates were far higher than the settlement average rates, while the garden assessments, based upon the value of the crop, were extraordinarily heavy; these last are not now in existence, having been wholly struck out of the list of rates and the lands assessed at dry rates only. Even the heavily reduced rates which immediately preceded the new settlement were in many cases higher than those which replaced them.

Probable results had permanent settlement been granted.

It will be shown below that whereas in 1851-55 the average assessment per occupied acre was R2·44, in 1898 the average was R1·87. But the average of the former period was only arrived at after numerous reductions in every district; 25, 33, 37 per cent. at a single stroke, were granted as general reductions in some districts during the first half of the century, while there were many less prominent ones in addition to "permanent remissions," cowles, etc. Hence it is obvious that the original average rates in general

Comparison of assessment in 1851-55 and now.

MADRAS. must have been much higher than those of the new settlement, while it is known that wet and garden rates were altogether excessive. As an example, North Arcot, a typical ryotwari district, may be taken; in this district in 1805 the *average* assessments per acre were R11-1.0, R3-10-0, and R21-9-0 for wet, dry, and garden lands respectively in the Southern division, and R15-3-0, R3-12-0, and R18-9-0 in the Northern Division; the maximum rates were of course far higher; apparently, however, no charge was made for a second crop if grown, but no reduction was made if it was not grown. These enormous rates, which threw all the higher assessed and best lands out of cultivation, were incessantly under heavy reduction up to 1864, but the reductions were only temporary expedients, while the areas and rates were doubtful and unequal, the areas being in many cases much against the ryot, as in Palmaner taluk, where the true area was found to be 33 per cent. *less* than the nominal area. Hence the new survey and settlement which began in 1871, the result of which is an assessment averaging R4-15-2 per acre of wet land *plus* one-half extra for a second crop when grown, and R1-4-2 on dry land, in which latter are included all the gardens which bore the immense assessments mentioned above. The contrast is noteworthy; it is unlikely that the ryot would, even at present prices, assent to a permanency of the original rates, which is what is claimed not by him but for him.

The original figures for South Arcot are not very dissimilar from those for North Arcot; and though there were continued reductions in this district also, yet it was the weight and inequality of the assessments which led to the new settlement being introduced into two taluks of this district earlier than in any other district, *viz.*, 1861-62. It is noteworthy that though the assessment in these two taluks, which were settled under the ideas prevalent in 1860, bore the proportion of 31 per cent.—on the wet land—to the gross produce *at commutation rates*, yet these assessments were an actual reduction from rates which were themselves heavily reduced from paimash (original) rates.

MADRAS.

The district of Salem was assessed at rates considerably below those of the Carnatic districts, yet the assessments were frequently revised, reduced or evaded, while the *taram kammi* reduction of 1859 amounted to about 10 per cent. on the *then* rates; the new settlement, completed by 1872, resulted in an increase of only 4 per cent. in the assessment, though the excess found by survey was 15 per cent., so that the rates per survey acre were considerably lower than the rates which immediately preceded settlement, though those rates had been considerably reduced from Colonel Read's or later ryotwari rates.

In a subsequent part of this resolution the great rise in prices since 1855 will be shown: if then at the prices of the latter half of the century the assessment is just—or, as stated by objectors, high—its effect upon the ryots at former low prices may be judged. Hence the (supposed) "standard" rates were not and could not be permanent in any sense.

Other reasons why permanent settlement was impossible.

13. *Point (e).—Partly owing to the weight of the assessment at the then prices and conditions, partly to the absence of a proper survey, permanency was never established as a fact but remained a mere intention or guiding purpose which was not binding in perpetuity but is alterable according to circumstances.*—The Board must also point out that not only was the ryotwari system not introduced into all districts, but that in many if not in most ryotwari districts there was no standard assessment which, not to mention its weight, could be taken as a permanent assessment; in almost every district such a standard was a mere expectation. In G. O. No. 951, Revenue, dated 14th August 1855, which practically originated the new Survey and Settlement Department, it is distinctly stated that "in this Presidency alone there has hitherto been no regular survey.* In some districts attempts were made in the years immediately succeeding the British assumption to establish something like a register of lands and fixed rates of assessment

*"Survey" in the parlance of that day included "Settlement."

MADRAS. founded on actual measurement and valuation. But these measures were in every case carried out in haste, with imperfect agency, and in many cases in a very defective manner . . . . . But even these defective and imperfect surveys extended to only a few districts, and there are many, even at the present day, where the land revenue is based merely on the unchecked statements of the karnam, who thus has vast opportunity both of making exactions on the ryots and, in collusion with them, of defrauding the Government." Government then proceed to give several instances as examples of the Presidency, and it may be added from a close perusal of the district manuals and many other records, all available to the public, that except in a few districts, there was no semblance of a fixed standard assessment based upon a survey, and that where there had been a survey it was not only imperfect in general or had been in a great measure lost, but that the rates fixed on the fields had been altered and lost either by authorised reductions or by fraud. In fact, the conditions which Munro postulated for the introduction of a standard assessment of some permanency were, in general, absent. Those conditions included an accurate survey of the area, its division into fields, an accurate knowledge of the productiveness of the respective areas, and a consideration of the economic position of the ryot based partly upon observation, partly on consideration of his average payments over a long series of years; in most, if not in all districts, no such conditions existed; this was admitted by Munro in 1824 (Minute on the condition of the country) and the Revenue history of subsequent years is the history of a groping after a standard.

Moreover, in several districts, as in Tinnevelly and Tanjore, the system admitted of no permanent money standard: a grain assessment was levied (at the nominal rate in Tanjore of 47 per cent. of the gross produce), and this was commuted at varying prices; in Tanjore there were several settlements (in 1820, 1827—32 and 1859) on varying principles; in Tinnevelly, the assessment was nominally fixed in grain and commuted each year at current prices.

MADRAS.

In fact, Munro's later writings show that the introduction of a standard rate and even of a settled *system* of assessment was, even then, still an expectation. In his Minute of 1824 he writes as follows :—"Whether the assessment be a fixed rent in kind, or a fixed share of the crop in kind or commuted into money, or a fixed or varying money rent, it makes no difference; it is still ryotwari. All these varieties of assessment prevail more or less in the provinces under Government ; but though they all come under the general denomination of ryotwari, their effects on the prosperity of the country are very different; and it is therefore an important object that the kind of ryotwari which is most conducive to improvement, namely, a fixed and moderate money assessment, *should be everywhere gradually introduced.* But before we endeavour to make such a change in any district, it is absolutely necessary that we should survey its lands, and ascertain as nearly as possible its average revenue for a long series of years." The pages of Mr. A. D. Campbell in his paper prepared for the Select Committee of the House of Commons in 1832, the reports and proceedings relative to South Canara about 1843, the evidence of Mr. Dykes before the Committee of 1852, and the papers read in G. O. No. 951 of the 14th August 1855, mentioned above, with many other records, show that the standard assessment and the settled ryotwari system was yet to seek in the Madras Presidency in general. In fact, the Board of Revenue in their Proceedings No. 6369, dated 8th September 1868, in which they warmly advocated a ryotwar permanent settlement, spoke of it as a policy of *the future* (paragraphs 22, 28, 30, and 43) to be introduced as the new survey and settlement "should be" introduced into each district.

Review of past discussions on the subject.

14. The Board will now respectfully criticize the remarks of the authorities quoted by Mr. Dutt, premising that in none of the papers is there to be found any grouping of facts to prove the correctness of the dicta; only opinion is to be found, however authoritative, and however decidedly stated that opinion may be. As regards opinions, the words of the very Board of 1857 whose proceedings are quoted by Mr. Dutt, are noteworthy; "what

MADRAS. may be the opinion of the Government or of the Board of Revenue one year may be quite at variance with the views expressed by the same authorities another year in consequence of those changes in office which cause official opinions to be in fact the opinions of individuals who, in matters of this kind, will seldom be unanimous. Even among the most experienced and careful this great contrariety exists"; they therefore submitted their views with much diffidence. The present Board will now add another reason for variety of opinions, *viz.*, that the ryotwari system was in a state of flux and that neither systems nor principles of settlement had taken a permanent shape; practice differed from period to period and district to district, so that it was impossible to predicate anything absolutely; perhaps the only distinct and settled fact was the perpetuity of the tenure, and that was fixed by history and by the courts. It is noticeable that the dicta as to the permanency of the *assessment* are only to be found in the brief period between 1857 and 1868, so that the *personnel* of the authorities is a factor to be considered; also that the dicta are the more curious since the very authorities in question had long agreed to and were then carrying out the new survey and settlement, which latter, in fact, had, by 1868, been introduced into the whole or part of five districts. The Board has the strongest reasons for believing that the authorities prior to 1857 were not conscious of such actual permanency in the sense of perpetuity or even that it was a necessary principle of the ryotwari system: the meaning attached to the word "permanent" by Munro has already been stated, while the Governments which, from 1845 to 1855, earnestly and sympathetically considered the state of the country, the character of the revenue system, and the necessity for a new settlement, did not even find it necessary to argue the point but unhesitatingly suggested the alteration of the old settlement and the introduction of periodical settlements, reassessments, and alterations of the commutation rate. The Board very specially commends for perusal the selection of papers "relating to the proposed General Revenue Survey," printed in 1855, and containing the individual minutes of the members of Government from 1848 to 1855; there is no trace of even a suspicion that a periodical settlement would be counter either to the existing principles or actual practice of the ryotwari system. It may be added that the well-known printed petition to Parliament of the Madras Native Association in 1852 betrays no knowledge of any such permanency, but seeks to have the individual ryotwari system abandoned in favour of a village system. **MADRAS.**

The Madras Government Order of 1862.

15. The whole of the opinions on which Mr. Dutt relies are contained in G. O. No. 241, dated 8th February 1862, printed on pages 164—171 of Mr. Dutt's book. and will be respectfully criticized in turn. Government observes that "one fundamental principle of the ryotwari system is that the Government demand on the land is fixed for ever." The Board has already admitted that this was undoubtedly a *proposed* principle, but has also shown that the conditions of the country had not permitted its introduction as a practice, and that it remained a proposal which might or might not be accepted by Government; in any case it was not a principle which had been formulated and authoritatively notified, still less established by law as was the zemindari permanent settlement. Even the Hon'ble Mr. Maltby, whose views are chiefly reflected in the Government Order in question, does not combat the Government right to make the new assessment with periodical settlements, but states that he himself is "strongly in favour of a permanent assessment" *on the introduction of the new survey*, giving practical reasons but not denying the Government right to make the new assessment. In fact, the country was not in a state for permanency, and the despatch of the Secretary of State, dated 9th July 1862, while declaring in favour of Mr. Maltby's proposal for permanency, expressly states that before the introduction of such permanency, it must first be considered whether "any particular district is in a condition to warrant the practical application of the measure," and that the Madras Presidency was in fact "not at present generally in a condition which would warrant" a permanent settlement, which could only be carried out very gradually,

MADRAS. and that "the result of the survey and settlement operations which had been recently commenced will show how far the districts have yet attained the condition contemplated by Sir T. Munro as warranting the establishment of a settlement in perpetuity."

Colonel Read's proclamation of 1796.

16. The Government then quote Colonel Read's well-known proclamation of 1796 in the Salem district, which recited that "the assessment of every individual field in it (holding), when at the full rate, is fixed for ever, etc." The Board must point out—

(1) that the assessments have never attained their "full rate," for they were ruinously high, and were subjected through long series of years ending, in 1859, to continued and heavy reductions and remissions, such as the *taram kammi* and other general reductions, the abandonment of the heavy garden tax and of the double assessment levied when topes were planted on wet land, etc.;

(2) that Colonel Read's proclamation was not merely unauthorized, but was contrary to orders, which were to form a settlement for five years only;

(3) that the proclamation was never fully approved of even by his own officers or confirmed by Government:

(4) that the essence of Colonel Read's permanent plan was that the assessment should be invariable on *both sides, viz.*, that "the Government is never to require more or *receive less*, nor you to pay *less* or more than the present rate," a reciprocity which has been forgotten; seasonal or other remission was also ruled out under this system;

(5) that in 1824 the Board observed that the plan of permanent pattas as tried by Colonel Read had been found impracticable and had been abandoned, Colonel Read himself stating (10th August 1799) that "the absolving the ryots from their engagements was not only indispensable to the future

welfare of the people, but to relieve the most indigent of them from the hardship which a fixed settlement imposed upon them and to prevent a decrease of cultivation" (Minute of the Hon'ble Mr. D. Elliott of 1st November 1852); **MADRAS.**

(6) that the settlement was practically cancelled by the introduction of the zamindari system, and that the permanency proclaimed by Colonel Read did not form a declared part of the renewed ryotwari system when reintroduced;

(7) that when arranging for the introduction of the new settlement, it was found that the remissions and changes necessitated in the original assessments had been effected to such an extent during the previous sixty years "that Colonel Read's settlement has been quite obliterated, his very accounts have been lost, and the state of the present assessment is the growth of various measures applied not a little according to the inclination of every village accountant" (Settlement officer in B. P. No. 6334, dated 4th October 1867).

Colonel Munro's views 1802-1806.

17. The second quotation by Government is from Colonel Munro's views as expressed in 1802 and 1806, on which the Board will merely refer to its remarks in paragraph 9 *supra* containing Sir T. Munro's statements when Governor in 1820 and in 1824 on the meaning of the word "permanent" as used by him and as applicable therefore to the ideal ryotwari system.

The Revenue Board's Minute of 5th January 1818.

18. The remark of the Board of 1818 in paragraph 140 of its Minute of the 5th January and quoted by Government, relates to the old ryotwari system of Read and Munro *prior* to its abandonment in favour of the zamindari and village rent systems; that the Board in introducing the revised ryotwari system, which was the ostensible object of their Minute,

MADRAS. did not intend to introduce permanency, is shown by the facts (1) that in paragraph 291 the Board, referring to Colonel Munro's intention of introducing a permanent field assessment, derided "permanent field money assessments incapable of being permanent"; (2) that in the draft Regulation which they at the same time prepared, they make no mention of permanency, but declared that it has been deemed expedient to make a new "assessment," and "that the variable money assessment now paid in money for land should be changed into a fixed field assessment" that is, fixed as opposed to variable.

19. The late Government mentioned no authorities between 1818 and 1855-56, but the Board has shown and could quote both authorities and an overwhelming array of facts to show that whatever the purpose or intention of the ryotwari system, that system itself had not even been fairly tried in any one district except perhaps Coimbatore, still less had it been possible practically to introduce permanency into the confusion of rates which generally existed, altogether irrespective of the ruin would have been effected by such permanency by reason of the heavy fall of prices in the first half of the century.

20. The next quotation taken from the Administration Report of 1855-56 may almost be passed over; the word "fixed" does not *per se* prove anything as to permanency; as the phrase stands, it simply means the assessment fixed, or determined, or established, or fixed as opposed to fluctuating, for the words "in perpetuity" or "for ever" are not added. The words "perpetual lease" apply solely to the tenure, and it may here be remarked that as in paragraphs 29 and 30 of B. P. No. 6369, dated 8th September 1868, and elsewhere, the undoubted permanency and inviolability of the *tenure* by which the ryot holds have been frequently confounded with the permanency of the assessment: the tenure may be perpetual, but the land revenue may vary. It is indeed obvious that Government could not possibly have reported in 1855-56 that the assessment was "fixed" in the sense of being perpetual, when that same Government—the same individually—

The Administration Report of 1855-56.

had, in August 1855, penned its order No. 951 which originated the new survey and settlement scheme, and laid down, *ex suo motu* and without the slightest sense that they were offending any principle, that a new settlement should be made, and should subsist, so far as the grain assessment was concerned, only for fifty years, and that the commutation rate of the same should be altered every *seven or ten years* (paragraphs 23 and 21). The true meaning of the word "fixed" as used by Munro and the early administrators, *viz.*, non-fluctuating and certain, or not provisional, has been mentioned above. **MADRAS.**

The Revenue Board's Proceedings of July 1857.

21. The next quotation is from the B. P. No. 2400, dated 15th July 1857. In paragraph 1 the Board used the following words: "A Madras ryot is able to retain his land in perpetuity without any increase of assessment, as long as he continue to fulfil his engagements." The discussion in which the Board was then engaged was not the *propriety* of a new settlement which had already been accepted by it, but merely certain conditions of it, and the particular point then under discussion was not whether a periodical revision was permissible, but whether the *holding* was permanent or terminated with each period of settlement which, in the very next preceding paragraph, the Board had "urged" should be a period of thirty years. Having decided upon this period, they remarked incidentally on the erroneousness of the opinion that the Bombay settlement period, also of thirty years, secures a greater permanency of tenure to the ryot than the Madras ryotwari tenure which, by reason of the assessment being fixed on the field, involves annual settlements (jamabandi), and they pointed out that the Madras tenure is, notwithstanding the annual settlements, a tenure in perpetuity. The Board evidently had in mind paragraph 28 of G. O. No. 951, dated 14th August 1855, which had originated the iscussion, where Government remarked that under the ryotwari system "many fields are held permanently, although the ostensible title is only the annual patta." In fact, in 1848 the Hon'ble Mr. J. F. Thomas, Member of Council, objected to the annual settlement

MADRAS. as tending to keep the people in "tutelage," looking only to the year's tenure and its outturn rather than considering the land their own for a "period," and he therefore recommended leases for terms of years. The point of the then Board's remark is the perpetuity of the *holding*: people in "England" thought that under the system of annual pattas a ryot's title was only good for one year and that he was liable to be ousted or his rent raised as in an ordinary annual tenancy, whereas in fact he held in perpetuity on a non-varying field assessment. That the word "perpetuity" referred to the holding and not to the assessment is shown by the context.

22. Government further remark (paragraph 13) that "in practice this leading principle (limitation in perpetuity of the demand) has never been infringed," and that the assessments have been reduced, "but in no instance have they ever been raised, nor in the recent pressure for money has so obvious a source as increasing the land tax been even suggested as being open to Government." The Government, in giving this as an argument, must surely have forgotten the course of the revenue history and of prices; there was, it is true, no general attempt at or even idea of raising assessments, for the simple reason that they were already so unbearable that, with prices continuously falling for forty years until 1855, the only possible action of Government was reduction and remission and again reduction.

23. With the utmost respect for the late Government, the Board would observe finally that that Government seems to have been consumed with rightful anxiety lest, as a result of the discussions then going on, a permanent assessment of the zamindari order should be thrust upon the Presidency, and that the most was consequently made of the old ryotwari *idea* of permanency in order to show that permanency already existed in the ryotwari system, and that therefore no further permanency was required. The Board most willingly admits that nothing is more certain than that the ryot's title to hold the land is indefeasible, and that he cannot be ejected so long as he pays the fixed assessment, but it cannot admit that the word "fixed" means unalterable in

perpetuity, or that any assessment on ryotwari land has ever yet **MADRAS.** been so fixed, or that any district has ever yet arrived at such a condition as would, if ever, warrant a permanency of any sort, and it would quote the authority of Sir T. Munro in 1824 as to the precise meaning which he, as founder of the system, attached to the word permanent and the meaning which should therefore be attached to it up to the date of the decision to systematize a settlement previously either unorganized or disorganized.

In concluding this part of its resolution the Board would refer to the views expressed on page 298, Vol I, of Baden-Powell's Land Systems of British India.

Limitation of enhancements to rise in prices. Discussion of 1882-85.

24. *Point 2 in paragraph 3 supra.*—Mr. Dutt's paragraphs 6 and 7 relate to the principles on which the revision of assessments is to take place; he recites the despatch of Lord Ripon' dated 17th October 1882, which, according to Mr. Dutt, "laid down the principle that in districts which had once been surveyed and assessed by the Settlement department, assessments should undergo no further revision except on the sole ground of a rise of prices" and the "decision," says Mr. Dutt "was accepted by the Madras Government in 1883." Mr. Dutt then expresses his regret that the Secretary of State vetoed the proposal in his despatch of 8th January 1885 which, he considers, "reopened the question which had been wisely solved after years of mature deliberation," and which he characterizes as "one of the saddest documents ever issued from London," in having "thrown back the Madras cultivators into another era of uncertainty, needless harassment and unjust enhancements." Mr. Dutt therefore proposes (paragraph 13) that "this qualified permanency of assessments" may be conferred on the Madras peasantry, presumably by a formal and binding declaration of policy.

25. The Board cannot accept Mr. Dutt's history, his reading of the Secretary of State's despatch of 1885, or his proposals. The simple answer to Mr. Dutt is that the Madras settlement principles till 1883 were settled and consistent on the question of the mode of revision, and that the Secretary of State's despatch of

MADRAS. 8th January 1885 so far from rejecting or vetoing Lord Ripon's proposals, accepted, as sound in principle, the bulk of them, expressly including, for ryotwari areas, the particular one now in discussion. In the same despatch, however, the Secretary of State enunciated the further and general principle that no Government could be permitted to tie the hands of its successors by pledging them for ever to a particular line of action, and he therefore objected to any hard-and-fast rules being laid down by way of pledge or promise. Hence the result of the despatch, *quoad hoc*, is to leave the Madras Government at liberty, if it sees fit, to revise its settlements solely on a consideration of prices; it is neither compelled nor forbidden to do so. As the question is important, the Board will summarize the history of the matter and the contents of the despatch.

History of Madras settlement principles from 1855.

26. As already shown, the ryotwari system was, till 1855, in a state of flux, when the inequalities and weight of the assessment and the incessant but unsystematic reductions, compelled the Madras Government to introduce a new survey and revised assessment, chiefly with a view to ease the ryots. Owing largely to the uncertainty as to prices, Government originally proposed a grain assessment for fifty years with frequent changes of the money commutation rate, but in 1855-57 it was finally determined that the settlement should be for thirty years in money, and that the assessment should be fixed for thirty years; in 1858 the Madras Government published a notification to this effect. In 1862, however, the then Secretary of State, Sir C. Wood, declared that, where possible, the assessment might *eventually* be rendered absolutely permanent, but he took care to insist on the necessity for complete previous investigation and revision of the settlements for the imposition of a "full, fair and equable rent on all lands"; and he further decided that, in this Presidency, the general conditions were not ripe for any such permanent settlement. But this qualified decision had hardly been passed, when it was further limited by successive Secretaries of State, and in 1869, in his despatch to Madras, No. 7, dated

8th April, the Duke of Argyll, in reply to a Madras despatch of 1868, wrote as follows:— **MADRAS.**

Duke of Argyll's despatch of 1869.

".II. Whether, with respect to the despatch of Secretary, Sir Charles Wood, of the 9th of July 1862, to the Government of India, the grain assessments under the revision of the land-tax now in progress may not be declared to be permanent, and the money rates changed, if thought advisable by the Government of the day, every thirty years?

5. I will consider this last proposal first. I find that since 1856 the question of declaring the grain assessments permanent has frequently been referred for the decision of the authorities in this country, and it has been decided, both by the Court of Directors and by the Secretaries of State, that the settlement should be a money assessment founded upon due consideration of all the circumstances of the district, and revised after a term of years, and that your Government, so far back as 1858, directed the issue of a notification to this effect. Her Majesty's Government must adhere to that decision, nor do they see, as Your Excellency in Council seems to do, in the despatches addressed to the Government of India in and from 1862 to the present time on the general question of permanent settlement throughout India, anything inconsistent with this view. It seems to me impossible to read paragraphs 66, 67, 69 and 70 of the despatch of the 9th July 1862, some of which are quoted by your Government, without being impressed with the conviction that it was thought highly improbable that either your Presidency or that of Bombay, but particularly the former, should be brought, or at all events not for many years to come, within the terms under which alone it was permissible to confer a permanent settlement upon the land-owners. Your Excellency in Council distinctly states, in the despatch now before me, that "the time is probably still very distant when any measure limiting the maximum amount of the Government revenue, under the conditions laid down, could be adopted without serious injury to the interests of the community and of the State as representing the community, or with any real benefit to small sections of the community or to individuals," and it certainly is not the desire of Her Majesty's Government to force on any immature concession of this nature. They concur with you in the expediency, and indeed the necessity, of keeping in the hands of the Government such a legitimate source from which to supply the increasing wants of the State for the benefit of the people, as the extension of cultivation among waste lands. They are also happy to agree with your Government in opinion that, under the principles of the revised settlement now in progress for adjusting the

MADRAS. assessment and fixing it for a term of years, the share taken by the Government is kept within limits which are perfectly equitable to the cultivator. But they are unable to see that it is therefore necessary to make a declaration to the landholders that the grain assessments are to be permanent. On the contrary, they feel themselves precluded, for the same reasons which Your Excellency in Council has urged in your 18th paragraph for retaining the waste lands, from sanctioning the surrender of such a legitimate source of revenue as the Government share of the increased value which has been conferred on the land by improved administration, the construction of public works, especially works of irrigation and railways, together with the improved price of agricultural produce.

The Government of India's proposals of 1883.

27. He therefore directed "that the previous decisions of the Home authorities by which the assessments were to be revised after a period of thirty years, be adhered to." Here the matter rested for Madras till 1883, the principles confirmed by the above despatch remaining the guide for action in the settlements then in progress: for Madras the question was a settled question, its principles being consistent from 1857 to 1883. But in 1883 the Government of India addressed the Government of Madras on the tentative proposal made in the despatch of 17th October 1882—regarding the settlements of Upper India—to eliminate from future settlements the elements of uncertainty and inquisitorial enquiry, and to give to the ryot thereby an assurance of permanence and security while not depriving the State "of the power of enhancement of the revenue on defined conditions." The Government of Madras in G. O. No. 775, Revenue, dated 13th August 1883, accepted the proposal that "in districts in which the revenue has been *adequately* assessed" the element of price should alone be considered in subsequent revisions, such districts being those duly surveyed and settled.

The Secretary of State's final orders of 1885.

28. After considerable correspondence, in which apparently Madras took no part, the matter was disposed of by the Secretary of State, in his despatch of the 8th January 1885 on the above question, as discussed for the North-Western Provinces. In this despatch he fully accepted the principle that it was

desirable to simplify procedure and avoid unnecessary harassment **MADRAS.**
in the resettlements, and the rules taken from his despatch are as follow:—

(1) The permanent settlement idea is formally abandoned;

(2) The State shall still retain its claim to share in "the unearned increment" of the value of land to which there is a tendency in a progressive country;

(3) That a general and permanent rise in the prices of produce is one of the principal indications and measures of this increment;

(4) that it is nevertheless desirable to modify the existing system of revision of the temporary settlements of land revenue with a view of rendering it less arbitrary, uncertain, and troublesome to the people;

(5) that the modifications should be effected at least in the following particulars:—

(*a*) The repetition of field operations (survey, valuation, minute inquiries into assets, and the like) which are considered to be inquisitorial and harassing to the people, should be, as far as possible, dispensed with;

(*b*) enhancement should be based mainly on considerations of general increase in the value of land;

(*c*) the assessment will not be revised *merely* with a view to equalizing its incidence with that of the assessments of other estates;

(*d*) improvements made by the land-holders themselves should not be taken into account in revising assessments; but improvements made at the cost of the State should be taken into account, and also, to some extent, increase of cultivation.

29. These principles, though of general application as a whole, were laid down only for the circumstances of the North-West Provinces in the despatch of 22nd March 1883; they were repeated in that of 8th January 1885 with addenda, *viz.*, that assessments should not necessarily be uniform, since some estates (or tracts, in ryotwari provinces) might require lenient assessments or even reductions, while others, as where railways had been opened, might readily bear considerable enhancements; that no rules could be framed which would enable a land-owner to forecast enhancements; and as regards the proposal that "enhancements should be determined solely on the ground of a

MADRAS. general rise in prices," it was declared that "in ryotwari provinces the rule proposed is in principle sound, although there are considerable difficulties in applying it"; it was added that "the principle has been decided to be sound as regards Madras and Bombay" (paragraph 11).

30. But in the latter part of the despatch in criticising other proposals by Sir A. Lyall, the Secretary of State laid down principles, evidently for general guidance, in the following words:—

> My principal objections are . . . secondly, that it involves what I cannot but consider the dangerous policy of pledging Government for ever to a particular line of action.
>
> 20. On the latter point I entertain a strong opinion. Some of the principal administrative difficulties which now exist in India arise in a measure from such pledges having been given on former occasions. I consider that there is a great difference between making a public declaration beforehand of what its future action shall be, and its laying down from time to time the principles which shall regulate its action. The latter is necessary for the guidance of its officers and to secure uniformity and continuity in administration, while the former would bind its hands for its successors, when circumstances may have greatly altered. In my opinion, no hard-and-fast rules on the subject of the present discussion should be laid down; no such pledge or promise as that enhancements shall not exceed 15 per cent. should be given to the people. All the benefits anticipated from the scheme will accrue in due time if the new rules are promulgated simply by administrative order. When the people see that these rules are really acted on, this will give more confidence than any prior declarations. Besides, however good the scheme may be, it is certain that there will be points on which experience may enable the Government to introduce improvements, and it would be a grave mistake, by making promises now, so to tie up the hands of the administration as to prevent such improvements in the process, or the amendment of such flaws in it, as may become apparent.

Danger of pledging Government for ever to particular method.

31. The Secretary of State then mentioned general principles for the conduct of operations, excluding backward localities and suggesting that prices, land-owners' actual rentals, and the sale value of land should be factors in deciding revisions, care being taken not to raise the assessment unduly, finally observing that "a procedure such as is here sketched, if introduced with care and

applied with discretion, may be expected to diminish, if not altogether to remove, the evils of the present system of periodical resettlement, whilst it would not unduly sacrifice the claims of the State to profit by the increasing value of the land." **MADRAS.**

32. From the above it is clear that no settled question was "reopened" by the Secretary of State's despatch, and that the contents of the despatch itself do not bear the character which Mr. Dutt has assigned to it in his seventh paragraph and in pages 11 and 12 of his book.

Advantages of a free hand.

On the contrary, the Board believes the policy which leaves Government free to choose from time to time and from district to district the particular method of resettlement, to be a wise policy, wise both in the interests of the State in general and of the ryot in particular who is thereby saved from the dangers of novel forms of taxation; especially wise in the circumstances of a country in which improvement has but just begun and is still irregular, so that the increment which modern policy desires to draw, in part, to the State—especially when such increment is largely due to the direct action of the State—is not only necessarily large, but is necessarily needed for the due continuance and for the further development of improvements. Taking communications alone as an example of the improvements by which an increment arises to the agricultural population in addition to that due to a general rise in prices; there are districts in the Presidency in which, when the new settlements were introduced, railways, and often a full provision of roads, were either wholly absent or only just begun; in Anantapur there was, for instance, when the settlement scheme was first proposed, only one railway on one edge of the district, while in the last 12 years, with a view to its development and to its protection from famine, two new railways have been added; in Salem and Coimbatore, as elsewhere, land within easy reach of the railways has, to the Board's knowledge, increased tenfold in sale value since the building of the Madras and South Indian Railways, while no one can fail to note the increased area of valuable products, such as turmeric, plantains, fruit, etc., in those

MADRAS. tracts, products which are in demand, thanks to the railways, in Madras, Bombay, and other distant markets. "To move is to produce" said Mill, and it would be unjust to deny to Government, or rather to the State, some share in that increased production and in that increased value, whether of produce or of land, which is due not to a mere general rise in prices or fall in money, but to the effect of railways, a share which must be looked to for the partial recoupment of that loss which is apt to be caused to the State when railways are first driven through an unproductive and backward tract.

33. Railways are but an item of improvements which raise indefinitely the value of land and its produce far beyond the increment due to a rise in the price of staple food-grains with regard to which the land is now assessed, and the Board would protest against an absolute hard-and-fast limitation such as that proposed by Mr. Dutt for the permanent fettering of future administrations by the present. Should it be found possible at any resettlements and in given areas to apply the rule mentioned by Mr. Dutt, it is open to Government to do so, and such method would be as welcome to Government and to the Settlement Department as to the ryots. But it would be as impolitic as unnecessary to transform an elasticity of method into the rigidity of permanent shackles. The history of the new settlements in general as given above proves with what care the Government, though unfettered in its discretion, has applied the methods at its disposal, and that the ryots *are* protected, if not by a hard-and-fast (and one-sided) rule, yet by the care with which the system is worked against "excessive enhancements" (page 157 of Mr. Dutt's book). Where enhancements have necessarily been considerable owing to previous leniency and to the heavy rise in prices, as in Tanjore and in the Trichinopoly resettlement, the land-owner's profits have *pro tanto* been retrenched and a portion of the unearned actual or prospective increment of the sale value of his land has been appropriated by Government; this, however, is merely to say that the new settlements, like other levies, have done their unavoidable work of which land-owners and mortgagees have long had notice.

MADRAS.

34. *Point 3 in paragraph 3 supra.*—In his paragraphs 8 and 9 Mr. Dutt proposes to deal with "the manner in which assessments are now revised at each recurring settlement in Madras." The examination, however, is confined to two points, *viz.* (1) the method of calculating the cultivation expenses, which he believes to be so faulty that the estimate of the "net produce" arrived at thereby is unfair and untrustworthy, and tends to ruin the cultivation of the poorer soils (paragraph 8): (2) the supposed rule that the assessments shall not exceed or shall approximate to one-third of the gross produce (paragraph 9). From his last sentence in paragraph 8 it would seem that Mr. Dutt infers that the erroneous calculation of the net produce and consequent faulty assessment cause "three millions of acres of cultivable lands to be" out of cultivation in Madras; this inference will be dealt with separately.

Present method of assessment.

35. The Board would first point out that the net produce is *not* "ascertained by deducting from the gross produce the estimated cost of cultivation." The *normal* gross produce, *i.e.*, the gross produce struck on a comparison of good and bad years, is valued by a very favourable commutation rate which is usually considerably below the average of the previous 20 years, from which, moreover, all years of scarcity and high prices are excluded; from this sum from 10 to 27 per cent. is deducted for merchant's profits and distance from markets; another deduction is then made of from $6\frac{1}{4}$ to 25 per cent. for vicissitudes of seasons and unprofitable patches of soil, the allowance on dry lands being never less than 15 per cent. and now usually 20 to 25 per cent.; it is from this that are deducted the estimated expenses of cultivation, and the *remainder* is taken as the average net produce; of this a nominal half, usually rounded to a convenient *lower* figure, is taken as the Government assessment. But this again is subject to considerable reduction under the system of village or irrigation source grouping in which the circumstances, position, etc., of villages or the nature of the sources are taken into consideration, and,

Calculation of average net produce.

MADRAS. finally, the result is compared with existing rates and lowered if relatively too high. The results for the ten districts wholly or partly settled by 1878 and referred to by Mr. Dutt will be found in the table printed at page 394 of appendix, Volume III, to the Famine Commission report (1880), quoted from the replies of the Board to the Commission. It will be seen that for dry and wet lands the net produce obtained as above, average R3-3-3 and R11-13-6, whereas the assessment, nominally considered as half the net, was only R1-3-7 and R5-5-1, respectively, or much below the assumed half.

Cultivation expenses.

36. The Board does not propose to enter into a lengthy discussion of the details of cultivation expenses; they are to be found in the records from Munro onwards, and in the settlement reports and district manuals as well as in other printed sources of information. Nor does it assert that the gradation of expenses in proportion to produce is absolutely accurate in all details. It must be perfectly obvious to all that cultivation expenses differ not merely from soil to soil, but from man to man, from crop to crop, and from year to year; in one field a man will spend ten, twenty or more rupees on manure—according to crop, etc.—while his neighbour may spend little or nothing: one man cultivates his land with his own hands, drives a plough cut from a tree in his own field with a team he has bred on the land, and weeds and harvests with the labour of his own family, while his neighbour, perhaps a Brahmin, a merchant, or other non-cultivator, hires labour and buys material at every step. But since it is necessary to allow for the cost of raising a crop, the Settlement Officers prepare tables based upon many years of enquiry and experience and apply them to the soils in rough proportion to their productiveness, knowing full well that the less productive lands do, as a matter of fact, generally get far less spent upon them than the more productive; it is not that expenses on the poorer lands would not be as great or greater if they were highly cultivated, or that they would not cost more than good lands if they had to be raised to a given productiveness or to yield a given produce, but

that in fact they are *not* so highly cultivated and are not so productive; the best lands get the most attention, the most manure, the most labour; the ryot prefers to spend less upon the less productive and more precarious lands. Consequently the gradation, though only a generalized approximation, has a real foundation in fact. **MADRAS.**

37. That the poorer soils are comparatively neglected is a matter of the most ordinary observation and experience, and is recorded in many papers, whether in the settlement reports, the district manuals, or the reports of agricultural experts. Wet lands, when assessed at low rates, are usually at the tail of the irrigated area or are on a high level, or are of poor soil: these lands are usually tilled last, and get such labour, manure, and water as are available; hence a very great reduction in expenses, and the six rupees an acre mentioned as insufficient by Mr. Dutt would certainly cover them in a vast number of cases. In the case of dry lands it is notorious that immense areas of poor land get no manure, but are fallowed every third year or oftener, and that the manure available is kept for the better soils and especially for the "gardens" (dry land watered by wells). So also it is the better lands, the black cotton soils, the red loams and so forth, which get the thorough cultivation, and the crops the thorough weeding, necessary for good outturns, while on millions of acres of dry soils, assessed at from two to eight annas, in districts of scanty rainfall, with a rocky or unwholesome sub-soil and only a few inches of stony surface soil, the land is barely scratched and sown with castor, horse-gram, or millet: in most such cases R1 to R2 per acre would be an outside figure No one regrets this more than the Board: it is a miserable fact that millions of poor acres get miserable cultivation, but it *is* a fact, and the supposition that R6 per acre "does not cover the cultivation of any kind of cultivable soil in India" is a grave mistake. Possibly Mr. Dutt refers to wet lands only in the above quotation, which, however, is universal in its terms, and, as has been shown above, is incorrect even for wet lands.

MADRAS. 38. In considering the relation of the estimate of expenses to the outturn and to the consequent position of the cultivator, it must be remembered that these scales are maxima: not that they are not often exceeded whether according to the year, the crop, or the ryot, but that they are all calculated as though paid for in money, as though labour, cattle, manure, etc., were all purchased, a hypothesis wholly different from fact but differing wholly to the benefit of the ryot. The cost of bullocks is calculated at a certain rate as though they were always bought, whereas in very many instances they are bred by the ryot and brought up wholly on the straw of the farm crops or on wild pasture: moreover, the calculation usually allows for a minimum of acreage tilled and of duration of the cattle, whereas on dry land a pair will ordinarily last five years and more and till 14 acres or more per annum, besides doing much other work and yielding manure: hence the average rate of cost given in the tables is a maximum. So also in probably nine-tenths of the area, at least of dry lands, the labour expended is only that of the owner and his family, for the farms are of very small size; it is not mainly *paid* labour, though often mutually borrowed as when men plough, harvest, etc., in their neighbours' fields in return for similar assistance in their own. Manure again is largely the produce of the cattle of the farm, or picked up by the children or women in the waste lands, or is cut, as green manure, from the jungle. The feeding and housing of the bullocks which Mr. Dutt observes has not been allowed for, are omitted because straw does not enter into settlement calculations, though of great feeding or selling value; in the old reports, early in the century, it was often set against the whole cultivation expenses, and in the present day sub-tenants are willing to cultivate good lands on receipt of one quarter of the gross outturn of grain if they are allowed the whole of the straw also.

A vernacular proverb is to the effect that, if the cost of cultivation be counted up in *money*, not even the value of the goad will remain, whereas in fact not only does the ryot live, but most of his land has a good sale value; remembrance of this proverb would save many a fallacy. **MADRAS.**

39. It must also be remembered that the rates thus formed are checked by the existing rates, and that, should they prove excessive, they are reduced, so that the ryot "may run no risk"; there is visible in Madras, says Baden-Powell (Land Systems of British India, Volume I, page 298), a distinct tendency in revision settlements not to alter rates found to work well.

40. The Board must also point out that, if the actual cultivation expenses are really larger than are allowed for by the Settlement Department, the gross produce must, for many districts, be more valuable than is calculated by that Department. For since most lands, both wet and dry, will always let at least on the half-share system, and in the case of wet lands, often on a much higher landlord's share, it follows that, at most, half, and on the better lands two-fifths or one-third or even one-quarter, of the gross value must pay both the cost of cultivation and the livelihood and the profits of the actual cultivator. Now as regards wet lands: calculation will show that in some districts, as in the lower class soils of Bellary, Anantapur, in all but the highest classes of Trichinopoly (settlement just expired), etc., the cultivation expenses allowed are *more than* or nearly equal to half the gross produce at commutation rates: in most, if not in all, districts the amount left to the cultivator of the lower grade soils on the half-share or in the better lands on the one-third share, after paying the theoretical cultivation expenses, is so small that no cultivator would take up the lands on those conditions. Taking Salem as an example, since it is a well-known ryotwari district of which the initial (new) settlement is still current, the following table for all wet lands gives particulars; the commutation rate was 32 Madras measures—48 imperial seers per rupee. Land, both dry and wet, is habitually leased on the share principle; the share is here taken as one-half, but

Proportion of cultivation expenses to value of gross outturn.

MADRAS. the cultivator frequently gets less, especially on the high class river-channel lands :—

SALEM DISTRICT—*Wet.*

Class of soil.	Sorts.	Grain outturn, Madras measures (120 tolas).	Value at commutation rate.	Half-share.	Cultivation expenses according to settlement.	Balance to cultivator on half-share.
			R	R	R	R
II . .	1	1,080	33¾	16⅞	11⅞	5
	2	960	30	15	10⅞	4⅛
III . .	1	720	22½	11¼	9	2¼
	2	600	18¾	9⅜	7½	1⅞
	3	288	9	4½	3½	1
IV . .	1	960	30	15	10⅞	4⅛
	2	840	26¼	13⅛	10½	2⅝
	3	360	11¼	5⅝	4⅛	1½
V . .	1	720	22½	11¼	9	2¼
	2	600	18¾	9⅜	7½	1⅞
	3	360	11¼	5⅝	4⅛	1½
VII . .	1	284	26¼	13⅛	10½	2⅝
	2	720	22½	11¼	9	2¼
	3	360	11¼	5⅝	4⅛	1½
VIII . .	1	720	22½	11¼	9	2¼
	2	480	15	7½	6	1½
	3	288	9	4½	3½	1

For dry soils, cumbu in the northern portion of the same district may be taken; the commutation rate was 32 Madras measures or 48 seers per rupee. The assessments given are those of the first group only, but there are three lower groups in which the assessments in these classes range from R2-8-0 to As. 4: MADRAS.

SALEM DISTRICT—*Dry*.

Class of soil.	Sorts.	Grain outturn, Madras measures.	Value at commutation rate.	Half-share.	Cultivation expenses.	Assessment.	REMARKS.
			R	R	R	R	
III . .	1	336	10½	5¼	5¼	1¾	It will be noticed that on the "poorer class (sorts) of lands" the cultivation expenses allowed are relatively larger than on the better classes. Also that in every case but one the cultivation expenses allowed are equal to or exceed the whole half-share.
	2	288	9	4½	4¾	1¼	
	3	192	6	3	3¾	½	
IV . .	1	408	12¾	6⅜	5½	2⅛	
	2	336	10½	5¼	5¼	1¾	
	3	216	6¾	3⅜	4¼	¾	
V . .	1	288	9	4½	4¾	1¼	
	2	264	8¼	4⅛	4¾	1	
	3	192	6	3	3¾	½	
VII . .	1	336	10½	5¼	5¼	1¾	
	2	288	9	4½	4¼	1¼	
	3	168	5¼	2⅝	3¼	⅝	
VIII . .	1	288	9	4½	4¾	1¼	
	2	264	8¼	4⅛	4¾	1	
	3	168	5¼	2⅝	3¼	⅝	

41. Similar tables are as follow for Coimbatore where (see paragraph 52 *infra*), above one-seventh of the lands, wet and dry, were cultivated under the sharing system in 1877. The soils in the table are placed in the second grade only: the commutation rate for paddy was above 25 Madras measures or nearly 38 seers per rupee, and for cumbu 27 Madras measures or above 40

MADRAS. seers per rupee. The share system has been taken as one-half only, since only second-class soils have been entered :—

COIMBATORE DISTRICT—*Wet.*

Class of soil.	Sorts.	Grain out-turn Madras measures.	Value at commutation rate.	Half-share.	Cultivation expenses according to settlement.
			R	R	R
III	1	900	36	18	12⅛
	2	800	32	16	11⅛
	3	700	28	14	10
	4	500	20	10	8
	5	400	16	8	7¼
IV	1	1,000	40	20	12⅛
	2	900	36	18	12⅛
	3	800	32	16	11⅛
	4	700	28	14	10
	5	500	20	10	8
V	1	800	32	16	11⅛
	2	700	28	14	10
	3	500	20	10	8
	4	400	16	8	7¼
	5	300	12	6	4¾
VI	1	900	36	18	12⅛
	2	800	32	16	11⅛
	3	700	28	14	10
	4	500	20	10	8
	5	400	16	8	7¼
VIII	1	800	32	16	11⅛
	2	700	28	14	10
	3	500	20	10	8
	4	400	16	8	7¼
	5	300	12	6	4¾

The next table shows particulars for cumbu, which in this table is placed throughout in the first group; class IV is practically the same as class III, and class VIII as class V:— **MADRAS.**

Coimbatore District—*Dry.*							
Class of soil.	Sorts.	Grain outturn. Madras measures.	Value at commutation rates.	Half-share.	Cultivation expenses according to settlement.	Assessment.	Remarks.
			R	R	R	R a.	
III	1	250	$9\frac{1}{4}$	$4\frac{5}{8}$	$3\frac{3}{8}$	2 0	The relatively liberal rate of cultivation expenses on the poorer lands is well marked.
	2	225	$8\frac{3}{8}$	$4\frac{3}{16}$	$3\frac{3}{8}$	1 8	
	3	200	$7\frac{1}{2}$	$3\frac{3}{4}$	$3\frac{3}{8}$	1 4	
	4	175	$6\frac{5}{8}$	$3\frac{1}{4}$	$3\frac{1}{8}$	1 0	
	5	150	$5\frac{5}{8}$	$2\frac{3}{4}$	$2\frac{7}{8}$	0 12	
V	1	200	$7\frac{1}{2}$	$3\frac{3}{4}$	$3\frac{3}{8}$	1 4	
	2	175	$6\frac{1}{2}$	$3\frac{1}{4}$	$3\frac{1}{8}$	1 0	
	3	150	$5\frac{1}{4}$	$2\frac{5}{8}$	$2\frac{7}{8}$	0 12	
	4	125	$4\frac{3}{8}$	$2\frac{3}{16}$	$2\frac{5}{8}$	0 8	
	5	100	$3\frac{3}{4}$	$1\frac{7}{8}$	$2\frac{1}{4}$	0 6	
VII	1	225	$8\frac{1}{2}$	$4\frac{1}{4}$	$3\frac{3}{8}$	1 8	
	2	200	$7\frac{1}{2}$	$3\frac{3}{4}$	$3\frac{3}{8}$	1 4	
	3	175	$6\frac{1}{2}$	$3\frac{1}{4}$	$3\frac{1}{8}$	1 0	
	4	150	$5\frac{5}{8}$	$2\frac{5}{8}$	$2\frac{7}{8}$	0 12	
	5	125	$4\frac{3}{8}$	$2\frac{3}{16}$	$2\frac{5}{8}$	0 8	

42. It is clear by the above tables that either (1) the commutation rate is, at all events at present prices, too low, or (2) that the grain outturn is estimated too low, or (3) that the cultivation expenses are estimated too high, or (4) that the straw is of such value as to make up for the loss or small profit in grain, or (5) that the cultivation expenses are really not money expenses at all in most items, but only labour which is supplied by the cultivator, or (6) that the actual cultivator is ground down to the barest subsistence by the ryot land-owner. Everyone of the first five hypotheses is in favour of the Government ryot and against the Government; the sixth is a well-known characteristic of peasant landlords. For the Presidency in general, however, it is

MADRAS. clear that cultivation expenses in general are sufficiently well allowed for by the Settlement Department, and that it is precisely "on the poorer class of lands" that the cultivation expenses are most liberal and *not* most "ruinous."

Proposed assessment on gross produce.

43. It will further be clear that since the settlement allowance for cultivation expenses and the consequent calculation of the "net produce" are not "ruinous to the cultivation of the poorer class of lands," no sufficient ground has been made out by Mr. Dutt for his suggestion (paragraph 13) that in future revisions "one-fifth of the gross produce, and not one-half of the net produce, be accepted as the maximum of rent" or rather "assessment." For 36 years without interruption the "half net" principle based upon years of discussion and ordered both by the Court of Directors and by successive Secretaries of State as being *more fair* to the poorer lands, has been adopted, and the settlements of every district are now based upon it: to go back to the method of taking a share of the gross would be exactly to re-introduce uncertainty. In 1856 the Court of Directors declined to accept the Madras Government's proposal to take 30 per cent. of the gross produce as the basis of the maximum demand, observing that "in lands of a high degree of fertility, possessing every means of communication and in the neighbourhood of good markets, 30 per cent. of the gross produce may fall considerably within the limits of the rent or net produce; in lands less fertile and less favourably situated a much smaller share of the gross produce might considerably exceed it. The natural and inevitable consequence, as it appears to us, of apportioning the assessment to the gross produce is to favour the most fertile lands, and to press with increasing severity on the poorer lands, in an inverse ratio to their fertility." They consequently ordered that the assessment should be based not upon a share of the gross but upon a share of the net produce. In confirmation of the Court's observations it will be seen from the dry land tables for Salem and Coimbatore given above, that on the "half-net" system the poorer

lands are more favourably treated than the higher lands, *i.e.*, that **MADRAS.** the cultivation expenses are more liberal in proportion to the produce ; also that the assessments based on half the net produce are in almost all cases below, in many cases far below, one-fifth of the (nominal) gross produce even *at commutation rates.* In Coimbatore, for instance, the cultivation expenses allowed are R3-6-0 on land producing R9-4-0 and R3-2-0 on land producing R6-8-0, and so forth; only in III (1) does the assessment (R2) exceed 20 per cent. of the nominal gross produce taken as R9-4-0; in III (4) and (5) the assessment is R1 and As. 12 as against R1-5-0 and R1-1-0 at 20 per cent. of the gross ; in V (1) and VII (1) it is R1-4-0 and R1-8-0 as against R1-8-0 and R1-10-0 at 20 per cent., while in V (5) and VII (5) it is only As. 6 and As. 8 instead of As. 12 and As. 15. Moreover, with grain at its normal price, for the last decade, of 24 seers per rupee, the existing assessments of 2 and 4 annas which are arrived at on the half-net produce system, represent only three and six seers respectively, which, at 20 per cent. of the produce, represent a gross outturn of 15 and 30 seers per acre, which is an impossible *normal* outturn on any land.

44. It is thus clear not only that the ryot is assessed much below 20 per cent. of the gross produce on by far the greater bulk of the dry soils—for the highest classes of soils are not very extensive—but that the lowest classes of soils enjoy progressively lighter and lighter rates of assessment under the half-net system. In other words, the cultivation expenses on dry soils and consequently the net produce system are more favourable to the poorer than to the richer lands, and Mr. Dutt's reason for altering the method of settlement is therefore unnecessary and even inadvisable.

45. *Point (4) in paragraph 3 supra.*—In paragraph 9 Mr. Dutt deals with the proportion of the gross produce which he supposes is taken by the Madras Government as the assessment. His views are stated as follows :—

Another rule which regulates the assessments made in Madras is that the rent or revenue fixed by such calculations *should not*

MADRAS. *exceed one third of the gross produce of the soil* where the land is not irrigated at Government cost. I have had occasion to point out in another place that this proportion is excessive, and will necessarily impoverish the peasantry of any part of India. In Bengal the cultivators do not pay more than *one-sixth* the gross produce to their landlords in any district, if the district average be taken. And in Northern India, according to Sir A. Macdonnell's evidence before the Currency Committee, the cultivators pay abont *one-fifth* of the gross produce of the soil to their landlords. I hold it, My Lord, that where the British Government stands virtually as landlords, the Government should be less exacting, and not more exacting, than private landlords in India. And I also hold it that cultivators living directly under the British Government should be treated more leniently, and not less leniently, than cultivators living under private landlords. I feel confident that these views will commend themselves to Your Lordship and that Your Lordship will condemn both the rule of levying *one-half the net produce* as revenue, and the rule of making that revenue approximate *one-third the gross produce.* There is not a cultivator in India who does not recognize 3 annas in the rupee of gross produce as fair rent. And there is not a cultivator in India who does not consider 5 or 6 annas out of each rupee of gross produce to be an oppressive and impoverishing rate of rent.

In another place he says that the rule is that the demand "shall not exceed one-third or two-fifths of the gross produce" (page X of the preface to his book).

46. The Board is not aware of any rule as stated by Mr. Dutt: the rule "which regulates the assessments" is that oft he "half-net" and that only. Apparently Mr. Dutt refers to certain remarks in G. O. No. 951, dated 14th August 1855 (originating the new survey and settlement), in which (paragraphs 17 to 19) Government observed that the then existing rates were based on an *assumed* proportion of 50 per cent. of the gross in the case of wet lands and 33 in the case of dry lands: Government considered that these rates were excessive, and that the assessment should not exceed 30 per cent. of the gross "under the most favourable circumstances," a proportion subject to progressive deductions according to the absence of advantages. But the Court of Directors in their reply, dated 17th December 1856, declined to accept this rule of assessment upon the gross, and, in view of probable inequalities of the assessment, ordered that

it should be a proportion of the net. The matter was subsequently discussed with the Home Government, and in 1864* it was finally decided that the rule should be one-half of the net produce. In the note to the table of proportions of the assessment to produce on pages 202 and 203 of the Board's Proceedings in reply to the Famine Commission of 1878, it is clearly stated that the 30 per cent. scale was finally abandoned in 1864. Mr. Dutt's supposed 30 or 40 per cent. of the gross produce as an existing rule therefore disappears, and with it his strange development of it into an assertion that the rule is one of "*making* the revenue approximate one-third the gross produce." There is no such rule and no such attempt at approximation. **MADRAS.**

47. But Mr. Dutt evidently believes not only that there is such a rule, but that the assessment is comparatively near to the proportions of 30 per cent., since he pleads (paragraph 13) that one-fifth of the gross produce be hereafter laid down as the maximum, and he repeatedly quotes in his book the Board's table of proportions above mentioned as representing existing facts: "on an average," he says (page XI), "the State demand *represents* 12 to 20 per cent. of the gross produce for dry lands, and 16 to 31 per cent. of the gross produce on wet lands"; and again "the land revenue *realized is* between 12 and 31 per cent. of the gross produce in Madras" (page 18); this is repeated on pages 98 and 108 (note) and in every case as an existing and realized present proportion.

Actual proportion of revenue to value of real gross produce.

The Board observes that, though the figures are correctly taken from the table, the result is misleading as a general presentation of Madras district assessments: the only case where the assessment is given as 31 per cent. is that of two taluks (Chillambram and Mannargudi), the earliest ever settled, and settled (1860-61) when 30 per cent. was considered a low rate: moreover, the irrigation (Cauvery river channels) of the taluks is amongst the finest in the Presidency. Omitting this small area, a truer idea is given by the figures 12

MADRAS. to 28 per cent., and here again the highest rate is for one district only (Trichinopoly), settled in 1864-65. The *average* of the districts mentioned in the table is 15 per cent. for dry and 20 per cent for wet: see detailed table on pages 202 and 203 of the Board's Resolution. It may be added that both the Trichinopoly district and the two taluks of South Arcot were resettled before Mr. Dutt wrote, and that the proportions mentioned no longer exist.

this rate, as found by calculation for paddy, was only R85 per garce of 4,800 seers, being the average of 52 very low-priced years prior to settlement, but the commutation rate taken was still further reduced to R67, while the average price of the quinquennium which included the actual settlement years was no less than R168. This by itself shows that the proportion borne by the assessment to the real gross produce was far below that given in the table as the proportion borne to the nominal gross produce "at commutation rate." For full details, see appendix III. **MADRAS.**

49. Further, the commutation rate is fixed solely on the values of the chief food-grains, including horse-gram, of a district, whereas the real gross produce includes very large areas of far more valuable products, such as sugar-cane, turmeric, chillies, plantains, betel-leaf, tobacco, cocoanuts, areca-nuts, palmyras, indigo, ground-nuts, cotton, etc. Most of them, except cotton on red soils, palmyras, indigo, and ground-nuts, are grown on good lands in a superior manner and produce crops in many cases valued at between R100 and R200 per acre. Moreover, while the second crop on wet lands produces as a rule much more than half the first crop, it is never charged at more than half the single-crop rates, and may be compounded, when the water-supply is more or less precarious, at rates falling to one-sixth of such rates. Nor is any charge made on wet lands for a second crop raised without Government water on single-crop land, though this, as in the Kristna delta where sunn hemp is largely grown as an extra crop or as in the Godavari delta where green gram is frequently and lucratively grown, is often very extensive, nor for any third crop of any sort on any wet land, even if irrigated, as in parts of Tanjore. Nor is there the slightest charge made for second crop on the dry lands: these, though not general, are not infrequent on ordinary lands, while on the vast area of land irrigated from private wells—about a million acres—two and even three crops per annum are habitually grown, but pay no assessment whatever beyond the ordinary single-crop "dry" rate. Hence the proportion of the assessment to the real gross produce is much below that entered in the table.

MADRAS. 50. It is then a mistake to believe that since 1860 Madras settlement assessments in general ever bore to the *real* gross produce the proportions given in Mr. Dutt's quotations, but it is still more so to believe that they represent existing proportions: the new settlement assessment never did, and certainly does not now represent any such proportion of the real produce. For since 1855 prices have steadily and heavily risen, and, as shown in the second column of the Board's table which Mr. Dutt has omitted to notice or to quote, the proportions for the districts mentioned averaged, just before the famine, from less than half to about two-thirds of the rates quoted by Mr. Dutt: at that time the ratios for dry land were all between 6 and 13 per cent. and for wet between 10 and 17 per cent. of the gross produce calculated as common food-crops, and subject therefore to the remarks contained in the last paragraph; the average ratios were below 9 and exactly 13 per cent., respectively. Wet rates are higher than dry rates, as is usual, owing to the effect of the charge for water; in the old settlements of Munro and others the wet assessment was taken at 45 to 50 per cent. of the gross, being the ancient sharing system which still obtains between landlord and ryot on wet areas in many of the zemindaries under the permanent settlement, while the proportion on dry land was usually taken as 33 per cent.; for wet lands, however, there are rules for granting remission whenever a crop fails or land is waste from want of water or from floods, and the application of these rules forms a main item in the annual jamabandi. For the decennium ending with 1899, omitting the years of scarcity and famine, the ratios of assessment to gross produce would have ranged from 4 to 9 per cent. for the dry and from 8·5 to 13 per cent. for the wet land for the ten districts. For data regarding existing rates and their relation to the estimated gross produce, Appendices III and V must be consulted.

Rise in value of produce since 1855.

The matter may be put in another way. Let it be assumed that, as alleged in Trichinopoly, in 1861-62, the settlement assessment formed 30 per cent. of the gross produce at commutation rates; each ryot then retained R70 out of every R100. But let a rise in prices be assumed, as actually happened; then as soon as prices increase by 30 per cent. the ryot is practically, save for sundry cash expenses, as well off as he would have been previously without any Government assessment, for he will enjoy R100 net on the same amount of produce; when prices have increased by 75 per cent., he will enjoy R145 instead of his previous R70. Such a rise actually happened after 1855, and *quoad* the assessment, the ryots of the earliest settled districts, such as Trichinopoly, obtained by reason of the low commutation rates the full or the greater part of the benefit of this rise, and have enjoyed the same until now; in other words, for the thirty years of the settlement they obtained more, often much more, for their net produce after paying Government assessment, than they would have obtained when the settlement was formed had the assessment been abolished *in toto*. **MADRAS.**

Another illustration on hypothetical data may be given. Let it be supposed that in 1850 ten million acres produced crops worth, at then prices, 15 crores of rupees, and paid Government three crores as assessment: the ryots would then have retained 12 crores net. But in, say, 1875, under the effect of risen prices, let the produce on the same acres be worth 25 crores, the assessment thereon remaining practically constant; the ryots then would retain not 12 but 22 crores for themselves. The above figures are merely hypothetical and illustrative, but are within the facts, as may be seen by the figures recorded in paragraph 57 *infra* and in Appendix II. The year 1875 has been mentioned because it immediately preceded the famine of 1876—78, one main cause of which is apparently supposed to be the assessment.

Rise in selling value of land.

51. One of the best gauges, however, of the assessment in general is the sale or mortgage value of lands. The Board cannot here deal in detail with this interesting subject, but merely subjoins a few statistics. The aggregate figures for

MADRAS registered sales and mortgages, including those on buildings, for the last ten years in this Presidency are as follows :—

Sales.		Mortgages.	
Number.	Value in lakhs of rupees.	Number.	Value in lakhs of rupees.
2,543,117	5,038	3,624,396	7,079

The increase since 1878, during which period many of the new settlements have been introduced, is shown by the following figures :—

Sales in				Mortgages in				Leases in			
1877-78.		Annual average of the present decade.		1877-78.		Annual average of the present decade.		1877-78.		Annual of average the present decade.	
Number.	Value in lakhs.	Number.	Value in lakhs.	Number.	Value in lakhs.	Number.	Value in lakhs.	Number.	Annual rent value in lakhs.	Number.	Annual rent value in lakhs.
	R		R		R		R		R		R
75,864	254'66	254,302	503'71	131,082	393'59	362,428	707'77	44,662	39'76	92,888	54'10

In this table leases are comparatively few in number, since they are seldom registered; the immense mass of ordinary leases cannot be gauged from these figures. Whatever the full meaning of these numerous transactions, it is obvious that land has in general a very great value in exchange or on rent after the Government assessment has been deducted: two-and-a-half million sales for 50 crores in ten years, and more than three-and-a-half million mortgages for 70 crores, are eloquent figures, while the immense increase since 1878, though partly due to better registration, is significant. The value of each such sale averaged R198, and that of each mortgage R195, but the value per acre is not known. **MADRAS.**

The Board does not propose to enter here upon the acreage price of land which may be gathered from many public reports, but would observe that the prices of many millions of acres are high and, in general, rising, and that they vary from a comparatively small sum on ordinary dry lands to above R1,000 per acre on the productive and highly assessed wet lands of the Tambraparni valley in the Tinnevelly district. Several district manuals, the settlement reports, those of the Registration Department, and Mr. S. Srinivasa Raghava Iyengar's memorandum may be consulted on this important point.

Comparison of revenue and rent rates.

52. Mr. Dutt's main point seems to be that Government *makes the revenue approximate* to one-third of the gross produce and thereby impoverishes * the ryots, and he recommends as an example the rates of rent payable in Northern India by ryots to their landlords: in paragraph 13 he suggests a maximum of one-fifth of the gross produce. The figures already given by the Board show that this proportion is nowhere taken from the ryots "if," as Mr. Dutt says, "the district average be taken." The Board deals with this more completely in a later part of this resolution, but would here say that, if Government took one-fifth of the real gross produce from its ryots, it would fully double its present land revenue exclusive of cesses but inclusive of the total charge for water. The Government is, as a rule, far less exacting than private landlords, and the Board is unable to understand Mr. Dutt's statement that "there is not a cultivator in India who does not consider 5 or 6 annas out of each rupee of gross produce to be an oppressive and impoverishing rate of rent" or that three annas in the rupee is a "fair" rent. Probably there is no system so universal, so customary, and so generally accepted as the sharing (váram, batái, métayage) system, in which the half share

* In England it is often said that the farmer expects to produce "three rents," *viz.*, one for the landlord, one for the expenses of cultivation, and one for his own living and profits on stock.

MADRAS. is the rule for ordinary lands, but where lands are valuable, the half share becomes two-thirds, and even three-quarters of the gross produce as regards grain; in these métayage cases the land-owner (ryot) pays the assessment, and the cultivator (tenant) pays the cultivation expenses, but also generally obtains the whole of the straw. The Settlement Commissioner has recently made enquires in Chingleput, Tanjore and other districts, where all these rentals are found, and it is a source of surprise to the Board that the Government demand in general should be compared with the rents taken by wet land ryots from their sub-tenants. On ordinary dry lands a common rate of rent is twice the assessment, but this frequently runs up to five times, and in the case of rich produce, to ten times the assessment, as is also the case in wet lands. The district manuals and settlement reports may be consulted for rentals both on wet and dry lands: in the Coimbatore manual (page 300, volume II, revised edition) a table is given from the settlement report showing that above one-seventh of the whole of the lands, wet, dry and garden, in 592 villages (124,646 acres out of 844,314) were found to be rented to sub-tenants for half or a larger share of the gross produce, and on pages 301 and 303 other tables are given showing the rates taken from registered documents; the latest registered money rentals for wet land in that district range, except in one small area, from R28 to to R72 per acre, so large an area as 1,157 acres paying an average of R45. That these rents are "fair" in the sense of light, is not alleged, but they are regular and general contract rates. The Government assessment is low in comparison with the rentals taken by Government ryots from their sub-tenants.

In zamindari areas the rentals are often extremely high as compared with the neighbouring Government assessments owing to the fact that having been permanently settled in 1802, they either retain the "paimash" rates similar to those of the Government areas at the period, including the now obsolete garden tax, or, where untrammelled by such rates, they are able to make their own bargains with their tenants. or they have commuted the amounts due under the sharing system into money at their own rates. In a zamindari now under the Court of Wards **MADRAS.** the Board has found that the highest wet rates are R45 per acre for which, however, the ryot may raise two crops if he can; the garden rates run up to R15 per acre; these are maximum rates, but are actually being paid. The rate payable for betel-leaf gardens is fixed at R32 per acre. The maximum wet rates for Government lands in the three neighbouring districts are R10, R3 and R7-8, respectively, with the addition of one half extra when a second crop has been raised. The moderation of the Government assessments may be gauged from these figures. In considerable areas in the Godavari delta good zamindari lands are rented to tenants for growing paddy at R25 to R30 *plus* the Government water-rate, and at much higher rates for sugarcane. The Board is not defending these rentals, but they are payable and being paid.

Growth and pressure of the Revenue demand examined.

53. The Board will now deal in some detail with the questions raised by Mr. Dutt of the weight and amount of the assessment, and the supposed enhancement of revenue "at each recurring settlement," by which it is assumed that the ryot "has been reduced to a state of poverty and indebtedness which makes him an easy prey to famines" and owing to which some "three millions of acres of culturable lands are out of cultivation in Madras." It will be shown by statistics that the land assessment proper has not increased during the past fifty years even in proportion to the additional area brought under holding, that the tax per acre has decreased, and that the actual weight or proportion of produce taken has immensely diminished—practically by one-half—owing to the rise in prices. It is to be remembered that the new survey and settlements began in fasli 1271 (1861), and that the assessments at that date had been heavily reduced from the original settlements—so called—of the beginning of the century.

54. A statement appended, Appendix I, shows the areas of ryotwari land actually occupied in each year from fasli 1261 (1851-52) up to the latest year for which figures are available

MADRAS. the assessment thereon; the net demand for land revenue shown in the accounts as ryotwar, after eliminating the remissions granted; the amount of remissions granted each year with reference to the state of the season; the amount of the cesses or other contributions levied for local purposes, and for the payment of the village establishments; the gross demand ryotwar and cesses; and the average price of grain in each year. The following is an abstract thereof. In all cases, the figures for Malabar and South Canara are omitted :—

(*In columns 2 to 9,—00,000 are omitted, i.e., the figures represent lakhs.*)

PERIOD.	Occupied area.	Assessment thereon.	Total ryotwar demand	Cesses and merahs.	Gross demand.	SEASON REMISSIONS. Waste.	Others.	Total.	Average price of grain per garce.
1	2	3	4	5	6	7	8	9	10
	Acs.	R	R	R	R	R	R	R	R
Fasli 1261-65 .	124	302	270	4	274	12·2	20·2	32·4	107
„ 1266-70 .	141	320	304	5	309	10·7	20·5	31·2	144
„ 1271-75 .	168	320	336	7	343	9·1	11·3	20·4	194
„ 1276-80 .	185	324	351	(c) 22	373	8·9	10·5	19·4	194
„ 1281-85 .	190	322	361	(d) 42	403	6·3	9·1	15·4	155
„ 1286-90 .	188	323	348	40	388	14·4	17·6	32·0	216
„ 1291-95 .	185	322	364	44	408	5·3	8·2	13·5	148
„ 1296-1300 .	199	(a) 353	391	58	449	3·8	5·0	8·8	157
„ 1301-1305 .	209	(b) 382	(e) 426	58	484	6·2	7·7	13·9	194
„ 1306 .	215	400	440	56	496	8·5	22·5	31·0	212
„ 1307 .	216	403	474	54	528	3·4	7·0	10·4	262
„ 1308 .	216	405	485	55	540	2·0	2·7	4·7	199

(*a*) Water rates on wet land in Godavari and Kistna first included in th assessment during the period.

(*b*) Includes Tanjore settlement increase (12 lakhs) and Trichinopoly re-settlement ($4\frac{1}{2}$) as well as one taluk brought under ryotwari newly, and a large area of inams resumed. Full explanations are given below.

(*c*) Land-cess for local purposes first included.

(*d*) Village-cess levied in lieu of *merahs* to village servants first included.

(*e*) This figure, 426 lakhs, includes about 182 lakhs as the price of water, included in the land assessment or otherwise charged.

The figures in column 4 are arrived at by adding to those in column 3, the amount of a large number of *miscellaneous* charges—see paragraphs 63 to 65 *infra*—and deducting from the sum the remissions granted, particulars for which so far as they relate to the changing character of the seasons, are shown in columns 7—9.

55. In the next table the actual averages for each quinquennial period given above are compared with the averages for the five years ending with fasli 1265 (1855-56) which are represented as 100; the other figures therefore show the percentage increase or decrease from that level. The average rates of assessment per acre on the area occupied are also shown :— **MADRAS.**

Period.	Occupied area.	Assessment thereon.	Assessment per acre.		Demand ryotwar.	Demand ryotwar and cesses.	Season remissions.	Average price of grain.
			Amount.	Ratio.				
1	2	3	4	5	6	7	8	9
			R					
Fasli 1261-65 . .	100	100	2'44	100	100	100	100	100*
" 1266-70 . .	114	106	2'27	93	113	113	96	135
" 1271-75 . .	135'5	106	1'90	78	124	125	63	181
" 1276-80 . .	149	107	1'75	72	130	136	60	181
" 1281-85 . .	153	106'5	1'69	69	134	147	47'5	145
" 1286-90 . .	152	107	1'72	70'5	129	142	99	202
" 1291-95 . .	149	107	1'74	71	135	149	42	138
" 1296-1300 . .	160'5	117	1'77	72'5	145	164	27	147
" 1301-1305 . .	168'5	126'5	1'83	75	158	177	43	181
" 1306 . . .	173'5	132'5	1'86	76	163	181	96	198
" 1307 . . .	174	133'5	1'87	76'5	175'5	193	32	245
" 1308 . . .	174	134	1'87	76'5	180	197	14'5	186

Leaving out of consideration the last three years of the table, it will be seen that whilst the area in the occupation of the ryots under the ryotwari system increased during forty-five years by 68·5 per cent., the assessment thereon increased by only 26·5 per cent., and that for the first thirty years there was practically little or no increase in the assessment, although new settlements had been effected in the whole or greater part of twelve districts. The increase appearing during the quinquennium ending in fasli 1300 is mainly due merely to a change in the method of accounting for part of the water-rates levied under the

* *N.B.*—During the decennium immediately preceding this, the average market prices were 20 per cent. cheaper or only 80 per cent. of the level for this period.

MADRAS. Godavari and Kistna anicuts, which were first included with the assessment from fasli 1297 when twenty lakhs were added to the accounts of the assessment. The further large increase shown in the next quinquennium is due partly to the extension of irrigation and the increase of the charge for water in those districts (about three and a half lakhs), partly to the increased charge imposed at the settlement of the Tanjore district (twelve lakhs), and partly to the revision of the assessment in the Trichinopoly district (four and a quarter lakhs), besides other smaller items of which the increase by a million acres in the area occupied accounts for the greater portion.

56. The large increase in the area occupied does not, however, wholly represent an extension of cultivation or holdings, for in many districts the regular survey disclosed the fact that the original accounts understated the actual areas in occupation. Considerable areas of inam, or favourably-assessed, lands have from time to time fallen in to Government, or have been resumed; and areas which were formerly rented out at lump sums have been brought under a ryotwari settlement; still, by far the greater part of the increase represents an actual expansion of cultivation. This expansion has no doubt, in many cases, brought the poorer and therefore lower assessed soils under the plough, but against this cause of a reduced acreage assessment must be placed the addition of water rates to the assessments in the Godavari and Kistna deltas, and the revision of the old assessments in Tanjore and Trichinopoly.

Decrease in rate per acre in forty years.

57. If these facts be borne in mind, the comparison of the average rate of assessment per acre, which is made in columns 4 and 5 of the table above, may be taken to show the relative amount of the assessment on the land at each period. The figures show that the rate per acre has fallen on the average by 25 per cent. in forty years. But in considering this fact the course of prices must also be considered, and for this purpose it is necessary to examine further than the information given by the last column of the table allows. Accurate data regarding prices during

MADRAS.

the first half of the century are not forthcoming, but sufficient information is available to show that the fifteen years ending in fasli 1262 (1852-53) was a period of great depression, which culminated about 1843. The depression has been attributed to deficient supplies of currency, but whatever the cause, the rates for the quinquennium which ended in 1853, were much below those of the earliest years of the century*; statistics of prices for the agricultural year or *fasli* show that during that period the average market price for the principal food-grains of the Presidency was only R77 per *garce* of 3,200 Madras measures.† The course of prices for the ten years preceding and since that quinquennium is shown by th figures in the margin The figures (for details see Appendix II) quoted for years prior to fasli 1285 (1875-76) cannot be regarded with so much confidence as those for later years, but are sufficient to indicate the general course of prices. In fasli 1263 (1853-54) there was a sudden rise in prices to an average of R116 per garce, which was at first attributed to the character of the season, but when it was found to be maintained and continued, though the subsequent seasons were much more favourable, it was put down to the greater abundance of currency owing to large expenditure of borrowed money and to large demands for export produce. From 1268 to 1285, the average of prices was double that of the quinquennium for 1258-62, with a still greater increase for

Period.	Average price per garce. R	Ratio.
Fasli 1248-49	108	140
„ 1250-54	75	97
„ 1255-57	114	148
„ 1258-62	77	100
„ 1248-62	88	114
„ 1263-67	128	166
„ 1268-72	162	210
„ 1273-77	216	281
„ 1278-82	162	210
„ 1283-85	161	209
„ 1286-89	259	336
„ 1290-94	145	188
„ 1295-99	157	204
„ 1300-1302	209	271
„ 1303-1305	179	233

Decrease in pressure due to rise in prices.

* *Vide* table on page 58 of *Progress of the Madras Presidency during the last forty years* by S. Srinivasa Raghava Aiyangar, Diwan Bahadur, C.I.E., 1893.

† A Madras measure holds 62·5 fluid ounces of water or 120 tolahs of cleaned rice.

1273-77 during which period the famine of 1866 occurred. In 1286 (1876-77) the great famine began, and prices remained at an excessively high level for four years, after which, with good crops and a smaller population, they fell greatly, but have since recovered. In faslis 1301 and 1302 severe scarcity existed over a wide area, and prices have not since then returned to the level that prevailed from 1855 to 1875. They have, in fact, during the last half of the century, been almost uniformly double the rates which prevailed before the Government decided, partly on the ground of the low prices, on a general scheme for survey and settlement which was then expected to result in general reductions such as had been frequently given before that period, but on no settled system.

58. It will be seen, therefore, that while the *incidence* of the land assessment per occupied acre decreased by 25 per cent. over the whole period of forty years, and by 29 per cent. during the first thirty, the *pressure* of these reduced assessments was still further and very largely decreased owing to the doubling of the value of the chief products of the soil.

59. The explanation of this striking general result is to be found in the extremely low estimates of the value of the gross produce, and the very small proportion thereof which has, on the average, been taken as the land-tax. The proportions of the gross produce, as estimated for settlement purposes, which the settled rates presented *at the commutation rates* adopted, are noted in the margin for a number of districts (for details see Appendix V).

	Settlement date.	Dry.	Wet.
Trichinopoly .	1864-65	13	28
Ganjam .	1878-84	14	23
Coimbatore .	1878-82	15	22
North Arcot .	1881-86	17	19
Madura .	1885-93	16	19
Anantapur .	1891-98	6 to 11	14·5 & 15
Tanjore .	1893-94	16	26 & 20

But it must be remembered as previously mentioned (see paragraphs 35 and 48; also Appendix III), that the commutation rates adopted were, except in part of Kistna, Ganjam (wet land) and Madura, not only much lower than the average prices from which those rates were derived, but were, as a rule, from 25 to 50 per cent. lower than the prices that ruled during the period in which the settlements were actually made. Prices during the last decade have again been much dearer in almost every case than they were when the settlements were introduced. Consequently the proportions given in the margin are far higher than the ratio actually borne by the assessment to the real money value of the gross produce. MADRAS.

60. From the figures above quoted, it will be seen that in respect of the dry land, to which the State does not supply the valuable commodity—water—which it does to the wet land, in no case does the assessment fixed represent more than a bare sixth of the *nominal* gross produce, and this although the customary State share of the produce was commuted at the settlement at rates which yield the cultivators an enormous profit on the transaction; this advantage to the ryots has continued since the settlements. Besides this, it may here be mentioned that, taking the country as a whole, it could be easily shown, did space permit, from the facts and statistics of actual consumption and otherwise, that the estimated normal rates of outturn adopted for settlement purposes, from which, moreover, deductions are made to allow for the vicissitudes of the seasons, are less than the average yield of a series of years; hence the ryot obtains a double advantage. Again, in determining the assessments no cognizance is taken of the more valuable products, such as indigo, tobacco, oil-seeds, sugarcane, cotton, etc., which the ryot may and does cultivate largely without any additional payment, except where he uses on dry land water supplied from a public source. As regards second crop and produce which uses water enough for a second crop, it must be pointed out that in a large number of cases special concessions have been granted to the ryots to induce them to compound for the charges imposed for water so used; save in a few exceptional cases this second crop charge is normally one-half the single assessment, and the ryots may compound for this, except under the largest irrigation works on which Government has invested capital, at rates ranging from one-sixth to one-third of the single assessment. No charge whatever is levied for second or third crop raised on dry land; in fact, so long as the ryot pays the assessment fixed for his land, he is free to do what he pleases therewith.

MADRAS. When these great advantages are allowed for, the proportions mentioned in the marginal table above will be seen to be very greatly reduced; certainly, even on wet lands where part of the assessment is the price paid for water supplied at the cost of Government, much below the one-sixth share which is admittedly due to the State.

61. The precise effect of the settlement of each district during the period in question is shown in Appendix IV to this resolution. The general result was that the assessments imposed on the lands in occupation at the time when the settlements were made, were increased in bulk by 9 per cent. including that portion which was levied with reference to areas which had previously escaped taxation but were discovered by the scientific survey, which, in the case of 19 districts, resulted in an increase of 8 per cent. Of the gross additional amount imposed during the period under reference (31½ lakhs), the chief items are noted in the margin.

	Lakhs.
Gódávari . .	+ 3·84
Trichinopoly . .	(− 3·88 + 4·10)
Kistna . . .	+ 4·68
Coimbatore . .	+ 2·05
Tanjore . . .	+ 12·02

In Trichinopoly, the settlement of 1864-65, which had resulted in the large reduction of 3·88 lakhs, was revised, and though on a much extended area, the revision only resulted in a recovery of the revenue given up at the settlement of nearly forty years ago.

Results of resettlements.

The first survey in this district revealed a deficiency of 7 per cent. in the areas previously reported. In Gódávari, one of the districts first settled, the original settlement enhanced the demand by 22 per cent., but in that district there had previously been no record of the measurement of the holdings; at the resettlement of this district, which has only recently been carried out after more than thirty years' interval, the increase imposed has been 24 per cent., whilst average prices have doubled in the period. In Kistna, where also the original settlement has partially expired and is being revised, the first survey disclosed a deficiency of 7 per cent. in the area previously recorded, but the first regular assessment showed an increase of 16 per cent., although the commutation rate was taken as more than 50 per cent. below the prices ruling at the time of the settlement; the increase at settlement is attributable mainly to the low revenue demand of the joint-rent system previously in vogue. In Tanjore, the increase by settlement is mainly due to the fact that the commutation rate on which the previously existing rates had been based was extremely low, *viz.*, R56 per garce, as compared with the average commutation price of R142 and R121 per garce, the commutation rate adopted; and partly to the high average class of the irrigation and the high average quality of the alluvial soil of the delta. The combined effect of these factors would have been to raise the assessment even higher were it not for the liberal allowances made in respect of cultivation expenses and other items. **MADRAS**

Expansion of irrigation.

62 It has already been mentioned in the note to the table in paragraph 54 *supra*, that of the gross ryotwar demand from fasli 1301 to 1305 (426 lakhs) about 182 lakhs represent in reality charges for water supplied, which are either included in the land assessments or are otherwise levied. These charges have, during the period under reference, greatly increased, owing chiefly to the great expansion of irrigation under works on which Government has expended capital. So far as works of this class are concerned, the expansion of irrigation may be judged from the figures noted in the margin showing the calculated amount of the revenue solely due to irrigation during the last half century. Part of the increase in this revenue during the period, *viz.*, 70 lakhs, is due to the expenditure of capital on the development of an increasing

Period.	Lakhs.	Proportion.
Fasli 1261-65	31'40	100
„ 1266-70	42'36	135
„ 1271-75	48'77	155
„ 1276-80	57'10	182
„ 1281-85	64'07	204
„ 1286-90	70'16	223
„ 1291-95	73'16	233
„ 1296-1300	84'86	270
„ 1301-1305	101'06*	322

* This sum includes 48'23 lakhs which are credited annually to the old works on which the Government has expended capital in their development or supersession. Of this, about 37'13 lakhs are credited to old works superseded in by those which had already been taken up for development in the first period (F. 1261-65).

MADRAS. number of works, some of which previously existed; but practically the whole of the increase must be put down to the expenditure of public funds. The charge is generally, according to the custom of Southern India, included in the land assessment, so far as the first crop is concerned, though some portion is, as shown below, otherwise levied. Consequently the gross apparent increase of land assessment is *pro tanto* no real increase at all, but is a payment for a valuable commodity or instrument by which produce and its value and the value of land, are enormously increased.

Miscellaneous revenue.

63. It will have been observed that column 4 of the table in paragraph 54 above, shows that the total charge appearing in the accounts against ryotwari holdings in almost all the more recent years, exceeds the assessment considerably and sometimes largely. The excess represents what is known as "Miscellaneous revenue," of which the following items are the chief :—

Particulars of Miscellaneous Revenue.	Lakhs.			
	Average. 1301-1305.	1306.	1307.	1308.
	R	R	R	R
Charges for water not included in the assessments	19·27	20·22	22·11	25·26
Charges for land temporarily occupied .	8·39	7·68	9·04	8·88
Charges on minor inam or favourably assessed land in Government villages including water-rates.	27·28	34·80	36·81	36·91
Tree revenue	3·76	3·60	3·38	3·24
Charges for water in permanently-settled estates	7·08	8·69	9·04	10·75
Other charges	9·22	9·21	11·69	9·93
Total .	75·00	84·20	92·97	94·97

Remissions.

Against charges such as these are set off remissions granted with reference to the state of the season, or for items of charge included in the assessments which really represent cesses for local or village purposes, or are old endowments of religious institutions. Changes have been made from time to time in the manner in which some of these charges are shown in the accounts, so that it is not possible to exhibit the exact incidence during the whole period on the land liable for ryotwari assessments; for instance, in fasli 1304, ten lakhs which had previously been treated as a local cess were added under the third head above. **MADRAS.**

Increase in total revenue demand in forty years.

The total revenue demand thus arrived at has, however, increased by about 156 lakhs, or 58 per cent., in forty years, of which 80 lakhs occurs under the regular land assessment and has been already explained. No inconsiderable portion of this increase is due to the decrease in the average amount of remissions granted from year to year; such remissions having been, fifty years ago, a regular and recurring incident of the annual settlement which, owing to the weight of the assessment and to the want of a proper survey, were allowed or were schemed for in every possible way. In favourable years now-a-days, such remissions, notwithstanding the greatly-increased area in occupation, do not amount to one-third of what was normal formerly. This decrease results partly from the policy resolved on in 1855 with a view to remove temptation to bribery and corruption and to protect the ryots from the continual interference of petty officials, partly from the decreased weight of the assessments, partly from the greater attention paid to the upkeep of minor irrigation works. The evils attendant on the old system were fully described by the Government when it resolved on carrying out a scientific survey and a regular system of land assessment.

64. The table given above shows that the greater portion of the miscellaneous revenue is derived from charges for water supplied, the amount of these charges for the quinquennium ending with fasli 1305 being about 36·75 lakhs.* About 7 lakhs of this

* The exact amount cannot be shown, as a change in the method of recording the charges was made in fasli 1303.

MADRAS. amount is for water supplied to land on which the revenue charge is permanently settled, and should therefore be eliminated from the charges on ryotwari villages. This amount, like all other charges for water, has been increasing with the expansion of irrigation under works on which Government has expended capital.

65. When the Government resolved on carrying out a regular survey of the Presidency, it was also decided to inquire into the titles and to determine the areas and conditions on which the inam (favourably assessed) lands of the Presidency were occupied. In many cases such inams were enfranchised at enhanced rates, since the village officers are now paid regular salaries. These operations resulted in an increase of the revenue under the third head mentioned above by at least 4 lakhs, whilst by a change in the system of record in fasli 1304, about ten lakhs additional were transferred to this head. According to the latest statistics, the total area of minor inam lands in ryotwar villages is about 4,244,000 acres, and this should be added to the area which contributes towards the ryotwar demand which now includes the quit-rent levied on those lands.

In addition to this area, that occupied from year to year for temporary occupation must also be included, on which about 8 or 9 lakhs of rupees are annually levied. Some of this area is so poor that it cannot be continuously cropped; some lies in localities where the rainfall is so precarious that it is only occasionally that circumstances allow of its being shown: some represents land reserved for public or communal purposes, the occupation of which is objectionable. During the quinquennium from fasli 1301-1305, the average area of this fluctuating cultivation was 723,000 acres per annum. This area does not appear in the accounts of "occupied" land, although the assessment levied on it does appear in the accounts of revenue collected.

66. From the figures above given, it will be seen that the average amount of 426 lakhs of ryotwar land revenue—less 7 lakhs levied for water supplied to permanently-settled estates and a

number of minor items which cannot be separated—was really paid, not for the 20,900,000 acres of ryotwar holdings, but by the occupiers of 25,900,000 acres of ryotwar, inam, and miscellaneous land. Above 40 per cent. of the gross charge is made for water supplied, but, even including this, the incidence per acre is really R1·64 and not R2·01 per acre on the land by which the revenue is paid. MADRAS.

67. It does not appear profitable to pursue the analysis of the statistics further. They show that the area in occupation has, notwithstanding the set-back of the great famine of 1876-78, increased very largely; that the assessments on the land have not kept pace with this expansion, and that much of the more recent increase is due to the inclusion of charges for water and to the resettlement of the very rich district of Tanjore; that the assessment per acre is far lower than it was forty years ago, though, for the reasons just stated, it has somewhat increased of later years; that the pressure of the assessments has, owing to the doubling of prices, immensely decreased; that the total ryotwar land revenue demand is spread over a far larger area than at first sight appears; and that the incidence thereof represents a demand of from 30 to 40 seers of grain per acre only, on the average prices of the Presidency during recent favourable years, even when the whole charge for water supplied is included. On the poorest classes of dry land the assessment represents from three to six seers of dry grain when prices are twenty-four seers per rupee, which is the average for the decade 1885 to 1895.

Cesses.

68. It must, however, be remarked that, as shown in column 5 of the statement in paragraph 54 *supra*, during the last 30 years two new local cesses have been levied in addition to the land assessment, *viz.*, the land cess and the village service cess. In fasli 1275 (1865-66) a commencement was made in levying a land-cess for local purposes, which is now collected at the rate of one anna in the rupee on the gross land revenue demand. This is expended on purely local requirements, and so much as is not spent on primary education and medicine is spent on improvements

MADRAS. which directly increase either production or the profits of the ryots, *viz.*, communications and public markets. The village service cess, though new, is not an additional charge at all; from time immemorial, the custom has been for the ryots to remunerate the officers of the village communities by a proportion of the produce of their lands; these fees (merahs) were paid direct by the ryots to the village officers and servants, and did not, in general, appear in the Government accounts. In the early years of the period covered by the statistics under discussion, only a small proportion of those fees had been commuted into money payments and was collected with the public revenues, but in fasli 1281 (1871-72) a village service cess was imposed to take the place of these fees which were then abolished, and the village establishments were reorganized. This cess, therefore, does not represent any increase of taxation though it appears as an increase in the accounts of revenue.

Proportion of revenue to real gross produce.

69. The Board will now show the proportion borne by the land revenue mentioned above to the real gross produce. In the statement given as Appendix VI an estimate of the value of the crops produced in the ryotwari villages only of the Presidency, *excluding* Malabar and South Canara, has been framed. In regard to these estimates, it is perhaps sufficient to note that the rates of yield adopted represent the average outturn of a series of years, those for food-grains having been adopted from an estimate prepared for an entirely different purpose two years ago, and that the settlement rates of outturn considerably understate the yield obtained in a series of ordinary years. The valuation of food-grains adopted is approximately the average of the recorded prices for the whole Presidency during recent *normal* years. Mr. Dutt's criticisms on pages 97 and 98 of his book do not apply to Madras, where the acreage actually cultivated, the nature of the crop on each acre, and the exact area of waste or of withered crops, are recorded every year with great accuracy for ryotwari areas.

MADRAS.

70. The estimate may be summarised as follows:—

	Lakhs of rupees.
Food-grains of all sorts	29,23
Oil-seeds	3,68
Drugs and narcotics	2,87
Condiments and spices	2,39
Cotton and other fibres	1,93
Sugars	1,46
Orchard and garden produce . . .	1,45
Indigo and other dyes	1,06
All other crops	37
TOTAL .	44,44

Besides the above, there is the income derived from the live-stock of the country which, for the ryotwari area of the Presidency, excluding Malabar and South Canara, cannot be put at less than the number noted in the margin. The horned cattle produce manure, hides, horns, bones, milk and ghee, and a certain amount is realised by sale to butchers; the sheep yield some wool and with the goats produce manure, milk, ghee, meat, and skins for tanning. Taking all these items together, and considering the immense consumption of milk and ghee, the total value of all animal products cannot be less than ten crores per annum.

	Millions.
Horned cattle .	13½
Sheep and goats	14

In the case of ryots living near towns and on lines of traffic a great deal of money is realised by the sale of straw and fodder, dung for fuel, and firewood from private lands; the value of straw has not otherwise been included.

Taking all these items into consideration, the gross agricultural produce may be estimated at above 55 crores of rupees from the portion of the Presidency alluded to.

71. Taking now the gross land revenue including all cesses and charges for water, and averaging—for the four years ending with 1898-99, exclusive of the year 1897 as a famine year—5·26 crores, it will be seen that this is well below 10 per cent. of the value of the gross produce; if, however, the 119 lakhs due as the average annual charge for water supplied by works paid for out of

MADRAS. Government capital (paragraph 62) during the same years, be deducted, the proportion falls to 7·4 per cent., or slightly above one-fourteenth. If the whole charge for water (206 lakhs) be deducted, the proportion sinks to about 6 per cent. or about one-seventeenth, and even this includes the two cesses mentioned in paragraph 68.

If a deduction of 15 per cent. be made from the above estimate of gross produce as a margin on account of village prices, errors, etc.,—a deduction, however, which is hardly necessary, since grain prices, as tabulated in this department, are chiefly those of rural parts, while the crop estimates for other products are generally low and straw is omitted,—the proportions borne by the assessment will be about 11 per cent. or one-ninth if all charges for water and both cesses be included; 8·7 per cent. or one-twelfth, if the charges (119 lakhs) for water under specially developed works be excluded; and 6·8 per cent. or one-fifteenth, if all charges for water be omitted. Hence the one-tenth of the gross produce elsewhere mentioned by Mr. Dutt as a proper district average is beyond or above the sum taken as land revenue in this Presidency considered as a whole, if the cesses are deducted, and much beyond it if the charge for water is deducted.

Enough has been stated to show that the real proportion of the Madras ryotwari land revenue taken as a whole, to the real gross produce, has been wholly misunderstood.

It will be noted that if the Government demand in any district be assumed at one-eighth of the gross produce, each acre can, on that assumption, produce only 30 seers of grain for every two annas of the demand when grain is taken at an assumed village price of 30 seers per rupee. In other words, land assessed at from 2 to 8 annas per acre, of which there are millions of acres in the Presidency, produces, *on the above assumptions*, only from 30 to 120 seers of marketable grain per acre. Whether it is correct or not that millions of acres produce or can only produce, if cultivated, less than one-eighth of the produce of the average English acre taken as 32 bushels, it is clear that it is not in the reduction of the assessment, but in the development of cultivation that hope and amelioration are to be found; more produce, better and closer markets, cheaper and safer credit, a larger share of the sale values of produce, are the *desideranda*, not, except in occasional cases, reduction of assessments. **MADRAS.**

72. The detailed estimate of the value of the crops will be found in Appendix VI.

The Irrigation Act of 1900.

73. *Point 5 in paragraph 3 supra*, viz., *the Irrigation Act of 1900 and its provisions.*—The Board's Resolution has already run to great length, and it will therefore content itself on this point with remarking that local knowledge would explain to Mr. Dutt the reason for and scope of the new law. The law, however, does not "enable Government to levy a compulsory water-rate on all lands within the wet cultivation area" but only on such lands as necessarily, by their position, receive a sufficient supply of water successfully to grow an irrigated crop: critics have forgotten that the basis of the Madras assessments, especially on wet lands, is a share of the crop, and that if, owing to the action of Government, a ryot is enabled to raise a wet crop, whether he has asked for water or not, Government is entitled, as of immemorial right, to a share in the increased outturn or value of the produce. It will be noticed that in giving his assent to the Act, His Excellency the Viceroy confirmed and emphasised the declaration of the Madras Government that the long-standing practice of exempting from water-rate, irrigation obtained from wells which are fed by percolation, shall be adhered to, and that in other cases of irrigation of lands by percolation, water-rate is to be levied only when a full and constant supply of water is assured, so that the Madras cultivator is *quoad hoc* precisely in the same position as before the Act was passed.

74. Several other mistakes also need correction, but the Board will only mention those directly connected with settlement operations which are the objects of Mr. Dutt's animadversion.

75. On page X of the preface to his book Mr. Dutt, writing about Madras, says " the revenue . . . . is fixed at each recurring settlement, and settlements are often made for shorter

MADRAS. periods than 30 years." Not one single settlement has been made for less than 30 years.

76. In paragraph 8 of his letter, Mr. Dutt says, " over three millions of acres of cultivable lands are out of cultivation in Madras," the inference being that they are waste because of the weight of the assessments. As a matter of fact, the waste assessed area is larger than here stated, but though assessed, the assessment is often nominal and the area uncultivable; such are the large areas of hill and forest in Malabar, Coimbatore, etc., the swampy and saline soils of Kistna, Trichinopoly, etc. Much, moreover, of the assessed waste lies in the well known " famine zone " and consists mostly of a very poor class of shallow, stony, arid soils bearing a very low assessment (much of it from 2 to 6 annas per acre), and unoccupied by reason of the comparative sparseness of the population. In the Anantapur district, for example, there are now 867,000 acres of unoccupied dry land, the *average* assessment on which is As. 3—5 (3·4 annas) or slightly over 5 seers at the average price of the decade 1885—1895, while of the total area unoccupied at the close of the recent settlement 44 per cent. was assessed at two annas, 39 per cent. at four annas, 9·8 per cent. at six annas, and 2·8 at eight annas, leaving only 4·6 per cent. at higher rates; the population in 1891 was 708,549 and the area occupied at the introduction of the settlement just closed was 1,228,000 acres; it is now 1,286,000 acres, showing that it is not the settlement assessment which keeps land out of cultivation.

West assessed area.

77. The main answer to Mr. Dutt, however, on this point is the area taken up since the new settlements began; in 1855, 12,400,000 acres (round figures) were under ryotwar holding in the Presidency, exclusive of Malabar and Canara and exclusive of minor inams; in 1898 the area was 21,600,000 acres, being an increase of 9,200,000 acres or 74 per cent., about 1,400,000 of which, however, is only nominal, being due to excess found on proper survey, so that the net increase is about 7,800,000 or 63

Increase in occupation since 1855.

per cent. This increase has been regular and continuous save for the check due to the great famine of 1877-78, and has never been checked by settlement operations, a sufficient proof that the assessments are moderate. The figures for 1855 also include land which was held on cowles and so-called grass rents or other favourable terms, so that the area was greater especially under the influence of the *dittam* and other methods, than would have been held at the actual assessments: all these artificial modes of keeping up large holdings and consequently the revenue, have long been abolished. Mr. Dutt's mistake consists partly in looking at the area now waste absolutely instead of comparatively by periods, partly in not examining the waste district by district, and in not making local enquiries about it. **MADRAS.**

Sales and relinquishments.

78. On page 96 of his book he speaks of "the ten thousand cultivators of Madras who are annually driven from their homes and lands for being unable to pay the State demand." Poor ryots, seemingly many in number but relatively few—about one in 417—lose their lands, or some of them, partly for reasons mentioned by Munro in his Minute of 1824 quoted below; but many sales are solely due to the revenue rules which absolutely forbid the cancelment by the Revenue officers of a puttah, or of entries of fields therein, except on personal relinquishment or by revenue sale: absence, death, incapacity etc., frequently cause failure to relinquish, and sale follows: in fact *sale* is a necessary corollary of the permanence and completeness of the ryot's tenure of his land. Much poor and valueless land, moreover, is taken up, as in Anantapur, for mere catch crops in good seasons, and the cultivator having reaped and carried his crop allows process against the land. Many of the revenue sales are therefore nominal; some are, of course, due to failures in farming: some, to the Board's knowledge, are collusive.

79. The Board has now dealt with Mr. Dutt's chief criticisms, but is conscious that though its remarks are lengthy, the ground has, partly from the brief time allowed, partly from the complexity of the subject, been imperfectly covered: the subject embraces

MADRAS. the history of the land revenue and much of land economics for the past century. Mr. Dutt may be referred for a detailed study of this subject to the numerous reports and histories even now available: in particular the District Manuals and settlement volumes would enlighten him as to the history of the ryotwar system, and the consequent necessity for, the objects, and the results of the new settlement system; the Manual of Mr. Baden-Powell, and the Memorandum of Mr. S. Srinivasa Ragava Iyengar on recent progress in this Presidency, present matters in an admirable form. The Board may also refer on economic and agricultural matters as well as on revenue, to the District Manual of Coimbatore* prepared by the present Settlement Commissioner, where every point, except the first, touched upon by Mr. Dutt, has for a typical ryotwar district, been handled by anticipation in a non-controversial manner, long before the present discussions arose. The Board would also refer to the resolutions of a former Board contained in its Proceedings (Land Revenue), No. 414-A., dated 2nd October 1894, especially paragraphs 28 to 35, and No. 308, dated 15th September 1897, especially paragraphs 23 to 26. These Proceedings dealt with the criticisms of Mr. Rogers on the Madras Settlements.

General remarks and conclusion.

80. In its present resolution the Board has shown that no "rights" of the ryot have been confiscated by Government as supposed by Mr. Dutt; that the new survey and settlement was established not to enable Government to enhance assessments, but to ascertain, equalise and *reduce* them; that notwithstanding the great rise in prices which enabled Government in general to avoid reduction, the average rate per actual acre of the area originally held has, as a rule, barely, if at all, increased, except in Tanjore, while the present average rate per acre held, including all charges, is considerably lower than the rate per acre held in 1855; that in most cases the increase in the total assessment of the district has not

* New Edition, Volume II, for Economics: Old Edition for Revenue History and Agriculture.

kept pace with the increase found by survey; that excessive rates have been cut down, though unduly low rates may have been enhanced; that no change is needed from the half-net system to that based on a percentage of the gross; that the 30-year period of settlement has, since 1855, always been that sanctioned for this Presidency; that revision on the sole ground of prices may not yet be desirable though permissible; and that neither is there any rule to make the assessment approximate to 30 per cent. of the gross produce, nor does it anywhere, *in general*, approximate to such ratio, while the aggregate land revenue is far below that proportion. **MADRAS.**

81. The *gravamen* of Mr. Dutt's indictment apparently is that by the "enhancements" to which the ryot is "subject at each recurring settlement," he "has been reduced to a state of poverty and indebtedness which makes him an easy prey to famines in years of bad harvests" (paragraph 5): the supposed confiscation of a right to an unaltered or unalterable assessment, the equally hypothetical increase, inequality, and weight of the assessment, are, however, the only arguments adduced to support the above important inference. These arguments have been shown to be based on error, and the conclusion founded on them cannot therefore be accepted, nor can the Board enter into the question as to the alleged impoverishment and liability to famine of the ryot upon mere general assertions.

82. It may be remarked, however, that in so far as Mr. Dutt's conclusion is based on the weight of the assessments, it would follow that famines should, if this were a chief cause, have been absolutely chronic during the first half of the century, when the assessments were, acre for acre, actually larger in money, while their relative weight, rupee for rupee, was at least double their present weight owing to the lowness of prices, and when restrictions and compulsion in cultivation and collection, and taxation upon improvements whether in method or in crop, were universal: if the weight of the assessments did *not*, at that time, cause famine, then, *à fortiori*, such weight is not now an effective cause thereof.

MADRAS. 83. The Board's observation and experience, moreover, as to the impoverishment or even as to the poverty of the ryot forbid its acceptance of Mr. Dutt's suggestion; the experience of the past decade, indeed, leads rather to astonishment at the power of the ryot class of this Presidency to resist scarcities due to serious shortage in produce even in districts within the famine zone and in areas where, for several consecutive years, the extraordinary failures in the monsoons have resulted in grave and almost total loss of crop. Writers unacquainted with the Presidency or with the hard facts or looking at figures only and forgetful of the great masses of the labouring class as shown by the census, mistake for ryots a crowd of poor labourless coolies—some of them, indeed, owning a little poor land—who, in times of scarcity, clamour for work or for relief. That in grave famines such as in 1877-78 some proportion of the *small* ryot class must come upon the State is an obvious necessity, and would equally be the case in Europe under similar circumstances among similar classes and with similar absence of a permanent system of poor-relief. The Board, however, will not dwell upon this point even from its own most recent experience during the current year (1900) of scarcity due to grave loss of crops and to famine prices though it may say at once that practically the ryot class was not even represented on the works started, but coolies only.

84. A paragraph in Sir T. Munro's Minute of 1824 is sufficiently apposite to quote; the word "district" here means taluk; Munro is writing not about famines, but about ordinary years and conditions:—

Some men are apt to suppose, when they find in almost every district two or three hundred ryots who require remission for a part, for the half, or even the whole of their rents, that the assessment is too high, or that there is something wrong in the system, and they proceed immediately to recommend a change from the ryotwari to something else. But assessment, though it is often the cause, is not the chief cause of the failure of such ryots. Where the landed property of a district is distributed among many thousand ryots, and where there is no limitation to sub-division, except what is imposed by the produce of the land being inadequate to the subsistence of the ryot, it is evident that there will be many gradations of ryots, descending gradually from those holding the largest properties to those holding portions of land too small for their maintenance. It is evident that a lower assessment will not prevent this, or cause any other change than that of making the smallest portion of land on which the ryot can subsist somewhat smaller than before, without rendering him in any degree less liable to failure. There are many ryots who fail from another cause which no abatement of assessment can remove, and which it is not desirable should be removed; it is occasioned by a spirit of independence among the caste of husbandmen, which urges every labouring servant who can buy a pair of bullocks, to quit his master and to take land and cultivate for himself. In this undertaking many fail because the loss of a bullock, or an adverse season, destroys their small means; but by far the greater number finally succeed, and their success adds to the resources of the country. It is like the spirit of adventure in trade, which, though it frequently ruins individuals, yet promotes at the same time the prosperity of the country. We must, therefore, in a district containing two or three thousand ryots, always expect to find two or three hundred who are unable to pay their rent. **MADRAS.**

The quotation no longer wholly applies to present conditions, for, in ordinary years, few if any ryots need remission except where the irrigation sources have failed, and the proportion of ryots now "unable to pay their rent" is not 10 per cent. as Munro expected, but at the worst about 2·4 per mille or one in 417 instead of one in ten; or rather, as shown in B.P. No. 308, dated 15th October 1897, less than one in a thousand, since a very large proportion of sales is not the result of failure in cultivation, but of other causes, as pointed out above in paragraph 78. But the bases of the argument, *viz.*, the results of the law of inheritance, the ever-existing opportunity for mere labourers to attempt very petty cultivation on inadequate means and on the poorest soils, the result in adverse seasons, the occasional result in every season, and the remoteness of the effect of the assessments in causing failures, remain good.

85. Apart altogether from Mr. Dutt's criticisms and suggestions, there are many honest allegations and phrases now current with reference to the land and to the people, etc, of which some have the slenderest foundations, some are erroneous in fact,

MADRAS. some are mistaken in inference; these are passing uncontradicted into circulation and are gaining acceptance as axioms not from their value but from their mere currency; *decies repetita docent;* they are being treated not as matters for discussion but as established facts and, consequently, as the bases of perfectly honest attempts to alter or found a policy. It is time to ascertain and make public the true value of certain words and phrases which are rapidly shaping thought and may undesirably influence public sentiment.'

86. But while ready to point out any mistakes or mistaken inferences that students of the land question may make, the Board has no intention of denying that vast improvement is both possible and necessary—whether in the agricultural methods, in the economic position, in the financial safety and opportunity of the ryot, or in his general or technical knowledge, and would welcome assistance, whether by the collection or analysis of facts, or by more practical work in the fields indicated—towards the solution of problems essentially connected with agricultural stability.

APPENDIX I.

MADRAS.

Statement showing the ryotwari holdings, the assessment thereon, and the gross ryotwari land revenue and cesses for a series of years—areas and amounts being shown in lakhs (i.e., *00,000 omitted*)—*together with average prices of cereals. See paragraphs 54 to 65.*

Fasli.	Occupied area.	Assessment thereon.	Total ryotwar demand.	Cesses and merahs.	Gross demand.	Season Remissions.			Average price of grain per garce.
						For waste.	Others.	Total.	
1	2	3	4	5	6	7	8	9	10
	Acs.	R	R	R	R	R	R	R	R
1261 . .	123	298	276	4	280	13·6	12·9	26·5	75
1262 . .	128	302	274	4	278	11·1	13·0	24·1	73
1263 . .	123	300	247	4	251	17·5	34·4	51·9	116
1264 . .	123	298	270	4	274	11·1	19·1	30·2	134
1265 . .	125	312	282	4	286	7·9	21·5	29·4	138
Average .	124	302	270	4	274	12·2	20·2	32·4	107
1266 . .	133	323	294	5	299	8·9	16·9	25·8	112
1267 . .	137	329	284	4	288	16·8	31·0	47·8	140
1268 . .	141	329	319	6	325	10·0	22·5	32·5	165
1269 . .	146	311	315	6	321	6·4	14·0	20·4	145
1270 . .	151	310	309	6	315	11·3	18·3	29·6	158
Average .	141	320	304	5	309	10·7	20·5	31·2	144
1271 . .	158	320	322	7	329	8·7	16·5	25·2	169
1272 . .	164	323	338	7	345	6·5	9·0	15·5	173
1273 . .	170	321	343	7	350	9·2	9·3	18·5	182
1274 . .	173	318	336	5	341	10·5	10·9	21·4	207
1275 . .	175	319	341	*8	349	10·6	10·9	21·5	237
Average .	168	320	336	7	343	9·1	11·3	20·4	194

* Land-cess first appears.

MADRAS. *Statement showing the ryotwari holdings, the assessment thereon, and the gross ryotwari land revenue and cesses for a series of years —areas and amounts being shown in lakhs* (i.e., 00,000 *omitted*)— *together with average prices of cereals. See paragraphs* 54 *to* 65—contd.

Fasli.	Occupied area.	Assessment thereon.	Total ryotwar demand.	Cesses and merahs.	Gross demand.	Season Remissions.			Average price of grain per garce.
						For waste.	Others.	Total.	
1	2	3	4	5	6	7	8	9	10
	Acs.	R	R	R	R	R	R	R	R
1276 . .	178	318	352	15	367	5·5	5·7	11·2	264
1277 . .	182	323	330	18	348	15·2	22·3	37·5	190
1278 . .	184	324	340	22	362	12·0	15·1	27·1	188
1279 . .	188	327	360	26	386	8·0	4·7	12·7	180
1280 . .	192	330	371	29	400	3·9	4·7	8·6	147
Average .	185	324	351	22	373	8·9	10·5	19·4	194
1281 . .	189	322	356	*40	396	6·1	7·3	13·4	144
1282 . .	190	322	367	42	409	3·6	3·6	7·2	150
1283 . .	188	319	354	42	396	7·5	13·1	20·6	168
1284 . .	192	323	376	42	418	2·6	7·0	9·6	164
1285 . .	192	325	353	41	394	11·5	14·4	25·9	150
Average .	190	322	361	42	403	6·3	9·1	15·4	155
1286 . .	192	324	277	38	315	46·1	49·9	96·0	257
1287 . .	192	325	359	40	399	9·2	15·4	24·6	339
1288 . .	191	326	372	41	413	6·5	8·4	14·9	259
1289 . .	184	320	366	41	407	6·0	8·3	14·3	181
1290 . .	181	318	364	41	405	4·2	6·3	10·5	145
Average .	188	323	348	40	388	14·4	17·6	32·0	216

* Village service cess first included.

Statement showing the ryotwari holdings, the assessment thereon, and the gross ryotwari land revenue and cesses for a series of years —areas and amounts being shown in lakhs (i.e., *00,000 omitted*)— *together with average prices of cereals. See paragraphs 54 to 65*—concld. **MADRAS.**

Fasli.	Occupied area.	Assessment thereon.	Total ryotwar demand.	Cesses and merahs.	Gross demand.	Season Remissions.			Average price of grain per garce.
						For Waste.	Others.	Total.	
1	2	3	4	5	6	7	8	9	10
	Acs.	R	R	R	R	R	R	R	R
1291 . .	180	317	357	41	398	6·5	7·0	13·5	137
1292 . .	183	321	363	44	407	4·7	6·6	11·3	136
1293 . .	185	323	374	45	419	3·7	3·6	7·3	137
1294 . .	187	324	350	46	396	7·8	20·2	28·0	169
1295 . .	191	327	376	45	421	3·8	3·4	7·2	169
Average .	185	322	364	44	408	5·3	8·2	13·5	148
1296 . .	195	331	386	46	432	2·8	4·5	7·3	149
1297 . .	197	*355	390	59	449	2·1	1·6	3·7	145
1298 . .	198	357	392	57	449	4·1	5·7	9·8	158
1299 . .	201	361	396	65	461	3·8	3·7	7·5	165
1300 . .	202	363	390	64	454	6·1	9·4	15·5	175
Average .	199	353	391	58	449	3·8	5·0	8·8	157
1301 . .	202	365	368	66	434	16·9	20·0	36·9	233
1302 . .	207	371	403	68	471	5·6	9·0	14·6	220
1303 . .	210	388	439	†38	477	1·7	1·6	3·3	196
1304 . .	213	395	452	‡57	509	5·1	4·0	9·1	177
1305 . .	215	393	468	59	527	1·8	4·0	5·8	163
Average .	209	382	426	58	484	6·2	7·7	13·9	194
1306 . .	215	400	440	56	496	8·5	22·5	31·0	212
1307 . .	216	403	474	54	528	3·4	7·0	10·4	262
1308 . .	216	405	485	55	540	2·0	2·7	4·7	199

* About 20 lakhs charged for water in Godavari and Kistna transferred to assessments.

† Village service cess suspended for the year.

‡ Ten lakhs transferred to Land Revenue "Miscellaneous."

MADRAS.

APPENDIX II.

Statement showing the average prices of cereals for a series of years in the Madras Presidency.

Year.	Paddy. 1st sort.	Paddy. 2nd sort.	Cholam.	Cumbu.	Ragi.	Average. Imperial seers per rupee.	Average. Per garce.	Ratio of price per garce to the average for the quinquennium 1261-65.
	Rupees per garce.							
Average for— Fasli 1251-60 .	85	76	97	87	86	47'0	86	80
Average fasli 1258-62	76	68	88	76	76	53'0	76	72
Fasli 1261 . .	72	65	88	75	73	...	75	...
" 1262 . .	70	63	84	77	72	...	73	...
" 1263 . .	103	96	136	126	119	...	116	...
" 1264 . .	121	110	162	140	135	...	134	...
" 1265 . .	129	119	154	145	143	...	138	...
Average .	99	91	125	113	108	38'0	107	100
Fasli 1266 . .	111	100	123	111	114	...	112	..
" 1267 . .	173	122	153	149	144	...	140	...
" 1268 . .	158	143	183	173	167	...	165	...
" 1269 . .	141	130	161	143	150	...	145	...
" 1270 . .	153	140	172	165	160	...	158	...
Average .	139	127	158	148	147	28'0	144	135
Fasli 1271 . .	166	150	184	171	172	...	169	...
" 1272 . .	167	155	197	172	174	...	173	...
" 1273 . .	176	163	205	183	185	...	182	...
" 1274 . .	206	188	222	211	209	...	207	...
" 1275 . .	219	201	270	246	247	...	237	...
Average .	187	171	216	197	197	20'9	194	181
Fasli 1276 . .	258	231	316	219	297	...	264	...
" 1277 . .	1[illegible]3	164	209	191	202	...	190	...
" 1278 . .	191	170	201	185	194	...	188	...
" 1279 . .	181	163	196	183	175	...	180	...
" 1280 . .	146	131	166	149	143	...	147	...
Average .	192	172	218	185	202	20'9	194	181

MADRAS.

***Statement showing the average prices of cereals for a series of years in the Madras Presidency*—contd.**

YEAR.	PADDY.		Cholam.	Cumbu.	Ragi.	AVERAGE.		Ratio of price per garce to the average for the quinquennium 1261-65.
	1st sort.	2nd sort.				Imperial seers per rupee.	Per garce.	
	Rupees per garce.							
Fasli 1281 . .	144	130	159	151	135	...	144	...
„ 1282 . .	149	135	168	150	146	...	150	...
„ 1283 . .	156	140	197	180	169	...	168	...
„ 1284 . .	155	139	191	171	164	...	164	...
„ 1285 . .	137	126	171	158	157	...	150	...
Average .	148	134	177	162	154	26·2	155	145
	Imperial seers per rupee.							
Fasli 1286 . .	16·1	17·5	15·0	15·3	15·2	15·8	257	...
„ 1287 . .	12·2	13·6	11·2	11·8	11·2	12·0	339	...
„ 1288 . .	15·2	16·9	14·9	15·6	15·8	15·7	259	...
„ 1289 . .	21·3	23·5	22·0	22·8	22·8	22·5	181	...
„ 1290 . .	25·1	27·6	29·3	28·4	29·7	28·0	145	...
Average .	18·0	19·8	18·5	18·8	18·9	18·8	216	203
Fasli 1291 . .	25·8	28·5	31·7	30·3	31·9	29·6	137	...
„ 1292 . .	26·1	28·5	32·0	30·3	32·5	29·9	136	...
„ 1293 . .	25·8	28·2	31·7	30·3	32·3	29·7	137	...
„ 1294 . .	21·8	23·5	24·6	23·9	26·6	24·1	169	...
„ 1295 . .	22·3	23·7	24·2	23·7	26·6	24·1	169	...
Average .	24·4	26·5	28·8	27·7	30·0	27·5	148	138
Fasli 1296 . .	24·6	27·0	27·7	27·5	29·9	27·3	149	...
„ 1297 . .	25·7	28·0	28 6	27·3	30·9	28·1	145	...
„ 1298 . .	23·7	25·8	65·9	24·6	28·6	25·7	158	...
„ 1299 . .	21·6	23·5	25·6	24·4	27·9	24·6	165	...
„ 1300 . .	20·5	22·4	24·0	23·2	25·9	23·2	175	...
Average .	23·2	25·3	26·4	25·4	28·6	25·8	157	147
Fasli 1301 . .	17·0	18·3	17·0	16·5	18·0	17·4	233	...
„ 1302 . .	17·2	18·8	18·2	18·7	19·8	18·5	220	...
„ 1303 . .	19·2	21·3	20·1	20·	22 6	20·7	196	...
„ 1304 . .	20·6	22·6	23·2	22·8	25·5	22·9	177	...
„ 1305 . .	21·4	23·9	25·4	25·5	28·1	24·9	163	...
Average .	19·1	21·0	20·8	20·7	22·8	20·9	194	181
Fasli 1306 . .	18·2	19·9	18·0	19·5	20·6	19·2	212	198
„ 1307 . .	15·1	16·5	14·4	15·6	15·9	15·5	262	245
„ 1308 . .	18·9	21·1	21·2	20·0	21·0	20·4	199	186

MADRAS.

APPEN

Comparative Statement of

District.	Paddy.				Cholam.		
	Commutation rate.	*Commutation price.	†Price at time of settlement.	Average prices for 1890-99.	Commutation rate.	*Commutation prices.	†Price at time of settlement.
1	2	3	4	5	6	7	8
	R	R	R	R	R	R	R
1. South Arcot (Chidambaram)	72	78	157	177	116⅔	...	148
2. Godavari	72	76	137	174	84	95	171
3. Trichinopoly	67	85	168	184	100	118	194
4. Kurnool—							
Proper	110	112½			105	107	
Pattikonda	120	133	175	190	125	145	175
Cumbum and Markapur	120	133			125	145	
5. Kistna –							
Masulipatam portion { Delta	80	84			100	98	
Masulipatam portion { Upland	90	91	154	174	95	95	200
Guntur portion	100	118			112	133	
					(a)		
6. Salem	100	123	136	198	100	137	147
7. Nellore	107	125	143	192	129	143	194
8. Tinnevelly	108	125	195	213	...	...	...
9. Cuddapah	126	140	165	194	139	163	184
10. Chingleput	105	120½	133	200	...	...	...
11. Ganjam	80	90	100	142	...	...	...
					(a)	(a)	
12. Coimbatore	126	138	173	206	119	132	197
13. North Arcot	95	105	150	187	...	...	...
					(a)	(a)	
14. Madura	123½	123½	152	191	108½	108½	159
15. Vizagapatam	105	125	141	156	...	...	...
16. South Arcot	108	127	157	177	...	...	...
17. Bellary—							
Black cotton soil taluks	139	163	182	194	135	176	182
Five western taluks	141	166			125	147	
18. Anantapur—							
Gooty and Tadpatri	139	163	180		135	176	210
Four taluks	117	138	180	185	129	152	180
Hindupur and Madaksira	118	139	180		...	...	...
19. Tanjore	121	142	158	178	...	...	...
1. Trichinopoly	121	146	176	184	...	...	...
2. Godavari	118	139	194	174	...	...	...
3. Kistna	118	139	182	174	170	200	271

* These are average prices for the periods prior to settlement on which the in nearly all cases fixed much below the actuals of the period on which the rates

† Columns 4, 8, 12 and 16 give the average prices for the periods during which prices and rates, these prices show equally that the grains were undervalued at

(a) An average rate was adopted, being the average for all the staple dry

The figures in columns 5, 9, 13 and 17 represent the average of all recent

DIX III.

MADRAS.

Commutation Rates and Prices.

	Cumbu.				Ragi.				Black Paddy.	
Average prices for 1890-99.	Commutation rate.	*Commutation price	†Price at time of settlement.	Average prices for 1890-99.	Commutation rate.	*Commutation price.	†Price at time of settlement.	Average price for 1890-99.	Commutation rate.	Commutation price.
9	10	11	12	13	14	15	16	17	18	19
R	R	R	R	R	R	R	R	R	R	R
...	93	.	182	199	93	.	186	..	...	...
221	60	69	136	175	66	76	156	200	60	71
201	83	103	179	213	83	100	173	213	..	...
210	...	...	...	...	...	...	...	...	...	...
250	70	71	183	232	.	..	...	...	65	71
243	(a) 100	(a) 137	124	212	(a) 100	(a) 137	116	196	...	...
232	107	127	181	236	...	...	...	..	...	...
...	...	...	..	..	.	...	...	.	..	...
227	130	148	178	220	...	.	...	...	...	...
...	...	...	...	...	142	161	173	237	...	...
...	...	.	...	.	105	120	133	190	...	...
252	(a) 119	(a) 132	154	203	(a) 119	(a) 132	158	203	...	...
...	115	128	172	232	126	140	152	204	...	...
255	(a) 108½	(a) 108½	168	223	..		...	.	...	...
...	114	136	146	164	126	149	166	185	.	...
...	123	143	172	199	...	...	...	...	...	...
200	...	...	...	...	...	..	...	..	...	...
	...	...	..	...	...	...	...	...	..	...
} 206 {	...	..	...	..	...	...	...	...	...	...
	...	...	...	...	...	...	...	..	...	...
	...	...	...		100	118	174	168	...	...
...	134	158	205	206	130	153	187	201	..	...
Resettled districts.										
...	134	160	202	213	130	158	200	213	...	...
...	...	..	...	...	...	...	...	...	96	113
250	..	...	.	.	..	...	..	...	96	113

commutation rates are based and show that the commutation rates adopted were
were nominally based.
the settlement was being introduced. When compared with the commutation
the settlement.
grains of the district.
favourable years during the last decennium.

MADRAS.

APPENDIX IV.

Statement showing the Financial results of settlement operations in several districts.

DISTRICT.	Year of settlement.	* Revenue assessment.	Settlement assessment.	Difference.
1	2	3	4	5
		R	R	R
1. Godavari .	From 1862 to 1867 .	17,10,402	20,94,142	+ 3,83,740
2. Trichinopoly	" 1864 " 1865 .	15,82,074	11,94,018	− 3,88,056
3. Kurnool .	" 1865 " 1878 .	12,87,123	13,27,500	+ 40,377
4. Kistna .	" 1866 " 1874 .	30,00,939	34,69,248	+ 4,68,309
5. Salem .	" 1870 " 1874 .	17,29,016	17,97,381	+ 68,365
6. Nellore .	" 1873 " 1875 .	17,10,412	18,98,568	+ 1,88,156
7. Tinnevelly .	" 1873 " 1878 .	25,16,366	25,04,256	− 12,110
8. Cuddapah .	" 1874 " 1883 .	15,19,259	16,27,135	+ 1,07,876
9. Chingleput .	" 1875 " 1878 .	13,57,612	14,10,576	+ 52,964
10. Ganjam .	" 1878 " 1884 .	6,55,732	7,20,449	+ 64,717
11. Coimbatore .	" 1878 " 1882 .	24,51,880	26,56,792	+ 2,04,912
12. North Arcot	" 1881 " 1886 .	17,47,530	17,81,257	+ 33,727
13. Nilgiris .	" 1881 " 1890 .	33,632	68,559	+ 34,927
14. Madura .	" 1885 " 1893 .	15,97,950	16,12,680	+ 14,730
15. South Arcot	" 1887 " 1893 .	34,56,199	35,58,877	+ 1,02,678
16. Vizagapatam	" 1889 " 1890 .	3,53,770	4,06,393	+ 52,623
17. Bellary .	" 1890 " 1894 .	12,68,666	13,53,608	+ 84,942
18. Anantapur .	" 1891 " 1898 .	8,69,721	9,13,607	+ 43,886
19. Tanjore .	" 1893 " 1894 .	41,14,499	53,16,144	+ 12,01,645
	TOTAL .	3,29,62,782	3,57,11,190	+ 27,48,408
	Resettlements.			
Trichinopoly .	From 1894 to 1895 .	13,73,038	17,83,009	+ 4,09,971
Godavari . .	" 1899 " 1900 .	32,68,661	36,49,866	+ 3,81,205

*The "revenue assessment" here entered is the amount in the year prior to the introduction of the new settlement, not the original (paimash) assessment It is the original assessment less all the deductions due to reduction in rates and concessions granted from time to time from the introduction of the ryotwar system till the new settlement.

MADRAS.

Statement showing the Financial results of settlement operations in several districts—contd.

District.	PERCENTAGE OF INCREASE + OR DECREASE –.					
	Dry land.		Wet land.		Total.	
	Area.	Assessment.	Area.	Assessment.	Assessment.	Area by survey.
	6	7	8	9	10	11
1. Godavari	Not available.				+ 22	Not known.
2. Trichinopoly	+ 13	– 21	– 18	– 28	– 25	+ 7
3. Kurnool	Not available.				+ 3	+ 9
4. Kistna	Do.				+ 16	+ 7
5. Salem	+ 15	+ 2	+ 18	+ 9	+ 4	+ 15
6. Nellore	– 1	+ 1	+ 3	+ 22	+ 11	...
7. Tinnevelly	Not available.				– 0·5	+ 7
8. Cuddapah	+ 8	+ 9	+ 11	+ 4	+ 7	+ 8
9. Chingleput	+ 12	– 8	+ 11	+ 7	+ 4	+ 11
10. Ganjam	+ 28	+ 1	+ 13	+ 14	+ 10	+ 20
11. Coimbatore	+ 6	+ 8	+ 8	+ 8	+ 8	+ 7
12. North Arcot	+ 13	– 3	+ 11	+ 4	+ 2	+ 13
13. Nilgiris	...	...	...	...	+ 103	+ 75
14. Madura	+ 8	– 10	+ 9	+ 14	+ 1	+ 8
15. South Arcot	+ 8	– 3	+ 5	+ 9	+ 3	+ 7
16. Vizagapatam	+ 21	– 2	+ 17	+ 21	+ 15	+ 20
17. Bellary	+ 5	+ 6	+ 8	+ 9	+ 7	+ 5
18. Anantapur	+ 6	+ 9	+ 8	+ 2	+ 5	+ 6
19. Tanjore	+ 6	+ 8	+ 1	+ 32	+ 29	+ 2
Total	...	...	...	...	+ 8·3	+ 7·7
	Re-settlements—*contd.*					
Trichinopoly	– 2	+ 13	– 3	+ 52	+ 30	– 2
Godavari	...	+ 31	...	(a) + 7	(b) + 11·7	– 0·04

(*a*) 22·8 } On water-rate at R4 per acre which was the rate in force up to fasli
(*b*) 24 } 1304.

MADRAS.

APPENDIX V.

Statement showing the percentage of the value of gross produce which the assessments of dry and wet land represent at commutation rates *in the districts settled by the Settlement Department.*

District.	Year of settlement.	Dry. Value of gross produce.	Dry. Assessment.	Dry. Percentage of columns 4 on column 3.	Wet. Value of gross produce.	Wet. Assessment.	Wet. Percentage of column 7 on column 6.	Remarks.
1	2	3	4	5	6	7	8	9
		R a. p.	R a. p.		R a. p.	R a. p.		
South Arcot	1860-61	11 15 10	1 13 5	15	17 9 9	5 8 7	31	Chidambaram and Mannargudi taluks resettled as part of South Arcot in 1891-92.
Godavari	1862-63	10 4 8	1 6 2	13	...	...	...	Western delta.
	1866-67	10 14 9	2 2 1	20	...	...	...	Eastern and Central deltas.
	1866-67	8 5 9	0 15 6	12	18 14 9	4 1 3	22	Upland.
Trichinopoly	1864-65	7 0 6	0 15 5	13	15 2 8	4 4 2	28	
Kistna	1866-67	6 6 9	1 3 1	18	21 2 10	4 6 6	21	Masulipatam portion.
	1873-74	11 0 2	1 9 9	15	31 11 0	6 8 3	21	Guntur portion.
Salem	1870-72	9 14 6	1 5 6	13	24 10 6	5 1 9	21	South.
	1870-74	7 10 8	0 14 5	12	23 0 6	3 15 1	17	North.
Nellore	1873-74	5 12 0	1 0 6	18	23 7 7	5 4 10	23	Principal division
	1874-75	7 12 0	1 6 5	18	23 8 8	5 6 4	23	Sub-division.
Kurnool	1865-70	6 10 4	1 0 3	16	34 10 5	5 9 4	16	Proper.
	1872-73	5 3 9	0 11 3	13	31 6 2	5 7 0	17	Pattikonda.
	1874-75	8 13 9	1 7 6	17	43 1 10	7 13 3	18	Koilkuntla.
	1877-78	5 1 3	0 10 11	13	30 4 2	5 12 11	19	Cumbum and Markapur.
Chingleput	1875-78	7 8 6	1 2 8	15	17 5 9	3 8 4	20	
	1874-75	8 0 11	1 3 6	15	40 14 7	6 11 7	16	Three taluks.
Cuddapah	1877-80	6 15 9	0 15 6	14	36 9 3	6 4 1	17	Do.
	1881-83	4 6 3	0 7 3	10	45 6 1	4 9 6	18	Four taluks.
Coimbatore	1878-82	6 2 7	0 14 7	15	29 14 0	6 7 6	22	
Tinnevelly	1873-78	...	...	...	26 5 1	6 10 2	25	
Ganjam	1878-84	7 3 2	0 15 8	14	14 0 3	3 12 11	23	
North Arcot	1881-86	7 7 1	1 4 2	17	25 12 0	4 15 2	19	
Madura	1885-93	7 1 3	1 1 8	16	21 10 0	4 1 9	19	
Vizagapatam	1889-90	7 8 11	1 1 0	14	22 8 1	5 9 5	25	
South Arcot	1887-93	8 1 2	1 8 1	18	24 7 0	5 7 4	22	
Bellary	1890-92	5 5 10	0 15 7	18	37 0 5	6 14 11	19	Three taluks.
	1892-94	4 15 2	0 8 8	11	25 4 7	5 5 3	21	Five taluks.
Tanjore	1893-94	9 3 1	1 7 8	16	25 0 11	6 7 0	26	Delta.
					16 14 5	3 6 11	20	Non-Delta.
Anantapur	1891-92	6 14 3	0 11 9	11	30 6 6	4 6 8	14·5	Two taluks.
	1896-97	4 5 11	0 4 3	6	27 6 2	4 0 8	15	Four taluks.
	1897-98	5 2 5	0 6 4	8	29 5 6	4 6 11	15	Two taluks.

Note.—The gross value is exclusive of the value of straw. It is merely the estimated value *at the commutation rates adopted* in each case, of the estimated yield of food grains. These rates were, as shown in Appendix III, generally much lower than the price of grain prevailing at the time of, and for a number of years previous to, the settlements, whilst recent prices have always been far dearer. Hence the percentage in columns 5 and 8 is far from being the true percentage on the real gross produce.

APPENDIX VI.

MADRAS.

Estimate of the value of crops produced in ryotwari villages of the Madras Presidency excluding Malabar and South Canara.

Crops.	Thousands of acres.	Rate per acre.	Value.
		R	R
Paddy	5,300	at 30	15,90,00,000
Cholam	4,240	at 10	4,24,00,000
Cumbu	2,625	at 9	2,36,25,000
Ragi	1,570	at 10·25	1,60,92,500
Wheat, barley and maize	90	at 12	10,80,000
Other grains and pulses	5,570	at 9	5,01,30,000
Total Food-grains	19,395	...	29,23,27,500
Castors	700	at 20	1,40,00,000
Ground-nuts	190	at 35	66,50,000
Gingelly	720	at 20	1,44,00,000
Other oil-seeds	70	at 25	17,50,000
Total Oil-seeds	1,680	...	3,68,00,000
Chillies	152	at 100	1,52,00,000
Turmeric	12	at 250	30,00,000
Other condiments and spices	142	at 40	56,80,000
Total Condiments and spices	306	...	2,38,80,000
Sugarcane	55	at 200	1,11,00,000
Other sugars	69	at 50	34,50,000
Cotton	1,514	at 12	1,81,68,000
Other fibres	56	at 20	11,20,000
Indigo and other dyes	425	at 25	1,06,25,000
Tobacco	105	at 100	1,05,00,000
Tea, coffee and chicory	55	at 200	1,10,00,000
Other drugs, etc.	36	at 200	72,00,000
Orchard and garden produce	291	at 50	1,45,50,000
All other crops	368	at 10	36,80,000
Total	24,355	...	44,44,00,500

MADRAS. *Resolution by the Government of Madras (No. 191, Revenue, dated 13th March 1901.)*

The thanks of His Excellency the Governor in Council will be conveyed to the Honourable Mr. Nicholson for the able and careful report contained in the Resolution read above.

2. The report is, in the opinion of Government, a full and complete answer to the criticisms of Mr. Dutt. There are but two points on which His Excellency the Governor in Council desires to remark.

3. From a letter written by Mr. Dutt which appeared in the *Pioneer* of the 12th January last it is understood that Mr. Dutt found the authority for his statement that this Government had fixed "*one-third* of the *gross* produce as the maximum limit of rent [assessment]", in the compilation of Standing Information for the Madras Presidency published in 1879. It is true that the compilarion in question contains a mis-statement to the effect that "the land tax" was then being revised on the principle that it should in no case exceed 40 per cent. of the gross produce for land irrigated at Government expense. or one-third of the gross produce for land not so irrigated. This error appears to have been due to a misapprehension by the compiler of the correspondence (referred to in paragraph 46 of the Board's present resolution) which had previously taken place on the subject of the relation of the rates of assessment and the gross produce. The compilation of 1879 was, however, superseded by "The Madras Manual of the Administration" by the same author issued in 1885. In the latter work, the correct rule is given that the assessments are calculated so as to approximate as nearly as possible to *half* of the value of the *net* produce. The rule is also explained in other standard works of reference. such as Stack's memorandum on current settlements and Baden-Powell's Land Systems of British India.

4. The other matter on which His Excellency the Governor in Council wishes to comment is the estimate of the gross annual agricultural produce of the country contained in paragraph 70 of the Board's Resolution. His Excellency the Governor in Council

considers that in respect of several of the staple food crops the MADRAS Board's data result in an underestimate of the money value of the average yield per acre.

CHAPTER VIII.—BOMBAY.

From the Government of Bombay to the Government of India, No. 2181, dated the 30th March 1901.

I am directed to acknowledge the re ceipt of your office letter No 2044, dated 13th Oct ober 1900, and as desired in it to forward the accompan ying memorandum containing the views of this Government on the matter referred to in the letter, dated 6th April 1900, from Mr. R. C. Dutt, late of the Indian Civil Service, concerning land settlements in Bombay.

2. The Chief Revenue Officers have been consulted as desired, and the information embodied in the memorandum has been obtained partly from the records of Government and partly supplied by the Survey Commissioner and Director of Land Records and Agriculture, whose statements have been generally accepted by the Commissioners of Divisions. The delay in furnishing the memorandum has been due to the pressure of famine and other work.

Memorandum in reply to the letter of Mr. R. C. Dutt concerning Land Revenue Settlements in the Bombay Presidency.

Early position of Mirasidars.

1. The first statement in the letter with which it is necessary to deal is that in paragraph 2, where Mr. Dutt suggests that the Mirasi holder under native rule had his land-tax fixed in perpetuity and was in a more favourable position as a revenue payer than the survey occupant. In no reasonable sense can it be said that the land tax was fixed in perpetuity. The "Tanka" of Malik Amber, which was supposed to represent one-third of the whole produce, was fixed in the gross, its apportionment being left to the village community. The "Kamal" assessment imposed by the Marátha Government was much*

* Nearly double in Poona.

BOMBAY. higher, and, as it could not be levied it was farmed. The farmers could get profit only by imposing cesses,* which became an integral part of the demand. Leases to the heads of the villages were begun only in 1807-08. Instead of having a tax fixed in perpetuity, the Mirasdars as well as other landholders had to pay all that could be exacted from them, those who had the means having to supply the defects of those who had not. The assessment under the Marátha rule came to not less than one-half of the gross produce.

Increase in revenue demand in 1818 and later.

2. In paragraph 3 the statement is made that the land revenue was raised under British rule from 80 lakhs in 1817 to 115 lakhs in 1818 and to 150 lakhs in a few years more. The addition of 35 lakhs which accrued to the revenue in 1818 was entirely due to accessions of territory. The further increase mentioned was due partly to the same cause, partly to lapses of alienations, but not of course, to the existing system of settlement, which was not introduced into any district until 1839. How far, however, the introduction of that system was from causing an increase of assessment in every case may be gathered from the following figures regarding the full revenue demand at various periods in the táluka of Indápur, Poona District:—The Tanka, R1,22,000; (2) the Kamál, R2,22,800; (3) Mr. Pringle's survey R2,03,000; (4) original survey settlement, 1837-38, R81,000; (5) revised settlement, 1867-68, R1,25,800; (6) the same reduced, 1875-76, R1,13,000; (7) second revision, 1899-1900, R1,36,600. The assessment at the second revision of settlement is thus only 9 per cent. more than the Tanka and 40 per cent. less than the Marátha Kamál.

3. The revenues of British territories of the Bombay Presidency

* The Deccan Ryots Commission considered that much ancestral debt was due to these exactions, and Mr. Chaplin, reporting in 1822 on the newly acquired Deccan districts, wrote :—

"The rayats in many villages, though usually frugal and provident, are much in debt to savkars and merchants owing to the oppression of the revenue contractors; many of these debts are of long standing, and are often made up of compound interest and fresh occasional aids which go on accumulating so as to make the accounts exceedingly complicated; a rayat thus embarrassed can seldom extricate himself."

BOMBAY.

were compared in the year 1880, when it was found that the total demand on the eighteen districts comprising the territories acquired up to the end of the year 1878-79 was about 263 lakhs as compared with a demand prior to acquisition amounting to 256 lakhs of rupees and 63,585 khandis of grain. The Revenue demand, in other words, notwithstanding the vast development of the country, was little, if at all, in excess of what was assessed upon the same territory under Native rule. The demand in the same districts in the last normal year, 1895-96, amounted to R3,01,99,298, as shown in the margin. The increase as compared with the demand under Native rule amounts to about 15 per cent., and in consideration of the circumstances is clearly not excessive.

	Rs.
Northern Division . .	99,41,588
Central Division . . .	1,15,35,532
Southern Division . . .	87,22,178
	3,01,99,298

Cause of collapse of village system.

4. In his paragraph 3 Mr. Dutt attributes the break-up of the village community to the pressure of the land revenue assessments imposed by the British Government. The statement is without foundation. There is some doubt whether in the Deccan such a system was at any time in existence under the rule of the Maráthas. Sir B. Frere was of opinion that it was not. Other authorities such as Mr. A. Rogers (see pages 8—9 of his work on the Land Revenue of Bombay) considered that proprietory bodies did exist in ancient times. But he observes that the state of agricultural society had become completely disorganized in consequence of the revenue system adopted by the Maráthas, and such cohesion as may once have existed among communities had been entirely loosened. The collapse of the village system, if it did exist in the Deccan, thus at any rate, occurred before the introduction of British rule

Mr. Pringle's settlement.

5. *Paragraph 4.*—Mr. Dutt here alludes to the effects of Mr. Pringle's Settlement. As that Settlement was abandoned, the need for referring to it is not apparent. The Settlement was an acknowledged failure from the first, as the Revenue Officers anticipated, and as soon as

BOMBAY. the excessive character of the assessments was perceived, orders were given to reduce the assessments, and large remissions were granted for failure of crops. But the revenue administration had lapsed into a confused condition of which the native officials were not slow to take advantage. "Great part of the remissions allowed for failure of crops was systematically appropriated to their own use, whilst by their agency a system of unauthorized collections were generally introduced throughout the district. This latter practice is said to have been carried to such an extent that in many cases the unauthorised exceeded the authorized collections of the village. The Revenue Commissioner quotes a case in which the unauthorized collections amounted to R357 against the Government demand of R137 and another of R789 against R255."* It was mainly for the purpose of these unauthorized exactions that the torture referred to by Mr. Dutt was inflicted.

Principles and methods of Bombay settlements.

6. In his 5th paragraph Mr. Dutt states the principles of the Settlement as he understands them. He points out that the assessment is based on the individual holding, or field, that it is fixed for thirty years, and that its amount is determined with respect to the value not of the produce but of the land. This statement of the principles of the Settlement system is imperfect and it is in some important respects misleading. The basis or unit of assessment is the Survey number or plot of land of a size adapted for cultivation by a peasant with a pair of bullocks. The arable land, whether cultivated or waste but available for cultivation, was split up into these numbers, the area of which was accurately ascertained by survey measurement; of course regard was had to actual holdings, which were formed into one or more separate numbers provided the area was not less than a very low minimum. Then the soil of each number was valued according to its depth, texture, capacity for retention of moisture and other physical properties. Disadvantages or faults were taken into account as well as

The Survey Number.

Soil classification.

* Government Selection No. 379, page 41.

special advantages. The valuation was expressed in annas **BOMBAY.** of a rupee, sixteen annas representing generally the best soil. But as has been frequently pointed out before, these operations of measurement and of classification or soil valuation have nothing whatever to do with the pitch or amount of the assessment. They are only the methods by which the assessment is distributed over the numerous individual holdings of a ryotwari system. The classification is, no doubt, the cardinal factor by which the incidence of the assessment in each field is graduated. But the assessment as a whole is not based upon it. It is objected to by Mr. Dutt as unpractical, but it corresponds in method with the operations of a soil value in England and accords with the judgment of the people, whose estimates of the relative value of the different classes of soil were carefully taken into account by the framers and revisers of the system from time to time. It has been tested and improved by more than fifty years' experience, until a very remarkable degree of accuracy has been attained. At the beginning, however, undoubtedly mistakes occurred and imperfections existed. Poor soils were found to be relatively highly assessed, and the richer soils were found to have escaped too easily. The extreme importance of having a correct basis of distribution rendered it essential to correct the original valuations. The corrections were effected at the first revision settlements with the utmost care, fresh valuation, however, being performed only where the necessity for it was clearly indicated. It has been determined that when the relative valuation has been revised in accordance with the results of experience, it will be unalterable, so that, however the pitch or total amount of the assessments may be changed in future over any tract, their distribution as between field and field will be the same as at present, and this operation is now virtually complete.

7. The basis of the distribution of the assessment having been fixed as shown above, the next step is for the Settlement Officer to work out the rates of assessment. These rates are determined in the following manner:—The area dealt with, which is usually the sub-division

Assessment rates.

BOMBAY. of a district known as the táluka, is divided into groups homogeneous as to physical characteristics and economic advantages such as climate, rainfall, general fertility of soil, communications and the like. For each of these groups uniform maximum rates are fixed. These maximum rates are the sums which would be leviable upon a field the soil valuation of which is sixteen annas. Thus if the maximum rate be R3 per acre of sixteen-anna field, the assessment per acre upon a field the valuation of which was eignt annas would be R1-8-0, and so on. By applying the maximum assessment rates to the soil valuation the rate per acre on each field is arrived at. But before fixing the maximum rates the Settlement Officer considers what direction the revision should take. For this purpose he reviews fully every circumstance shown in the past revenue history, prices, markets, communications, rents, selling and letting and mortgage value of land, vicissitudes of season, and every other relevant fact indicating the incidence of the previous assessment and the economic condition of the tract, and upon this induction he bases his proposals for enhancement or reduction of assessment as the case may be. When he finds from the records of the previous Settlement that the assessment was designedly pitched low with the object of encouraging cultivation, or for other reason deemed sufficient at the time, and if he further finds from the land records of the period of the lease under revision that cultivation has in consequence largely expanded, that prices have risen, that the assessment bears a low proportion to the sale, letting and mortgage value of land, and that notwithstanding vicissitudes of season the assessment has been paid with conspicuous ease, he will probably propose an increase of assessment. This is what has happened recently in many parts of the Presidency, and in particular in the Deccan and Southern Maràtha Country. If, however, he should find that the condition of the country has been stationary, that prices have not risen and that the country has not been developed or any rise occurred in the value of land, he will not propose any enhancement. Cases of this description have occurred already in the Konkan Districts of Ratnágiri and Kánara. Again, if the assessment at the original Settlement was pitched high and the cultivation

BOMBAY.

has been contracted, or the revenue has proved difficult to collect, and the relation of the assessment to the value and rental of land is found to be high, the Settlement Officer will propose a reduction. Few instances of actual reductions have occurred up to the present. But reductions have been actually proposed and sanctioned in the Olpád Taluka of the Surat District, and it is not improbable that they may be proposed and approved for some talukas of Broach. The general result to be attained by the revision of assessment being decided on, the maximum rates are proposed which, when applied to each field by means of the classification, would bring about that result, higher rates being imposed on those groups which enjoy the greater advantages, and lower on the less favourably situated groups. In this way the total assessment, which it is reckoned that the sub-division will bear, is equitably distributed throughout each group, village, and field.

Mr. Dutt's proposals examined.

8. In place of the system described above Mr. Dutt would prefer to have a system based on the valuation of the produce of each field. But it would be impossible to complete investigations within any measurable period of time which would determine with any approach to accuracy the average produce of each individual field. If it is suggested that an estimate of the average produce in homogeneous tracts of similar soils might be accepted, then in the first place it may be pointed out that attempts at such estimates failed disastrously in the Pringle Settlement. In the next place it is to

Assessment on average produce.

be urged that the land is not distributed into considerable areas of equally fertile soil, and no assessment could be equitable which did not take account of the relative fertility of the several holdings.

Restriction of grounds of enhancements to rise in prices and increase of cultivation.

9. Mr. Dutt also objects to the consideration in the determination of assessments of some of the economic conditions enumerated in paragraph 7 above, and suggests the extension of cultivation and rise of prices as the only legitimate grounds of enhancement. The extension of cultivation,

BOMBAY. however, is not under a ryotwari system a cause of enhancement of assessment. It causes an increase of revenue because the available waste land is already assessed before it is taken up, and on each new number occupied the assessment becomes automatically leviable. But this increase of revenue is derived without any alteration in the rate of assessment. An occupant is at liberty to cultivate as much or as little of his holding as he pleases, and no extension within the limits of the holding will render him liable to increased assessment at the end of the lease. But as indicating the lowness of the subsisting assessment, the extension of cultivation during the currency of the lease has always been regarded as an economic fact of the first importance in justifying an increase of assessment. For the original assessments have been purposely kept low in order to encourage such extension, and there is no just reason why they should not be raised to a reasonable level after a considerable period of enjoyment by the occupant at low rates.

10. The general progress of the tract Mr. Dutt considers to be no fair ground of enhancement unless it be reflected in increased prices of agricultural produce. Now, as a matter of fact, up to the present time the general progress of districts in which enhancements have been made have been accompanied by considerable rises of price, which have been made the main ground for the enhancements taken. Indeed, the principle invariably recognised by the Bombay Government is that the enhancement should fall far short of the rise of price on which it may be based. Thus, in the Karmala Taluka of Sholapur a rise of 35 per cent. was taken against a rise of prices amounting to 100 per cent. Other similar instances could be cited. Where general progress has been taken as the justification for an enhancement, it has been only as one item of the evidence that the assessment, at the original settlement, have proved to be no less easy than was anticipated at the time and would therefore bear the enhancement which had always been looked forward to at the end of the lease.

11. Mr. Dutt objects to the consideration allowed as a ground of enhancement to the improvement of communications apart

from the rise in prices which they may have been expected to produce. Now, if the prices in the villages could be made the basis of revision of assessment, it would not be necessary to take into account any improvement of communications. But that is impossible. The prices recorded are necessarily those of the market towns, and so long as these prices are taken, a decrease in the expense of conveying produce to market may be a fair ground for some increase of assessment. But generally improvement of communications is taken into account only through the effect on the prices on the basis of which the assessment is fixed. There are few other public improvements affecting the value of land not irrigated by water supplied at State expense, but such as there are afford, of course, a legitimate ground for a variation of the assessment when the time for revision comes. The method of charging for water supplied at State expense adopted in this Presidency does not appear to be impugned. **BOMBAY.**

12. The principles upon which revisions of assessment are to be effected were prescribed afresh by law in 1886, after the most careful consideration, in the following terms: see section 107 of the Land Revenue Code :—

> "In revising assessments of land revenue regard shall be had to the value of land and, in the case of land used for the purposes of agriculture, to the profits of agriculture: provided that if any improvement has been effected in any land during the currency of any previous Settlement made under this Act, or under Bombay Act I of 1895, by or at the cost of the holder thereof, increase in the value of such land, or in the profit of cultivating the same, due to the said improvement, shall not be taken into account in fixing the revised assessment thereof.'

These principles have been strictly adhered to in all settlements, original or revised, and no closer definition of them is required or would be expedient. They afford ample security that the revenue will never be enhanced for insufficient reason; they appear to be perfectly equitable and have been already put into practice with success.

BOMBAY.

Imposition of judicial checks on enhancements.

13. Mr. Dutt's proposals regarding the imposition of judicial checks on enhancements will be recognized as wholly unpractical. The practice of leaving to the Executive complete freedom in determining the amount of the assessments leviable in accordance with the general principles laid down by law has been universally accepted throughout India. It is a necessary corollary from the principles on which taxation of every description is assessed throughout the civilized world, and is no way inconsistent with the delegation of authority to the Courts to settle disputes as to rents as between landlord and tenant, who stand to one another in a relation of private contract, or to determine with the aid of assessors the value of land taken up for public purposes. Even in England there is no proceeding in a Civil Court for the recovery of over-paid or over-assessed taxes; the aggrieved parties can only apply to the Commissioners appointed for the purpose, that is the Revenue Officers of Government. In certain cases a particular Court may be selected as the Appellate authority for certain appraisements, but the Court thereby becomes a Revenue Court for the time being and is virtually the assessor of the tax.

14. A perusal of the proceedings of the Legislative Council of India,* when the Bombay Revenue Jurisdiction Bill of 1876 was under consideration, shows that the agitation against this Act is based on misapprehension. The power of the Courts was always limited to the enquiry whether the action of the Revenue Department was within the discretion left to it by law. It was even urged that the Bill was unnecessary and might safely be dropped. The Bill was eventually passed, chiefly for the purpose of declaring the scope of the Court's interference and for preventing useless litigation. In dealing with a case about the time when the Bill was being discussed, the learned Chief Justice, Sir Michael Westropp, strongly repudiated, on behalf of the High Court, the assumption by the Civil Courts of jurisdiction to determine the propriety of Land Revenue Assessments. There

*Supplement to the *Gazette of India*, April 8th 1876, pages 405, etc.

was not, in the opinion of the Court, he said, the faintest desire on the part of the Legislature that the Civil Judges should, by the assumption of such jurisdiction, "be transformed into Revenue Commissioners or Collectors of a superior grade." Under no circumstances could he "deem the Civil Courts entitled to arrogate to themselves the duties of those offices." **BOMBAY.**

15. Mr. Dutt has been content to infer the excessiveness of the Bombay assessments from the fact of the enhancements which have taken place. He has not examined the assessments themselves in order to determine whether they are moderate or the reverse.

Enhancements at first revision settlements explained.

16. But, first, the occurrence of the enhancements, which Mr. Dutt rightly puts at about 30 per cent., is not wholly attributable to an estimated increase of 30 per cent. in the value of the produce, nor will a similar enhancement as he supposes be re-imposed at subsequent revisions. As pointed out by Sir J. Peile in 1886, when introducing the amendment of the Land Revenue Code, quoted in paragraph 12 above, the high rate of the enhancement taken at the revisions then current was due to the fact that they were *first* revisions of which enhancement is a natural feature, because in them are restored to their old level assessments which were at the original settlements adjusted to a low condition of agriculture and trade. Another cause was the correction at revision of the measurements of the original surveys, a measure which resulted in large areas being brought to account which had escaped assessment altogether at the original survey.

17. But, further, the assessments themselves, when examined, will be found to satisfy all the reasonable criteria of moderation in assessment. These criteria may be taken as four in number, *viz.*, (1) the effect of the assessment on cultivation; (2) the ease with which it is collected; (3) its relation to the net produce and to the value of the land as shown by rents, and sale and mortgage values; (4) its relation to the gross produce.

18. As regards the first criterion, it may be observed that under the Bombay ryotwari system the amount due from an occupant

BOMBAY. increases with every fresh piece of land which he takes up, and decreases with every acre which he relinquishes. So long as the assessment is not burdensome cultivation will expand until the whole of the culturable area has been taken up, but whenever the assessment is excessive, sooner or later cultivation will be curtailed, and the process of curtailment will commence before the total culturable area has been absorbed. The criterion is an almost infallible indication of the moderation of the assessment or the reverse. Accordingly, in those occasional areas where, owing to mistakes in the Settlement, over-assessment may have occurred, or where the assessment originally moderate may have become excessive owing to deterioration of the soil or other causes impossible to foresee at the introduction of the Settlement, the first indication is given by a diminution in the area under cultivation.

Increase of cultivation.

19. Applying now this criterion to the Bombay assessments it is found that in the forty years ending 1895-96 cultivation has increased from 14¾ to 23⅓ million acres, in other words, there has been an increase of about 60 per cent. as compared with an increase of population probably not exceeding thirty.* In several of the districts the whole of the culturable land has been practically absorbed.† But wherever waste remains to be taken up the process of expansion still continues. The excess of the rate of increase in cultivation over that in population shows clearly that the former increase is not due merely to pressure on the land of larger numbers requiring food. The figures in support of this statement will be found in tables A, B and C appended to this Note.

20. It is perhaps unnecessary to analyse tables A and B in detail. It is, however, remarkable that the highest assessed districts form no exception to the rule, and that the proportion of culturable waste has fallen in thirty-two years in Ahmedabad from 17 to 5·5 per cent., in Surat from 14 to 3¾ per cent., and in

* The excess between 1872 and 1891 is about 13 per cent.

† *e.g.*, in Ahmednagar, Sholápur, Poona and Satara, where the culturable waste amounts to less than 1 per cent. of the total culturable area.

Kaira from 21 to 9⅓ per cent. of the total culturable assessed area. **BOMBAY.** The proportion of waste in Broach, which is more highly assessed in relation to its population than any other district of the Presidency, is only a little over 3 per cent. It will, however, be observed that the rate of increase in cultivation is slower as the years advance. The reason of this, of course, is that the best lands were taken up first and most rapidly. It might be thought from inspection of the figures, that in some of the Deccan districts—Poona, Sátára, Sholápur—and some of those of the Karnátak—Belgaum, Bijápur, Dhárwár—there had been actual retrogression. It is to be observed, however, that in the districts in question almost all productive land had been taken up in the sixties or early seventies. In the year 1875-76 the maximum was reached and then ensued the famine of 1876-77, after which, temporarily, large areas of land were thrown up. Advantage was taken to include in forest a large proportion of the relinquished area, which was of very poor quality. This is the sole reason of such diminution as the figures show in the cultivated area. The people have never ceased to clamour for the restoration of the lands taken out of cultivation, and, as the figures given in the margin show, in all these districts the proportion of culturable land left unoccupied is of the smallest.

District.	Percentage of unoccupied to total culturable land.
Poona	·83
Satára	·75
Sholápur	·50
Belgaum	1·23
Bijápur	1·22
Dhárwár	2·00

Pressure of revenue demand judged by realizations.

21. As regards the ease with which the assessments have been collected, it will be sufficient to observe that in the year 1891-92, when there was a considerable failure of crops, no less than 99·2 per cent., and in the year 1896-97, a season of severe famine, 95·3 per cent. of the revenue was collected with an insignificant amount of pressure. The following figures for the latest year available, 1898-99, and the latest normal

BOMBAY. year, 1895-96, will show how little pressure is required in ordinary circumstances:—

			1898-99.	1895-96.
Number of holdings			1,217,109*	1,226,110†
Amount of revenue for collection			R3,11,90,322	3,01,99,298
Number of cases of distraint of moveable property and sale of immoveable property other than land .			3,323	359
Amount for which distraint of moveable property and sale of immoveable property other than land were resorted to			1,62,660	11,027
Number of cases of forfeiture and sale of occupancy			1,681	922
Amount for which forfeiture was resorted to		R	64,399	21,280
Occupancy of land declared forfeited .	Area	A.	46,972	11,632
	Assessment.	R	47,429	20,931
Occupancy of forfeited land sold . .	Area	A.	4,262	1,768
	Assessment.	R	4,418	2,948
Forfeited land returned to defaulters . .	Area	R	26,904	5,716
	Assessment	R	28,110	9,682

It may be observed that the amount of compulsory process in the year 1898-99 was much higher than the normal, owing to the pressure required to recover arrears of revenue incurred in the famine of 1896-97. Nevertheless, distraint was required for the recovery of little more than five in every thousand rupees for collection, and forfeiture of land for little more than two in every thousand. Although nearly 47,000 acres of land were declared forfeited about three-fifths of it was returned to the occupants.

Relation of revenue to net produce.

22. As regards the relation of the assessment to the net produce of the land, it is difficult to form a definite opinion. For the value of the net produce can be determined directly only by deducting from the gross produce the whole costs of cultivation, including wages, due to the cultivator and his household for

* Including 210,992 inam holdings.

† Including 211,474 inam holdings.

the labour bestowed by them on the land, the value of the manure applied, marketing expenses, and other numerous items. The best indication of the relation of the assessment to the net profits of agriculture is to be found in the comparison of it with prevailing rents. BOMBAY.

Produce rents.

23. To take first produce rents. According to information furnished by the Director of Agriculture and other good authorities, a common rent is half the gross produce. It was the standard also of the Kamal of the Maráthas. Now, as will be shown below, the assessment in the Deccan amounts to no more than one-fifteenth to one-twentieth of the gross produce in a normal year. It is evident that such an assessment must be moderate, even when allowance is made for every possible vicissitude of season. Even in such a calamitous succession of seasons as the Deccan has passed through this assessment is found easy. There have been three total failures in five seasons. Taking the other two seasons as normal, the assessment at one-fifteenth of the produce in a normal year will not exceed one-sixth of the gross produce on the series of years, or, in other words, one-third of the produce rent. But as a matter of fact the present cycle of bad seasons is without precedent. One bad year in three is the accepted standard of vicissitude in the Deccan, according to which the assessment does not on an average of years exceed one-tenth of the gross produce, and one-fifth of the prevailing produce rent.

Cash rents.

24. As regards cash rents such statistics as are available all go to prove that the letting value of land bears everywhere a high relation to the revenue demand. Very rarely has it been found to be less than twice the assessment. In many parts of the Presidency, and specially in the Deccan, it is a good deal higher, three, four, and even six to seven times the assessment being not uncommon.

BOMBAY. The following table gives the letting value as recorded in the assessment reports of all the tálukas settled during the last five years :—

District.	Táluka.	Average rate of assessment per acre in land sublet.	Average rate of rent.	Average multiple of rent as compared with assessment.
		R a. p.	R a. p.	
Kaira	Nadiád	4 7 10	13 8 2	3·9
	Ánand	4 3 4	11 5 11	2·69
	Borsad	4 11 10	22 4 6	4·69
	Kapadvanj	1 12 1	6 11 11	3·83
	Thásra	2 9 0	5 11 8	2·23
Surat	Chorási	4 6 0	11 13 8	2·70
	Olpád	5 8 3	10 12 9	1·95
	Bhárdoli	3 5 3	7 7 0	2·23
	Chikhli	2 12 4	4 12 4	1·74
	Jalálpur	3 13 9	8 13 10	2·29
	Bulsár	2 8 7	5 12 4	2·27
Thána	Murbád	0 14 2	2 10 9	3·0
	Kalyáan	1 12 2	5 5 5	3·03
	Bhiwndi	2 2 2	4 15 5	2·32
	Sálsette	3 9 11	13 13 11	3·8
	Bassein	2 15 8	7 6 0	2·47
	Váda	0 13 6	2 8 8	3·02
	Sháhápur	0 15 10	2 1 6	2·11
	Máhim	1 2 1	4 2 2	3·65
Poona	Indápur	0 7 7	1 6 11	3·0
Násik	Málegaon	0 14 2	2 14 4	3·0
	Nándgaon	0 8 7	1 15 6	4·0
	Báglán	0 7 2	1 4 8	3·0
Satara	Karád	2 5 1	9 13 6	4·0
	Pátan	1 12 0	5 11 9	3·0
	Válva	2 3 3	9 8 4	4·0
Khándesh	Nandurbár	1 5 1	3 9 7	2·0
	Chálisgaon	0 14 5	6 7 11	7·0
	Dhulia	0 15 5	4 8 1	5·0
	Shirpur	0 13 3	5 8 11	7·0
	Shábáda	1 1 5	6 8 5	6·0
	Taloda	1 7 10	4 12 9	3·0
Kolaba	Roha	3 15 3	8 9 0	2·15
Ratnágiri	Ratnágiri	1 2 8	2 4 3	2·0
Kánara	Yellápur	3 4 0	6 8 0	2·0
	Haliyal	2 0 0	4 0 0	2·0

25. It will be seen from the Statements D and E attached that land is generally sold for about 24·8 times and mortgaged for about 19 times the assessment. Having regard to the prevailing rates of interest in this country these values of land subject

to the full Government assessment are very significant and furnish **BOMBAY.**

Selling value of land.

a remarkable contrast to the selling value of mirás land, which in 1832 as reported by Mr. Chaplin (see page 26 of the report of the Deccan Riots Commission) did not exceed two or three years' purchase. There is the same authority for the fact that land yielding R200 gross produce could seldom be mortgaged for more than R100.

26. The rapidity with which the land is passing into the hands of the money-lending classes has sometimes been adduced as evidence of the burdensome character of the assessment. But as a matter of fact there is no better proof of the moderation of the assessment than the great demand which has arisen for it on the part of thrifty capitalists.

Relation of assessment to gross produce.

27. Regarding the relation of the assessment to the gross produce, a statement has been recently submitted by the Director of Land Records and Agriculture to the Famine Commission giving for each district, (1) the average price of an acre of food-crops, (2) the incidence of the land revenue upon the net cropped area, and (3) the percentage of (2) upon (1). The result is given in the table below:—

District.		*Average price of an acre's out-turn of staple food crops.	Incidence of land revenue per acre on cultivated, *i.e.*, net cropped area.	Percentage of (2) upon (1).
		1	2	3
		R	R a. p.	
Ahmedabad	Ryotwári	19·06	2 8 8	13·34
	Zemindári		0 12 5	
Kaira	Ryotwári	28·10	4 13 5	17·22
	Zemindári		2 5 11	
Panch Mahals	Ryotwári	20·24	1 1 9	5·43
	Zemindári		0 8 8	
Broach	Ryotwári	24·62	5 2 3	20·38
	Zemindári		0 13 2	
Surat	Ryotwári	43·10	5 9 0	12·91
	Zemindári		2 5 1	
Khándesh	Ryotwári	14·30	1 6 8	9·91

BOMBAY.

District.		*Average price of an acre's outturn of staple food crops.	Incidence of land revenue per acre on cultivated, *i.e.*, net cropped area.	Percentage of (2) upon (1).
		1	2	3
		R	R a. p.	
Nasik	Ryotwári	16·00	0 14 1	5·50
Ahmednagar	„	10·24	0 10 4	6·31
Poona	„	14·35	0 14 1	6·13
Sholápur	„	10·78	0 9 0	5·22
Sátára	„	16·26	1 3 0	7·30
Belgaum	„	18·30	1 3 11	6·80
Bijápur	„	8·45	0 9 10	7·2
Dhárwar	„	18·17	1 6 8	7·80
Thána	Ryotwári	47·44	2 1 11	4·47
	Zemindári		2 9 8	
Kholába	Ryotwari	48·79	4 1 1	8·37
	Zemindár		2 0 11	
Ratnágiri	Ryotwári	30·45	1 2 9	5·90
	Zemindári		...	
Kánara	Ryotwári	59·95	4 2 7	6·94

*NOTES.—The acre's outturn is for each crop the average estimated in the quinquennial tables furnished to the Director General of Statistics with the letter from this Government, No. 7274, dated 2nd October 1897.

The averages are based on various trustworthy sources of information such as the crop-experiments, the investigations of the experienced Survey Officers who drew up similar averages in the year 1884 and the more recent inquiries of the Deputy Director of Agriculture, Mr. Mollison, and the Director during the famine of 1896-97.

28. It will be seen that in Bijápur the assessment is equal to about one-fourteenth and in Sholápur to about one-nineteenth of the value of an acre of the staple food-crops. On the other hand, in the four highly assessed districts of Gujarat we find that the incidence of the assessment is as follows:—In Ahmedabad less than one-seventh, in Kaira rather over one-sixth, and in Surat, the most highly assessed of all, about one-eight, and in Broach rather more than one-fifth. It is to be remembered that these incidences apply to the acreage under the staple food-grains. The value of an acre of crops other than food-crops is generally of course larger than the value of an acre of food-crops. It may then be safely inferred from these figures that in the poorer parts

of the Deccan the assessment is not more than 5 to 7 per cent. of the value of gross produce of a cultivated acre in a normal year. It may be as high as 20 per cent. in the most highly assessed parts of Broach, Kaira, and Surat. But though the proportion of the produce taken is much higher in the more severely assessed districts of Gujárat than in the lightly assessed districts of the Deccan and Southern Marátha Coountry, the land of the former districts is no doubt more profitable to the cultivator. The reason is obvious. The surplus of produce left with the cultivator is notwithstanding the high assessment much larger. Thus, after paying the assessment, the cultivator in Sholápur, the most lightly assessed district, is left only R10·22 per cultivated acre, whereas in Surat the remainder to him is R37·5. **BOMBAY.**

29. The above statements of proportions of the assessment to the produce and letting value which have been given show that the assessment can seldom in the average approach the limit of one-half the net produce proposed by Sir Charles Wood, or, except in the case of exceedingly fertile land, the limit of one-fifth of the gross produce recommended by Mr. Dutt, and that there is no indication of so much as one-half of the landlord's assets, where land revenue is obtained from him, being taken as the State demand.

30. It has been shown in the preceding paragraphs that the enhancements were justified and that they have not resulted in an excessive assessment. The following facts and considerations indicate that they have not, as alleged by Mr. Dutt, increased impoverishment. Mr. Dutt cites the authority of Sir W. Hunter, who in the debate in the Supreme Legislative Council upon the Bill which became eventually the Deccan Agriculturists' Relief Act, gave expression, in the terms quoted by Mr. Dutt, to the fear that the assessments in the Deccan might not leave the ryot enough to live on. Sir W. Hunter's statements were not answered at the time by Sir T. Hope, who had

Connection between revenue demand and alleged impoverishment of Deccan ryot.

BOMBAY. charge of the Bill, for the sole reason that they were not relevant to it; they were based on observations of the Special Judge for the Deccan Agriculturists' Relief Act, who gave it as one of some general conclusions from information supplied by Subordinate Judges which he had not had time to digest. The business of the Subordinate Judges does not lie much with the ordinary ryot; the cases which come before them are cases of persons whose circumstances are exceptionally unfavourable, and they are not in a good position to generalize as regards the ordinary ryot. The assessment in the Deccan, which, as above indicated, ranges between 5 to 7 per cent. of the gross produce, is not such as could materially affect the sufficiency of the cultivator's food.

31. Moreover, the sole ground alleged by Mr. Dutt for belief in the increased impoverishment of the Deccan ryot is his incapacity to resist famine. But if there be one thing which has been proved conclusively by the occurrences of the last four years it is the increase in the resisting power of the Deccan ryot. In the famine of 1876-77 when the revenue was lighter the difficulties of collecting it were much greater. The cultivating classes came in considerable numbers on to relief works, large areas of land were relinquished, the owners emigrating and many of them disappearing altogether. Now, however, although this is the third famine in five years and in many places the intervening seasons were not favourable, little if any land has been thrown up by the cultivators of he Deccan. In 1896-97, notwithstanding a failure of crops in the worst-affected districts such as Sholápur and Bijapur, as complete and disastrous as could be conceived, the proportion of the cultivating classes which came on to the relief works never exceeded 12 per cent. of the total number of cultivators. In other districts the proportion was wholly insignificant. The figures for the past and current years are not yet available, but it is clear that the great bulk of the cultivators have had means, in the shape of either saleable assets, or credit to support themselves and their families through a second, and seem likely to be also able to support them-

selves and families through a third year of extensive failure of crops within a period of five years. The manner in which such an unprecedented recurrence of calamities has been withstood most cogently disproves the assertion that the ryots of the Deccan are now generally impoverished. It may reasonably be doubted whether in any country in the world so large a proportion of the population could have been thrown out of occupation and deprived of their ordinary means of livelihood for such lengthened periods with less disastrous results. BOMBAY.

J. W. P. MUIR-MACKENZIE,

Chief Secretary to the Government of Bombay.

---

sidency in 1866-67 and 1898-99.

...etails of Column 10.		Percentage of columns 8 + 9 on column 7.	Percentage of column 10 on column 7.	Area under non-food crops in 1898-99.
...vernment.	Alienated.			
11	12	13	14	15
Acres.				Acres.
1,406,366	439,678	5·55	94·45	343,447
442,814	365,785	9·47	90·53	43,972
440,093	173,224	9·86	90·14	21,287
468,987	193,229	3·13	96·87	192,687
655,637	110,002	3·77	96·23	106,526
841,534	148,352	4·65	95·35	17,740
4,255,431	1,430,270	5·95	94·05	725,659
2,559,026	641,114	0·9	99·1	265,461
2,892,643	401,929	7·72	92·28	1,239,443
2,009,133	393,231	2·25	97·75	233,958
1,887,493	641,956	0·83	99·17	162,324
1,401,557	875,276	0·75	99·25	134,684
2,085,390	377,951	0·5	99·5	218,968
2,835,242	3,331,457	2·48	97·52	2,254,838
1,168,963	985,202	1·23	98·77	254,226
2,138,074	1,050,357	1·22	98·78	517,051
1,591,630	761,107	2·0	98	551,508
332,888	585	13·62	86·38	15,963
689,308	23,945	0·84	99·16	1,850
1,584,928	222,354	0·74	99·26	9,796
7,505,791	3,043,550	1·73	98·27	1,350,394
1,596,464	7,805,277	2·87	97·13	4,330,891

...7 are not available.

BOMBAY.

Statement comparing the extent of fully assessed oc

1855-56.

DISTRICTS.	No. of Government villages.	OCCUPIED AREA. Total.	OCCUPIED AREA. Average per village.	No. of Government village
1	2	3	4	5
Northern Division.				
Ahmedabad	499	325,503	652	45
Kaira	495	262,528	530	52
Panch Mahâls	...	...	...	45
Broach	406	403,719	994	40
Surat	807½	413,362	512	86
Thána	(2,216)	(1,000,000)	(451)	2,21
Central Division.				
Khándesh	3,206½	1,294,644	404	3,85
Násik	...	...	...	...
Ahmednagar	1,879½	2,562,127	1,363	1,9
Poona	970	1,447,006	1,492	1,59
Sholápur	917	1,962,895	2,141	...
Sátára	1,180	1,428,086	1,210	1,0
Southern Division.				
Belgaum	1,320	1,226,129	929	8
Bijápur	...	...	...	1,02
Dhárwár	1,211	1,144,614	945	1,9
Koláha	...	...	...	9
Ratnágiri	1,279	(1,000,000)	(782)	1,2
Kánara	(1,416)	(320,000)	(226)	(1,4
TOTAL PRESIDENCY PROPER	17,802½	14,790,613	831	20,

NOTE (1)

STATEMENT C.

Population of each district of the Bombay Presidency proper in 1872, 1881 and 1891.

DISTRICT.	1872.	1881.	1891.
Ahmedabad	829,637	856,324	921,712
Kaira	782,733	804,800	871,589
Panch Maháls	240,743	55,479	313,417
Broach	350,322	326,930	341,490
Surat	607,087	614,198	[illegible]
Thána	847,424	908,548	819,580
Khándesh	1,028,642	1,237,231	1,460,851
Násik	734,386	781,206	843,582
Ahmednagar	773,938	751,228	888,755
Poona	907,235	900,621	1,067,800
Sholápur	662,986	582,487	750,689
Sátára	1,160,050	1,062,350	1,225,989
Belgaum	938,750	864,014	1,013,261
Dhárwár	988,037	882,907	1,051,314
Bijápur	816,037	638,493	796,339
Kánara	398,406	421,840	446,351
Ratnágiri	1,019,136	997,090	1,105,926
Kolába	350,405	381,649	594,872
TOTAL	13,391,954	13,267,895	15,163,506

BOMBAY.

STATEMENT D.

Abstract statement showing results of ordinary sales under Court decrees.

District.	Taluka.	Ordinary sales. Average rate of assessment per acre.			Average rate per acre for which sold.			Average number of years purchase of assessment represented by sales.
		R	a.	p.	R	a.	p.	
Kaira	Nadiad	4	2	11	189	3	0	45·22
	Anand	3	9	10	120	3	11	33·06
	Borsad	4	4	4	183	0	3	42·80
	Thasra	2	2	7	55	12	2	25·79
	Kapadvanj	1	12	4	57	6	6	32·71
Surat	Chorisa	5	6	6	133	13	5	24·74
	Bardoli	3	4	2	33	2	11	10·11
	Chikhli	2	15	3	34	15	0	11·81
	Bulsár	2	9	10	43	4	11	16·56
	Jalalpur	3	12	5	55	1	11	14·60
	Olpád	5	11	11	73	10	3	12·81
Thana	Kályan	1	12	5	26	0	7	14·67
	Murabad	1	1	9	20	3	4	18·2
	Bhiwndi	2	3	11	32	9	7	14·51
	Sálsette	3	10	2	108	3	10	29·7
	Bassein	2	5	1	56	10	0	24·18
	Mahim	1	5	7	47	12	1	35·13
	Sháhápur	0	13	3	15	13	6	19·08
	Vada	0	12	5	14	4	0	18·28
Násik	Nándgaon	0	7	2	8	14	2	20
	Málegaon	0	12	5	9	13	9	13
	Baglan	0	7	2	11	4	3	25
Poona	Indápur	0	1	5	9	7	9	18
Khándesh	Nandurbar	1	4	2	15	8	3	12
	Taloda	1	9	9	17	3	0	11
	Shirpur	0	13	6	32	6	3	38
	Sháháda	1	1	9	32	3	2	29
	Dhulia	0	11	9	18	2	11	25
	Chálisgaon	0	12	6	18	8	1	24
Sátara	Patan	1	14	1	67	9	4	36
	Karad	2	3	7	113	5	7	51
	Válva	2	2	3	86	12	5	40
Kolába	Roba	3	5	9	58	6	6	17·37
Ratnagiri	Ratnagiri	1	0	1	39	0	1	39
Kanara	Yellapur	3	4	7	56	8	6	17·2
	Haliyal	1	8	6	34	0	0	22

BOMBAY

STATEMENT E.

Abstract statement showing results of simple mortgages and mortgages with possession.

District.	Taluka.	Simple Mortgages.			Mortgages with Possession.		
		Average rate of assessment per acre.	Average rate per acre for which mortgaged.	Average number of years purchase of assessment represented by simple mortgages.	Average rate of assessment per acre.	Average rate per acre for which mortgaged.	Average number of years purchase of assessment represented by mortgages with possession.
		R a. p.	R a. p.		R a. p.	R a. p.	
Kaira	Nadiad	4 3 2	117 4 11	27·03	4 0 1	165 12 6	41·38
	Anand	4 7 9	108 4 1	24·13	3 15 11	129 11 9	31·44
	Borsad	4 8 9	113 10 3	24·91	4 4 1	143 6 5	33·68
	Thasra	3 4 4	53 0 8	10·19	3 1 11	59 2 11	18·94
	Kapadvanj	1 11 5	53 4 9	19·38	1 12 5	61 9 4	35·15
Surat	Chorasi	7 4 8	99 9 1	13·05	5 11 9	95 4 9	16·78
	Bardoli	3 3 9	21 0 2	6·49	3 6 7	28 10 0	8·34
	Chikhli	2 14 2	19 1 11	6·91	2 14 3	26 5 5	9·10
	Bulsar	3 12 5	14 10 5	3·88	2 9 2	31 13 8	12·37
	Jalalpur	5 2 11	118 9 0	21·88	4 9 8	69 12 5	15·14
	Olpad	5 7 11	53 2 1	9·66	5 7 9	57 2 10	10·42
Thana	Kalyan	2 0 2	26 6 10	13·14	1 11 6	19 10 9	11·43
	Murbad	1 2 2	14 5 8	13·1	1 0 10	17 11 1	16·8
	Bhiwndi	1 13 7	16 15 7	8·60	2 2 4	26 15 10	12·58
	Salsette	3 6 9	70 15 6	23·4	3 4 6	71 6 8	24·2
	Bassein	3 2 0	80 15 8	25·90	2 6 2	46 13 8	19·37
	Mohim	1 5 3	30 10 11	22·93	1 11 0	44 13 6	26·52
	Shahapur	0 14 2	13 3 2	17·35	0 14 3	14 1 1	15·82
	Vada	0 13 4	8 11 0	10·98	0 14 3	13 5 5	14·90
Nasik	Nandgaon	0 9 1	10 8 10	19	0 8 8	9 13 7	18
	Malegaon	0 11 10	7 11 11	10	0 14 7	9 14 7	11
	Baglan	0 6 11	7 12 7	18	0 13 0	15 7 6	17
Poona	Indapur	0 8 8	8 14 6	16	...	...	...
Khandesh	Nandurbar	1 2 9	15 12 9	13	1 1 3	12 0 2	11
	Taloda	1 8 9	13 15 3	9	1 12 5	7 13 10	4
	Sirpur	0 14 11	23 8 9	25	0 12 9	10 1 2	25
	Shahada	0 13 11	25 4 6	26	1 6 4	34 13 8	25
	Dhulia	0 12 11	13 1 6	16	0 10 9	11 12 8	18
	Chalisgaon	0 12 0	14 0 5	19	0 14 3	21 1 7	24
Satara	Patan	2 3 3	54 7 5	24	0 15 5	27 13 1	29
	Karad	2 14 2	64 0 1	22	2 8 2	90 12 11	36
	Valva	2 7 7	53 11 6	21	2 7 9	85 10 8	33
Kolaba	Roha	3 7 10	46 8 11	13·33	1 3 9	15 2 4	12·25
Ratnagiri	Ratnagiri	1 1 7	39 7 5	36	1 0 4	41 0 0	40
Kanara	Yellapur	3 7 0	47 8 1	13·8	3 9 5	70 1 11	19·6
	Halliyal	...	...	...	...	...	...

GLOSSARY OF VERNACULAR TERMS.

Assámí or **Asámí.** A cultivator; a tenant.

Batái. Division of the crop between the cultivator and the landlord.

Chaukídár. A village watchman; a member of the rural police.

Chaukídárí. Pertaining to the village watch and ward.

Cholam. The giant millet; *Sorghum vulgare.*

Cowl or **Kaul.** The document granted by the Collector, proprietor or receiver of the revenue to the subordinate payer of the revenue, stating the terms of the agreement and the amount to be paid.

Crore. Ten millions or one hundred lakhs.

Cumbu. The spiked millet; *Pennisetum typhoideum.*

Dittam. A preliminary forecast or estimate of the year's cultivation (Madras).

Faslí. Belonging to the harvest or season. The harvest or revenue year, usually commencing in July.

Garce or **Garisa.** A measure of grain equal to 185·2 cubic feet or 9,860 lbs. avoirdupois.

Gaontía. The village headman (Sambulpur, Central Provinces).

Hukmnámá. A written order.

Hakul Tahsil. *Hak-i-Tahsil.* The rate or fee of the officer employed to collect the Government revenue.

Harra. A species of myrabolam (*Terminalia chebula*).

Havelí. A palace; a mansion. *Haveli* lands, Crown lands; those reserved for the supply of the privy purse.

Inám. A holding free of land revenue or on a favourable assessment.

Jama. The total sum of the land revenue levied or assessed on any estate or holding.

Jamábandí. A village or district rent roll. The annual settlement of the land revenue made under the *ryotwari* system.

Kamál or **Kámil jamá.** The full (Maráthá) assessment of land.

Khalsa. A term employed to distinguish the royal demesne from that held by barons and chiefs. Government lands.

Khas mahal. Crown lands; originally, those devoted to the private profit of the ruler.

Khot. Originally a revenue farmer with hereditary right of office, now proprietor (Konkan, Bombay).

Khudkásht. A resident hereditary tenant under a Zemindar; land cultivated by a proprietor for himself.

Lakh. One hundred thousand.

Lagwán. One of the village accounts showing the total assessment and by whom to be paid.

Mahál. A village, estate, or group of lands regarded as a unit for land revenue purposes.

Málguzár. Payer of the mál or revenue; the village headman or proprietor.

Málguzárí. Pertaining to the tenure of the málguzár.

Málik-maqbuzá. Possessor in full proprietary right of a plot or holding within a village.

Maund or man. A measure of weight of 40 seers or 80 lbs. avoirdupois.

Merak. Fees, and shares in grain, etc., allotted to hereditary village artizans and servants from the common share (Madras).

Mirás. Inheritance; inherited property or right.

Mirasidar. The holder of hereditary lands or offices in a village.

Narva. The mode of distributing equally the total land revenue assessment of a village among the co-sharers. *Narva* villages are villages held in co-partnership (Guzerat, Bombay).

Paimásh (Faimáísh). Measurement; survey.

Patel. The headman of the *ryotwari* village in Central, Western and part of Southern India.

Patwari. A village accountant and keeper of the village records.

Powars. A clan or caste of that name.

Puttah or Pottah. A written lease or document given to tenants or occupiers or other land-holders.

Rabi. The spring harvest which ripens at the beginning of the hot season.

Ragi. A coarse millet (*Eleusine Corocana*).

Ryot. A tenant under a landlord; also a land-holder or occupant holding direct from Government and not under any landlord or middleman.

Ryoti, Ryotwárí. The system of settlement in which there is no middleman or landlord over the individual *ryots*, who are severally (not jointly) liable for the revenue assessment on the holding.

Sanad. A title deed, a patent of appointment to a grant title, dignity or office.

Sáhukár or Savkár. The village money-lender.

Seer. A measure of weight equal to 2 lbs. avoirdupois.

Serai. A rest-house.

Sír. The landlord's home farm.

Sír Khudkásht. The landlord's private lands cultivated by himself.

Siwai. Any addition to the standard or customary revenue; profits from the land other than those of cultivation, *e.g.*, fisheries.

Sunn or San. A fibre plant (*Crotolaria juncea*).

Tahsíl. A local revenue sub-division.

Takavi. Government loans to land-holders and cultivators.

Tálúk, Tálúká. A division of a Collectorate or District (Madras and Bombay). A landholding or tenure which is subordinate to a landlord or superior (Bengal).

Tálúkdár. A landlord or zemindar holding (originally) an estate or group of estates by special grant or on feudal tenure.

Tálúkdárí. The tenure or status of a Tálukdár.

Tanká or Tankhá. The Maráthá fixed assessment in money (as opposed to any former revenue assessment varying with the years crop).

Taram kammi. A reduction from *taram* assessment, *i.e.*, the assessment based on classification of soils.

Til. An oilseed (*Sesamum indicum*).

Tola. A weight of which about 2½ go to the ounce avoirdupois.

Váram. A share of the crop or produce of the field (Madras).

Zemindar. A landlord or proprietor receiving rent and paying revenue thereon direct to Government.

Zemindari. Pertaining to the tenure of a Zemindar.

INDEX.

[NOTE.—The Statistical information contained in the volume is indexed under "Statistics."]